A Theory of Freedom

*In memory of Paul Bourke,
and in appreciation of shared friends*

A Theory of Freedom

From the Psychology to the Politics of Agency

Philip Pettit

Polity

Copyright © Philip Pettit 2001

The right of Philip Pettit to be identified as author of this work has been asserted in accordance with the Copyright, Designs and Patents Act 1988.

First published in 2001 by Polity Press in association with Blackwell Publishers Ltd

Editorial office:
Polity Press
65 Bridge Street
Cambridge CB2 1UR, UK

Marketing and production:
Blackwell Publishers Ltd
108 Cowley Road
Oxford OX4 1JF, UK

All rights reserved. Except for the quotation of short passages for the purposes of criticism and review, no part of this publication may be reproduced, stored in a retrieval system, or transmitted, in any form or by any means, electronic, mechanical, photocopying, recording or otherwise, without the prior permission of the publisher.

Except in the United States of America, this book is sold subject to the condition that it shall not, by way of trade or otherwise, be lent, re-sold, hired out, or otherwise circulated without the publisher's prior consent in any form of binding or cover other than that in which it is published and without a similar condition including this condition being imposed on the subsequent purchaser.

ISBN 0-7456-2093-0
ISBN 0-7456-2094-9 (pbk)

A catalogue record for this book is available from the British Library.

Typeset in $10\frac{1}{2}$ on 12pt Sabon
by Graphicraft Limited, Hong Kong
Printed in Great Britain by MPG Books Ltd, Bodmin, Cornwall

This book is printed on acid-free paper.

Contents

Introduction   1

1   Conceptualizing Freedom   6
2   Freedom as Rational Control   32
3   Freedom as Volitional Control   49
4   Freedom as Discursive Control   65
5   Freedom and Collectivization   104
6   Freedom and Politicization   125
7   Freedom and Democratization   152

Conclusion   175
References   180
Index   188

Acknowledgements

I amassed many debts in the course of writing this book. My thanks to David Held for proposing the project and to Victoria McGeer for talking through with me both the initial plan of argument, and many later versions. My thanks to Michael Smith with whom I share many of the ideas on responsibility and freedom that appear here and who has always been a great source of challenge and insight on the matters covered in the book (see Pettit and Smith 1996). My thanks to those who read through an early version and were most helpful with their comments. Michael Ridge and Jay Wallace were of incalculable help – Michael for an extended set of discussions and Jay for long and detailed observations – and I also found the comments of an anonymous reader very useful. And my thanks, finally, to John Braithwaite and Geoffrey Brennan with whom I have had a long-sustained discussion – a discussion sustained over nearly twenty years – of many themes that are central to the book. The text derives from a graduate seminar course that I taught as a Visiting Professor at Columbia University in 1999 but it was written for the most part at my permanent base in the Research School of Social Sciences, Australian National University. I thank all of those who took part in the New York seminar and made it so enjoyable and fruitful for me, as well as the many colleagues with whom I was able to discuss the material covered in the seminar.

Introduction

This book differs from standard treatments of freedom in attempting to provide a connected discussion of free will issues and issues of political liberty. It looks for a theory of freedom in the classical, comprehensive mould exemplified by Thomas Hobbes in the seventeenth century, and Immanuel Kant in the eighteenth, as well as by their contemporaries and immediate successors. While Hobbes and Kant had distinguishable things to say about free will and political liberty, they clearly did not think of those topics as isolated and distinct. They derived their views in each area from deeper, common roots.

Why look for a theory in the classic, comprehensive mould? Why try to bring together themes that now belong to distinct bodies of literature, even distinct disciplines? I make two observations in explanation of the approach I have taken, one of them conceptual, the other methodological.

The conceptual observation is that the word 'freedom' as it is used in psychological and political contexts carries connected connotations and supports analogous implications. Thus, to mention the connotation that is prioritized in this book, the fact that someone is said to be free in either context normally means that they can be held responsible for what they do in exercise of that freedom. Suppose that someone is said to lack freedom of the will in a certain realm of activity. That implies straightaway that they should not be held responsible for what they do. Or suppose that someone is said, not to lack free will as such, but to lack some specific political liberty: say, the liberty to speak out against the government. Again that implies that the person cannot be held responsible – not at least fully responsible – for failing to speak out. In each case there is a tie between the ascription of freedom and the imputation of responsibility and no one can think that this is a mere accident. It testifies to a continuity of usage and meaning across the two domains of freedom talk.

But the fact that freedom of the will and political liberty are conceptually connected in this way – and connected, as we shall see, in many other ways too – does not argue in itself for treating them together. The compartmentalization that we find in the contemporary literature on freedom might still be useful and productive; it might still represent a profitable division of scholarly labour. It might. But I think it doesn't. The reason turns on my second, methodological observation.

The sort of theory pursued in philosophy, whether in the psychological or political area, inevitably seeks to regiment various intuitions so as to fit them together in an appealing general structure. It looks for what John Rawls (1971) calls a 'reflective equilibrium' between particular intuitions or judgements – the data of the theory, if you like – and the more general, systematized claims that the theory defends. The methodological observation I want to make is that it will often make good sense, under this conception of philosophical theory, to seek a single theory of two conceptually connected domains rather than a different theory for each. I think that this makes good sense, in particular, with the domains of free will and political liberty.

The argument for this methodological claim is that the data in each of two connected domains may leave the choice of theory in that domain severely underdetermined, while the data in the domains taken together do much to constrain the choice of a single, comprehensive theory. The data in each of the separate domains may be consistent with multiple, more or less satisfactory equilibria, and yet the data in the domains taken together be consistent with only one equilibrium, or with a small family of equilibria. When we put the domains together, then we constrain the views to be defended in each domain, not just by the intuitions available in that area, but also by the intuitions available in the other domain. We ensure that there are more constraints on a satisfactory theory and we may thereby reduce the number of equally plausible candidates to a very few, or even to a singleton.

The lesson of this observation is that while domain-specific intuitions may be consistent with many theories of free will, and domain-specific intuitions consistent with many theories of political liberty, the combination of those sets of intuitions is capable of significantly constraining the choice of a single, unified theory of freedom. And this in fact is how I think it is.

There are many theories of free will, and many theories of political liberty, and little prospect in either area of definitively eliminating any of those options. The intuitions that guide theories of free will bear on what it means to say that an agent could have done otherwise, on what is involved in thinking that an agent authors an action in his or her own name, on what it is for an agent to be responsible for an action, and so on. And those intuitions have proven capable of being multiply interpreted and more or less satisfactorily systematized. The intuitions that guide theories of political liberty relate to whether raising the cost of an option inhibits an agent in the same way as the removal of an option, on whether we can say that natural obstacles as well as human beings interfere with choice, on whether a person can be unfree without suffering actual interference, and the like. And again those intuitions have lent themselves to a multiplicity of theoretical constructions.

In face of this underdetermination of theory in the two areas, it makes good sense to go back to the conceptual connection between free will and political liberty and to look into the prospects of a single, unified theory of freedom in general. And that is what I do in this book. I try to construct a theory that will bear at once on issues of free will and political liberty, and on the connections between the two. I seek out a theory that construes free will in such a way that it supports a defensible line on political liberty, and a theory that interprets political liberty in a way that fits with the line defended on free will. I seek a theory, in other words, that is constrained in each of its parts by the implications of that part across all the areas, psychological and political, in which we use the language of freedom.

I hope that the theory developed in the book will testify to the attractions of this holistic methodology. I do not think that the views defended here are so richly constrained that there are no plausible alternatives available; philosophy rarely works like that. But I do think that it is harder to see how the sort of unified theory presented here can be varied without significant loss than it is to see how to vary any of the familiar, compartmentalized positions that are defended in respect of free will and political liberty. I return to the issue in the Conclusion of the book.

In speaking of free will and political liberty, I have been using the terminology that has grown up under the very compartmentalization I reject. The language I prefer, and the language I use in this book, does not mark a distinction between psychological and political matters in such terms. I speak of freedom in the agent, rather than of free will, thereby avoiding any suggestion that it boils down to a psychological power of self-determination. And I speak, not of political liberty, but of the ideal that freedom in the agent would support as a target for political action; while I describe this as a political ideal of freedom, and even as an ideal of political freedom, I renounce the suggestion that it represents an autonomous domain of theory.

Freedom in the agent, as I think of it within my unifying project, has three aspects. It covers, first, the freedom of the action performed by an agent on this or that occasion; second, the freedom of the self implicit in the agent's ability to identify with the things thereby done, rather than having to look on them as a bystander; and third, the freedom of the person involved in enjoying a social status that makes the action truly theirs, not an action produced under pressure from others. So construed, freedom in the agent has a social as well as a psychological aspect and the discussion of that freedom inevitably takes us beyond the realm of free will, traditionally conceived, and into politically relevant matters.

Freedom in an agent contrasts with freedom in the environment of an agent, where this is a function of how many and significant are the options made available by the impersonal parameters under which the agent exercises his or her freedom: say, the parameters dictated by a harsh natural order or a constraining social system. Questions to do with the environment of opportunity in which freedom is exercised come up only in the last couple of chapters of the book. In the earlier part I assume that the environment will make sufficient options available for people to have choices and I concentrate on the question of what it means, and what it is for them to enjoy agency freedom – freedom of action, self and person – in making those choices.

The book is organized in seven chapters and it may be useful to provide a brief overview of these. In the first I look at the concept of freedom, specifically as it is used on the side of agency, and I argue that it is unified by a connection with responsibility. To be free, in the most general sense, is to be fully fit to be held responsible; it is to be fully deserving of the sort of reactions, say those involving resentment or gratitude, that characterize face-to-face relations. The free action, the free self and the free person are nothing more or less than the sorts of action, self and person that are compatible with such fitness; they are, as I shall say, responsibility-compatible.

This characterization of the concept of freedom raises the question as to what it is – assuming that there is some single structure at work – that makes someone fit to be held responsible. Chapters 2, 3 and 4 explore this question in the context of individual as distinct from collective agents, looking at three theories of the capacity involved:

these associate it, respectively, with rational control, volitional control and discursive control. The theory of freedom as rational control begins from an account of freedom in action, the theory of freedom as volitional control from an account of freedom in the self, and the theory of freedom as discursive control from an account of freedom in the person, though each serves to generate an overall view of free agency. I argue against the first two theories and defend the theory of freedom – specifically, the theory of freedom in the individual agent – that associates it with discursive control.

So far as the theory of freedom as discursive control involves a view of the free person it already has a social and political aspect to it. But the last three chapters of the book go on more explicitly to social and political questions. Chapter 5 argues that collective agencies, not just individual subjects, can possess freedom as discursive control; it thereby extends the theory developed in earlier, individual-centred chapters as well as connecting with the more social chapters that follow. Chapter 6 argues that one such collective agency, the state, should be given partial responsibility for furthering people's enjoyment of freedom as discursive control and that the best conception of those requirements that the state can usefully monitor – the best political conception of freedom – is provided by the republican ideal of non-domination. Chapter 7 looks at the danger that any powerful state will itself represent for people's enjoyment of non-domination, and ultimately of discursive control, and argues that the remedy lies in democratization, where this is represented as involving two dimensions, electoral and contestatory. The book ends with a short Conclusion in which I show how the main features of the position defended reflect the holistic methodology discussed in this Introduction.

The upshot is a treatment of freedom under which there is one single theme involved in all freedom talk – that of fitness for responsibility; there is one general theory of what constitutes such fitness in agents – discursive control; and this theory provides a standpoint from which we can see how issues of freedom go in the context of collectivization, politicization and democratization. The general line of argument can be gleaned from reading the concluding summaries that appear at the end of the different chapters.

1

Conceptualizing Freedom

We saw in the Introduction that the language of freedom applies on the side of agency – the principal focus in this book – and on the side of the environment where agency is exercised. And we distinguished three domains in which agency freedom is at issue: those of the action, the self and the person. The approach taken presupposes that there is a single, unequivocal concept of freedom at issue when we speak of a free action, a free self and a free person, and the question to which we now turn bears on what this is. What is the concept, assuming there is just one, that unifies talk of freedom in these three domains?

The connotations of freedom

To predicate freedom of an agent, in particular of something an agent did, is to suggest that at least three different sorts of thing hold (O'Leary-Hawthorne and Pettit 1996). The first is that the agent can be rightly held responsible for what he or she did; if the action was free then there can be nothing against thinking that the agent should have to answer for it. The second is that the action freely chosen is one that the agent can own, thinking: this bears my signature, this is *me*. And the third is that the agent's choice was not fully determined by at least certain sorts of antecedents; it was not fully determined, for example, by a hypnotic suggestion or an unconscious complex or childhood conditioning.

Any account of the concept of freedom must look to these connotations of responsibility, ownership and underdetermination and ask after which of them, if any, is the most basic determinant of the way we apply the concept. The account offered must explain why each of the connotations holds, or appears to hold, in our ordinary usage of the term. It must explain how the concept of freedom in an agent can apply at the level of action, self and person. It must support the intuitions that we find broadly compelling in our view of human agency. And, ideally, it must fit with a plausible theory of what actually constitutes freedom in an agent. As I suggested in the Introduction, the account must look for a reflective equilibrium (Rawls 1971) – an equilibrium that may require reflectively developed adjustment on one or another side – between those different elements.

My plan in this chapter is to develop an approach that prioritizes the responsibility connotation. The approach goes back in recent thought to Peter Strawson's essay, first published in the 1960s, on 'Freedom and Resentment' and it has been taken up in different ways by a variety of authors since then (Strawson 1982; Watson 1982; Wolf 1990; Fischer 1994; Pettit and Smith 1996; Wallace 1996; Scanlon 1998). There are a number of considerations that favour the approach but the best argument in its support is that it leads us towards a satisfying view of the area overall. Since that argument is available only in light of what comes later, the commitment to analysing freedom in terms of responsibility should be seen as an assumption that will be tested in the long haul of the book, not just the short haul of this chapter. The theme has already been sounded in the Introduction.

In this chapter we will be looking further at what is involved in thinking of freedom from the perspective of responsibility and we will be identifying some considerations that support the approach. One initial reason for favouring it is that it promises to do better than alternatives in saving all three connotations. There is little or no reason to think that the underdetermined action, or the action that is wholly owned by the agent, has to be a matter for which the agent can be held responsible. But there is reason to think that any action for which the agent can be held responsible is going to be underdetermined in a significant way, and is going to be something that the agent can and must own.

Underdetermination will not connote responsibility, because a wholly chance event that occurs within me or by my hands will not necessarily be something for which I can be held responsible. Ownership will not connote responsibility, because I may identify as most distinctively and intimately mine a response or a state, a habit or a skill, that I cannot be held responsible for; it may be something that comes to me – happily, I think – by grace of genes or background. But the responsibility perspective saves those other connotations, because there is a certain underdetermination and a certain ownership implied in the very idea of being fit to be held responsible for something.

The connection with ownership appears in the fact that if I was fit to have been held responsible for doing A rather than B, and I did A, then that choice can be laid at my door – represented as mine – in a manner that connotes a degree of ownership. The self that is fit to be held responsible must be a self that is not alienated from the action of A-ing. The agent must be able to think of the thoughts that led to action, and of the action itself, in the first person: this is what I had in mind, and this is what I did.

The connection with underdetermination is a little less direct but still fairly compelling. If I was fit to have been held responsible for A-ing or not A-ing, then the awareness that I ought to A must have been capable of getting me to A, the awareness that I ought not to A must have been capable of getting me not to A. And that is to say that causal factors other than my awareness of what I ought to do cannot have fully determined what I did; they cannot have pre-empted my response. Those antecedents, however they are to be characterized, must have underdetermined my choice.

As the account given here of how we conceive of freedom starts from the responsibility connotation, so other accounts of freedom will start from the other connotations. We shall not be explicitly examining these rival approaches in this book, nor even looking at the objections that such approaches will sponsor to the conception of freedom as fitness to be held responsible. I put observations in place that pre-empt many obvious objections but I do not give much time to objections as such. The discussion of a number of themes will connect us with the literature developed in pursuit of those rival conceptions of freedom, however. In the discussion in chapter 3, for example, we shall be drawing extensively on Frankfurt's (1988) work on the analysis of freedom as ownership. But for good or ill the book develops the responsibility conception of freedom, and tries to make its appeal and merit clear, without entering into a sustained dialectic with the alternatives.

The conundrums of freedom

Depending on which of the connotations is given priority in the conceptualization of freedom – if indeed any is prioritized – the problematic of free agency will be given a different cast; a different conundrum, as we might put it, will take centre stage. Under the responsibility connotation, freedom is problematic so far as it is recursive in character; under the ownership, it is problematic so far as it has a first-personal aspect; and under the connotation of underdetermined choice it is problematic so far as it involves a certain modal possibility. I will look at these problems in reverse order.

The modal problem that underdetermination raises is to explain how it can be that for anything that is freely done, the agent must have been capable of doing something else instead. Under the most radical interpretation this means that at the moment of choice it must have been possible for the agent, regardless of the causal regime and causal history of the world up to that point, to have done otherwise (Sartre 1958; Van Inwagen 1983). Unless it is to be taken in a downbeat way that will scarcely attract defenders (Lewis 1986, Essay 25), this condition is in tension with a naturalistic picture of the universe: that is, with a picture of the universe under which every aspect of the world, including the freedom of agents, is fixed in place by the way the world is constituted, and the way it is organized by law, in the microphysical realm postulated in physics (Pettit 1993b; cf. Jackson 1998). Let the world be governed by deterministic law, and the condition is straightforwardly ruled out. Let it be governed by indeterministic law, and it is still unclear how agents are supposed to fill the gaps that such law leaves open; and if they do fill them, it is unclear why this does not compromise indeterminism.

There have been other interpretations of the modal condition, designed to make the underdetermination involved in freedom seem less problematic. These construe it as underdetermination by a select set of antecedents, not by everything that happens up to the moment of choice. They represent the capacity of agents to have done otherwise as their capacity to have acted, if not counter to all the causal influences on the action, at least counter to those particular antecedents. But these interpretations run into a variety of problems, as is now well known (cf. Berofsky 1987).

One line takes the condition to be that had the agent chosen, then he or she would have done otherwise (Moore 1911, chapter 6; Ayer 1982). But this is no good. Choosing or willing or any such cognate is an action, so that there will always be a question as to whether it itself satisfies that condition; this question will open up an indefinite regress. Another, more popular line takes the condition to be that had the agent not desired to act in that way, then they would not have done so (Davidson 1980, Essay 4). This proposal is not subject to the same difficulty as the last, since desiring is not an action and the question does not arise as to whether it itself is a free action. But it is problematic in another respect. For all the condition now stipulates, it may be that in order for the agent's desires to have gone the other way, the conditioning and drilling to which the agent was subject as a child would have had to be different from what it actually was (Chisholm 1982). It may be that the possible world where the agent's desires are different from how they actually are is a very remote world indeed; in order to get to it from the actual world we would first have to make the actual past different from how it is.

So much for the modal conundrum that the conceptualization of freedom in terms of underdetermination puts in centre place. The conundrum that the conceptualization of freedom in terms of ownership puts in that position bears on the first-personal aspect of freedom. This consists in the fact that with anything freely done it must be the case that the agent is able, indeed compelled, to see the action as his or her own. The agent cannot be detached from the action, or from the process leading to the action, in the way they may be detached from a reflex or a pathology or even an obsession or compulsion. The agent must not be a mere bystander or onlooker of what happens; they must identify with what is done by their hands.

This conundrum has been given particular attention since the work of Harry Frankfurt (1988) in conceptualizing freedom – strictly, as he would put it, freedom of the will – in terms of ownership. We naturally associate free agency with the operation of a certain process leading to action, and we naturally think that any objective process can be characterized in a third-person vocabulary. So how then can the agent be present in the first person; how can the agent see the action as distinctively his or hers? The question raises a serious challenge. Any objective process will lend itself to a third-person characterization – say in terms of a cause–effect sequence – that does not include mention of the self, only of events that occur within the self (*pace* Chisholm 1982). And so there will always be a question as to how the agent is able to see himself or herself in the process associated with free action, owning or claiming the action as something that bears their signature.

The conceptualization of freedom in terms of responsibility puts a different conundrum in centre position. This is associated with what I describe as the recursive character of responsibility. Suppose that I am responsible for an action. Presumably that will be so because that action is under the control of some other factor in me: say, my particular beliefs and desires. The recursive character of responsibility appears in the fact that, by ordinary intuitions, this means that I must be responsible in turn for those beliefs and desires. If I were not responsible for them, then presumably that would let me off the hook of responsibility with the action too: I could dismiss it as the product of something not within my sphere of responsibility. But if I am responsible for the beliefs and desires that are in control of the action, then presumably I am responsible for them in virtue of their being under the control of some further factor still in my make-up: say, my habits of forming and revising beliefs and desires. The recursive character of responsibility means that I must equally be responsible for those habits, for otherwise, once again, I would be off the hook. And so on, it appears, indefinitely. Let my responsibility be mediated by a certain sequence of controlling factors and it seems that I must be responsible for every link in that chain. I cannot be responsible for something in virtue of the operation of a controlling factor for which I am not also responsible. Responsibility is inherently recursive in nature.

The recursive nature of responsibility appears to entail an indefinite regress back along the lines of controlling influences in virtue of which an action is put down to an agent in the first place (cf. Klein 1990; Strawson 1994; Kane 1996; Hurley 1999). The problem is of a kind with the difficulties to which the other conceptualizations direct our attention. In each case free agency is associated with a condition that requires more than nature is apparently capable of providing; in each case free agency is depicted in a manner that makes it apparently inconsistent with a naturalistic picture of the universe.

Since we conceptualize freedom in terms of responsibility, we will usually focus in the discussion of free agency – particularly, in the discussion of free action – on the recursive conundrum. But the other conundrums will make an appearance too. The first-personal problem associated with the conceptualization of freedom in terms of ownership will come up here in the discussion of freedom in the self. And the modal difficulty that is associated with the conceptualization of freedom in terms of underdetermination will be explicitly addressed in chapter 4, when we defend the theory of freedom – particularly, the theory of free action – as discursive control. I will try to show at that point that the theory of freedom as discursive control provides resources sufficient to resolve the modal difficulty as well as the recursive problem.

Building on the responsibility connotation

The unity to talk of freedom, under the approach to be taken here, comes of the linkage between being free and being held responsible.

'Ought' implies 'can', so it has long been said, and whatever qualifications we may wish to impose on that principle, it gives nice testimony to the connection I have in mind. Wherever an 'ought' is addressed to a subject, it is assumed that there is a suitable 'can' present. Wherever there is an obligation imposed on a subject, it is assumed that the person has the capacity to discharge that obligation. You are a free agent and your action is a free action just to the extent that you are capable of being held responsible in the relevant choice. More specifically, you are free just to the extent that you are capable of being held rightly responsible, by the criteria implicit in the practice. You are free, so I shall say, just so far as you are fit to be held responsible.

The notion of fitness to be held responsible is grounded in the ordinary practice whereby we hold one another responsible for things we do, and proceed to impute blame for those actions we see as bad, praise for those we see as good. To be fully fit to be held responsible for a certain choice is to be such that no matter what you do, you will fully deserve blame should the action be bad and fully deserve praise should the action be good. How much blame or praise you actually get will vary, depending on orthogonal factors such as the expectations held of you and the performance of others; being fully fit to be held responsible means being fully qualified to receive whatever level of praise or blame is on offer. You will be a free agent so far as the way you are – in your self and in your person – allows you to make choices for which you are fully fit to be held responsible in this sense. And your action in a given case will be free so far as it materializes in a way that enables you to count as fully fit to be held responsible.

The practice of imputing praise and blame and holding people responsible is not an intellectual exercise in which we draw up an audit of one another's behaviour and then ponder on appropriate responses. It is written into some of our most basic reactions to one another, as when we feel resentment for the harm that someone does to us, or gratitude for a good that they provide. It appears also in the indignation that we feel on behalf of others who are maltreated by a third party or the approval that we feel on behalf of others who are treated well. But it is in every instance a matter of sensibility and affection as much as it is a matter of cognition and judgement. The practice is rooted deeply in the architecture of our psychology, engaging with some of our most robust emotions (Strawson 1982; Wallace 1996).

The picture adopted here is that when we think of an agent as free, we do so just to the extent that we think of them as worthy of this sort of reaction, be it a negative or a positive response. Being reaction-worthy in that sense is what it means to be fit to be held responsible. Not every free action will engage our reactions, of course; some may be neutral enough not to elicit resentment or gratitude, indignation or approval. But even such a neutral action, if it is the free initiative of a free agent, will issue from a choice such that had the agent done something good, our reaction would have been positive, and had the agent done something bad, our reaction would have been negative.

We see only human beings as worthy of reactions like resentment and gratitude. To feel such reactions towards natural phenomena like the weather or the business cycle, or even towards non-human animals and their doings is, so most of us think, quite inappropriate. Yet human beings and the choices of human beings are not inevitably reaction-worthy. We spontaneously identify people who are out of their mind or not themselves, in vernacular phrases, as inappropriate objects of resentment or gratitude. And we discriminate without difficulty between cases where ordinary subjects should be held reaction-worthy and responsible – if they do something bad then, as we say, there is little or nothing to excuse them – and cases where they should not.

The general idea behind the responsibility approach, then, is this. We engage with other human beings in a distinctive manner that involves the spontaneous attribution of responsibility, and we conceive of freedom as that property of human beings, and of the actions performed by human beings, that makes such an attribution appropriate under the rules of the practice. Our reactive attitudes are the lens in which the image of the free agent and the free action first takes shape and when we endorse the deliverances of that lens – when we think that the agent and the action are fully reaction-worthy – then we think that it is proper to predicate freedom. Being free is being such that the reaction is appropriate; it is being fit to be held responsible.

When will freedom in this sense fail? Intuitively, you will not be fully free in respect of a choice between A and B, if you are not aware of the availability of those options in your environment of choice, do not have the conceptual resources to evaluate them, or are not functioning in a way that would allow that evaluation to affect what you do. You will not be fully free if, as a self, you are subject to problems that make it impossible for you – or just particularly difficult for you – to claim A or B as something you did. And you will not be fully free if, as a person, you are the victim of an unwelcome form of pressure or duress or coercion that makes it more difficult to do one or other of those things. Such conditions generally serve to exculpate or at least excuse an agent; they remove or reduce the responsibility. And so if freedom is just fitness to be held responsible, they will also count as conditions that destroy or diminish the agent's freedom.

I speak for convenience, here and throughout the book, as if the practice of holding responsible always involves more than one person. But it should be clear that we also hold ourselves responsible for the things we do; we do not limit the practice to other people (Watson 1996; Oshana 1997). This shows up in the fact that we feel guilty about what we did in the past, and blame ourselves for our actions, as of course we may equally feel innocent and think that there is nothing to blame ourselves for. Feelings of guilt and innocence correspond in the first-person case to the resentment and gratitude that operate in the case of other people (Wallace 1996). The fact that I say little or nothing about that first-person case should not be taken to suggest that I do not think it is genuine or significant.

The primary form of fitness to be held responsible

But philosophy, like life, was not meant to be simple. And so, unsurprisingly, it turns out that our neat equation between freedom and fitness to be held responsible has to be qualified in a number of ways. Let us describe the sort of fitness to be held responsible that allows of the equation with freedom as the primary form. The practice of holding people responsible, and the associated conception of fitness to be held responsible, may depart from that primary form in any of three ways. Thus I now qualify my original thesis, and say that in order to be fit to be held responsible in the primary sense, people must meet three further conditions. They must count as fit to be held responsible from the perspective prior to choice, not merely after it; they must be fit in a personalized way to be held responsible, not just fit according to received social standards; and they must be properly fit to be held responsible, not just fit to be treated as if they were fit to be held responsible.

If an agent is fit to be held responsible in the prior-to-choice sense then they must be in a position such that no matter what is done, that position does not reduce their claim to be praised in the event of their action being good or to be blamed in the event of their action being bad. The agent must have the resources, prior to choice, that are required for taking any of the options. Some of the resources needed will be general or standing powers – they may engage with the agent's constitution as a self or status as a person – while others will involve the particular choice in question; they will include the agent's being aware of the available options, for example, and having access to standards by which to evaluate them.

The reason for this first qualification appears in the fact that we often praise people for actions – and in that sense represent them, *ex post*, as responsible for what they did – when they were not fully fit, *ex ante*, to be held responsible for their choice, and when it would be misleading to ascribe full freedom to them. The resistance agent who does not crack under torture may attract our lavish praise, for example, even though we would not say that the agent was fully fit, from the perspective prior to choice, to be held responsible for his or her actions. It is not the case that no matter what the person did in that situation, we would have taken them to be fully worthy of praise in the event of doing something good, fully worthy of blame in the event of doing something bad. We would not have thought them fully worthy of blame, had they actually cracked under the torture.

I said that in order to be fit to be held responsible in the primary sense, an agent must not only be fit in the prior-to-choice way but also fit in a personalized manner. The reason for this second qualification is that social considerations may often dictate that fairness in dealing with others, or indeed with ourselves, requires that we treat like people alike. Taking people who are operating in more or less the same situation, and who come of more or less the same background, we are hesitant to go too particular in determining whether or not each of them is fit to be held responsible; we are inclined to say that if one is held responsible then others should be held responsible too. In a word, we are loath to personalize the attribution of fitness to be held responsible. We do not deny that such personalization is possible; it's just that in many social contexts we will be pressed to standardize the norms by which we judge people.

It would be counter-intuitive to say that freedom is something standardized in this way, since that would imply that whether an individual was free in a certain choice might depend on who they were compared with. The obvious response is to say that the question of whether someone is free in a given choice is to be determined by whether they are fit to be held responsible in a personalized sense, not in a standardized one. This question will often be hard to determine, of course, and that is one reason why we are pressed to standardize; the more difficult it is to tell whether an exception is justified, the more disinclined we will be to make exceptions. But the fact that it may be hard to determine the answer to the question is neither here nor there. The important thing is that the notion of a personalized fitness to be held responsible makes good sense and provides us with a plausible candidate for being equated with freedom.

Being fit to be held responsible in the primary sense requires the fulfilment of a third condition as well. This is that the agent is fit to be held properly responsible, not just fit to be treated as if they were fit to be held responsible. We human beings are not just mutual observers, but interactants who influence one another actively. Thus we often treat others as fit to be held responsible, when in truth they do not actually display this fitness, because of the effect this will have on their performance. It may be required in order to induct others – say, children – into the practice, or it may help to encourage those already in the practice to become better able to satisfy its demands. It may serve a broadly developmental purpose. When I equate freedom with fitness to be held responsible, I assume that it is proper fitness to be held responsible that is in question, not fitness of this developmental kind.

We are moved by a developmental rationale when we hold food-processing companies legally responsible for any breach of health standards, even one that occurs as a result of bad luck: that is, when we impose strict liability. And we are moved by it when we tell our children that, accident or no accident, they will be subject to blame if anything is broken during a party, and they will merit approval and praise if all goes well. The developmental practice of ascribing responsibility is not premissed on the belief that the agents who are subjected to it will inevitably be fit, properly speaking, to be held responsible. It is premissed on the rather different belief that if those agents are treated as if they are fit to be held responsible – if they are told that blame or praise, penalty or reward, will ensue independently of knowledge and consent on their parts – then that will tend to make them fit to be held responsible. It will keep them on their toes, alert to every likely danger and every threatening consequence.

These are not the only cases where broadly developmental considerations affect our ascriptions of responsibility. For another example, consider the case where it may be hard to get people to be careful or conscientious about the performance of certain sorts of actions unless it is clear in advance who will be held responsible for things going wrong, or indeed for things going right: unless it is clear where the buck stops. The antecedent facts of the case will say that each party is fully responsible for his or her particular contribution but the developmental rationale will argue for locating responsibility for the total result in one or another person. That should ensure that there is one agent who will keep an eye on what is happening overall and who will guard against things turning out badly.

It should be clear that if freedom is to be equated with fitness to be held responsible, then the fitness in question must be fitness proper, not just fitness of a broadly developmental kind. Before leaving the developmental topic, however, I should draw attention to a problem that arises here. This is that the line between the developmental and the non-developmental way of holding people responsible is often going to be very blurred. Take a situation where I blame someone for doing something A rather than something B, though I know they did not actually notice that that was what they were doing; they failed to foresee the A-aspect of the action. In the developmental case I will hold the person responsible, more or less conscious that by doing so I can help them to learn to be responsible. In the other case I will treat them as a person with the capacity to foresee something like the A-aspect of what they are doing and I will hold that there wasn't anything about their position prior to choice – there wasn't anything about the factors that account for the non-exercise of the capacity or disposition – that reduces their fitness to be held fully responsible for A-ing. What is there, then, to distinguish the cases for me?

Nothing, I have to admit, but the standards implicit in ordinary practice. In the first, developmental case I will respond to complaint by saying: this is a lesson for you and I hope you will be more careful next time. In the second case I will respond by saying: you know the rules by which we operate in treating someone as a recognized or authorized respondent and there is nothing in those rules that would excuse you for having failed to foresee the A-aspect of what you did. In the first case I treat the person in a strategic way as a party in whom there is hope of inducing the habit of noticing something like the A-aspect of the choice taken. In the second I treat them more respectfully as a party that can be expected, under the design specifications for being an authorized respondent, to notice that sort of thing. The idea here is that if they fail to notice it, then that means that they are falling away from their own best practice. They are underperforming as a matter of contingent fact and if we are to mark the contingency of that fact – if, in other words, we are to recognize the agent as a proper respondent (Honneth 1996) – then we have to take the attitude that they ought to have done better. More on this idea in chapter 4.

To return to the main theme, I have urged that in equating freedom with fitness to be held responsible, we should be clear that this is fitness to be held responsible prior to choice, not after the event; personalized fitness to be held responsible, not fitness by some standardized convention; and fitness to be held properly responsible, not fitness to be treated as if one were fit to be held properly responsible.

I shall take these qualifications as understood in what follows. Their complexity makes for a bit of a nuisance but once recognized it need not continue to cause problems.

The main case for conceptualizing freedom as fitness to be held responsible

Although the case for equating freedom and fitness to be held responsible can only be conclusively assessed over the long haul, as I have emphasized, there are a variety of more or less persuasive considerations that can be marshalled in its immediate support. In this section I look at what I take to be the main argument for conceptualizing freedom as fitness to be held responsible and in the next I go through a long list of other advantages that favour the approach.

The main argument for the approach starts from the intuition that there is no sense in the thought that while someone did something freely, still they cannot be held responsible for it. The argument is that there is no possible way of saving that intuition other than by representing our concept of being free as the concept of being fit to be held responsible.

That freedom connotes responsibility means that there is an *a priori* connection – a connection that we all understand, without having to seek further evidence in its support – between being free and being responsible. It is not as if we know what being free is and we know what being responsible is and we find, on examination, that wherever the first obtains so does the second. Our very conception of what it is to be free makes a linkage between being free and being responsible. Someone who did not see why that connection had to obtain would fail to understand what freedom was or what holding someone responsible was.

How to explain the *a priori* connection between being free in doing something and being responsible for what one does? There is no problem under the supposition that we ordinary folk think of freedom as that capacity – whatever it amounts to in itself – that makes an agent fit to be held responsible for things he or she does. The supposition is that we live in a world where we continually address 'oughts' to one another – we operate within unremitting practices of holding one another responsible for things we do – and that we think of freedom just as the 'can' which such an addressing of 'oughts' presupposes. We may know nothing of the metaphysics of freedom, so it is suggested – we may know nothing of what freedom involves in itself – but we will be able to recognize that sometimes it is appropriate to address 'oughts' to others, sometimes not, and we will think of freedom as the capacity that makes the difference between such cases. Thus it will be no surprise if we take it for granted, as an *a priori* matter, that wherever there is freedom there is also responsibility.

The main argument for equating freedom with fitness to be held responsible is that while this *a priori* connection will be entirely unsurprising under the responsibility approach, it has to remain mysterious under other approaches. If we conceive of freedom as ownership or underdetermination, for example, how can we think that it is *a priori* – it is something we understand without having to look to empirical evidence – that if someone is free in doing something then they will be responsible for what they do? Being the owner of what one does, or being underdetermined in what one does, is one thing. Being responsible for what one does is another. So how can we ordinary folk find it compelling, independently of empirical inquiry, that freedom under either of those explications connotes responsibility?

But while the conception of freedom as fitness to be held responsible will make the connotation of responsibility unsurprising, this benefit may seem to come at too great a cost. For doesn't this way of thinking about freedom make it into a vacuous, non-explanatory capacity? Doesn't it mean that we cannot expect to know any more about freedom than Molière's doctor knew about the *virtus dormitiva* – the dormitive power – by which he vacuously explained the fact that opium puts people to sleep? Doesn't it mean that when we invoke someone's freedom in order to explain why we should hold them responsible, we are merely saying that their being fit to be held responsible explains why we should hold them responsible?

No, it does not. That a substance has dormitive power, in the sense of Molière's character, means that it will put people to sleep, and nothing more; that exhausts its implications and so exhausts the features by which we may know whether it is present or not. But that someone is fit to be held responsible means that he or she must be expected to satisfy a variety of constraints. Someone will count as fit to be held responsible for doing A rather than B in circumstance C – and as free, therefore, in doing A there – only if we find that a number of distinguishable conditions are fulfilled (Honoré 1999). The agent must have knowledge of the options, must have the resources to evaluate them and must be able to respond to the evaluation formed. The agent must be a self such that it is possible for them to see what is done as something done in their name and something they can endorse as theirs. And the agent must be a person such that what they do is not subject to the pressure or coercion of others.

While being free is just having the capacity associated with being fit to be held responsible, then, being fit to be held responsible is itself a condition – unlike having dormitive power – that breaks down into satisfying a variety of interconnected constraints. And so we can invoke the freedom of the agent to explain why we hold them responsible and still succeed in communicating an informative and falsifiable message: viz., that the agent satisfies the range of constraints associated with being fit to be held responsible.

Other advantages of conceptualizing freedom as fitness to be held responsible

But apart from securing the connotation of responsibility, there are a number of other advantages that come of thinking about freedom as that capacity, whatever it is, that underlies fitness to be held responsible. These are that by thinking of freedom in this way, we can preserve many of the intuitions about freedom that come naturally to us (Swanton 1992, 193–4). I shall rehearse ten advantages here, some briefly, others at greater length; a number have already been mentioned in passing.

The first advantage is that if we think of freedom as fitness to be held responsible then not only can we explain the connotation of responsibility, we can also give a certain credence to the connotations of ownership and underdetermination. We noted in the opening section that the action for which I am fit to be held responsible has to be, in an intuitive sense, an action that I own as mine, not an action that came upon me by dint of alien forces. And we also made the point that if I am fit to be held responsible in a choice between A and B, the action I take must be sufficiently underdetermined by other factors to leave room for the possibility that my recognizing that it is right will lead me to take it.

The second advantage of the responsibility approach to freedom is that it makes the concept of freedom something more than a philosopher's plaything. We saw that the practice of holding others responsible is deeply rooted in human life, as appears in the centrality of reactive emotions like resentment and gratitude, indignation and approval. The fact that fitness to be held responsible becomes salient to anyone involved in that practice, and that it represents what we think of as freedom in the agent, means that the concept of free agency is intimately woven into the tapestry of inescapable human sentiments and responses. This is as we should want it to be, I submit.

For among the various topics discussed in philosophy, none has such a deep resonance in ordinary reflection as those associated with freedom.

The third advantage of conceptualizing freedom as fitness to be held responsible is that it enables us to see, without any strain, why we should speak so readily of freedom in the three domains of action, self and person. An agent will be a free person to the extent that their position in relation to others allows them to choose in such a way that they are fully responsible for what they do. An agent will be a free self to the extent that their constitution – their relationship to their own psychology – allows them to choose in such a way that they are fully responsible for what they do. And an action will be free in itself to the extent that it materializes in a way that allows the agent to count as fully fit to be held responsible. The free person, the free self and the free action are, respectively, the sort of person, self and action that are consistent in themselves with full fitness to be held responsible. They are each, in the appropriate way, fully responsibility-compatible.

The fourth advantage of conceptualizing freedom as fitness to be held responsible is that the equation explains how freedom as we ordinarily conceive of it can come in degrees or be missing completely. We may think that someone is not responsible for anything – is not a responsible agent – or is not responsible in any sense for a certain action, or is responsible but only in diminished measure, or is responsible but under mitigating conditions. And this nicely explains why we think that similar points apply to freedom. We may think that an agent, say someone out of their mind, is not free in any sense. We may think that a free agent was completely unfree in relation to a certain option: it was not available to them. Or we may think that the freedom of the agent to choose that option was reduced but not entirely removed, whether by virtue of diminished capacity or mitigating circumstances. All of this is perfectly intelligible, under the perspective on freedom adopted here.

The fifth advantage of equating freedom with fitness to be held responsible is that it enables us to see why the freedom to do A rather than B should be different from the freedom to do A rather than B or C. There is a difference between being held responsible for A in relation to one set of alternatives and being held responsible for A in relation to another; one may be praised for doing A if the only option is B, whereas one may be blamed if C is also an option. And if freedom is constituted by fitness to be held responsible, then it is unsurprising that equally we find it intuitive to distinguish between cases of being free to do A, now in relation to this set of alternatives, now in relation to that.

This advantage suggests a natural comment on a case where we would treat an agent as responsible for a certain action, yet allegedly not regard that action as free. This is the sort of case where we are ready to hold someone responsible for doing something A when, unknown to the person, they would have had to do A in any case. Had they not done A of their own volition, they would have been forced into doing it, or they would have been hypnotically induced to do it, or perhaps an effective desire to do it would have been brought about within them by neuroscientific means (Frankfurt 1988, Essay 1). Though we would hold the agent responsible for having done A in such a case – they did it with full knowledge, full consent, full capacity and so on – some will say that we cannot think of their doing A as a free action. How could we think of it as free, so it will be asked, given that the agent could not have done otherwise?

In the case envisaged we treat the person as fit to be held responsible, not for doing A rather than non-A, but for doing A of their own volition rather than being manipulated into doing it: for trying to do A of their existing volition rather than trying to do anything else (Otsuka 1998; Fischer 1999, 117–19). And in that same sense we can also treat the person as free in regard to A. They were not free to do A rather than non-A, and this is what would normally be presupposed in the ascription of freedom. But they were free to do A of their existing volition or to be manipulated into doing it; they were free either to try to do A of their existing volition or to try to do something else (cf. Davidson 1980, Essay 4, 74–5; Frankfurt 1988, Essay 2, 24).

The sixth advantage accruing to our conceptualization of freedom as fitness to be held responsible is that notwithstanding the fact that we want responsible agents to do good and to avoid bad, so that there is an asymmetry built into the practice of holding people responsible, still the conceptualization allows us to think of freedom symmetrically. The reason is that there is no asymmetry in the notion of fitness to be held responsible for a given choice, once we abstract from what happens to be right and what happens to be wrong. To be fit to be held responsible is to have the capacity to do the option that is right, whatever that option should turn out to be. It is the capacity to do whatever should turn out to be right – be that A or B – not the more restricted capacity, given that A is right, to do A, or given that B is right, to do B. The more restricted capacity would be consistent with not being able to do B in the first case, A in the second, so that in either case there would be an asymmetry involved (see Wolf 1990). But the capacity to do whatever is right involves no asymmetry; it requires both the capacity to do A and the capacity to do B (Pettit and Smith 1996).

Consider a parallel. I may have the capacity to do what a dying relative requests, which is to think well of them, but I may not have the capacity to do whatever that relative requests in this regard, be it to think well or to think ill; I may have little or no capacity to think ill of the person. In such a case I will not be fully responsible for how I think. Full fitness to be held responsible requires that I be fully capable of doing whatever the dying relative requests, be that to think well or to think ill, not just fully capable of doing what he or she happens to request, viz. that I think well. More generally, then, for full fitness to be held responsible in respect of a choice between A and B, I must be fully capable of doing whatever is right, be that A or B, not just fully capable of doing what happens to be right, say A.

The seventh advantage of the responsibility perspective on freedom is that it enables us to see why it is so natural to think that offers may not affect an agent's freedom, while threats generally will (Nozick 1969). Take any capacity on the part of an agent to do A or B. The fact that one option is made easier will not reduce or remove that capacity, whereas the fact that one option is made more difficult may indeed reduce or remove it. If on any afternoon of the week I am capable of running ten miles or of cycling forty, then I will equally have the capacity to do one of those things or to do an easier version of the other, whereas I may not have the same capacity to do one of those things or to do a harder version of the other. This means, by analogy, that whereas fitness to be held responsible in a given choice may certainly be reduced by one or another option being made more difficult of access, it need not be reduced by one or another option being made easier of access: say, through the removal of barriers or the provision of extra incentives.

This observation explains why it is so natural to think that offers may not affect an agent's freedom to do something. We naturally think of offers as making one option easier without making any other harder. Or at least we do so with offers that do not count as palpably tempting or mesmerizing. But as against this it may be said that every offer necessarily raises the relative or opportunity costs of other options, as economists call them: it means that I will have more to forgo if I choose one of the less favoured options. This observation may lead us to give up on the ordinary practice of counting offers as often consistent with full fitness to be held responsible. But even if we do give up on the ordinary practice, we should continue to recognize a difference between offers and threats. This will consist in the fact that the costs associated with offers are likely to be much less serious, and much less inimical to responsibility, than the costs imposed by comparable threats.

The eighth advantage of conceptualizing freedom as fitness to be held responsible is that it explains why being free is an important good in human life. To be fit to be held responsible for doing something is to be a certain sort of person or self – to have a suitable personal status and a suitable self-constitution – and to perform that particular action in the manner proper to such an agent. In short, it is to be the sort of agent that can be incorporated with others within the practice whereby people hold one another responsible, and to act in the manner of such an agent. It is to merit in general, and to vindicate in this particular choice, perhaps the most basic form of recognition or authorization that others can offer (Honneth 1996). This explains the powerful intuition that whatever freedom consists in, it is something of value to human beings (Dennett 1984, chapter 7). It is something such that, other things being equal, one will regret losing it and one will resent anyone else for reducing it or taking it away. And it is something, indeed, that cannot be had on the cheap through adapting one's preferences to the circumstances on hand: prisoners cannot make themselves free, though they may increase their happiness, through schooling themselves to the enjoyment of life behind bars (Berlin 1969, xxxviii; Sen 1985b, 191).

The ninth advantage of conceptualizing freedom as fitness to be held responsible is that it explains a general presumption that is otherwise likely to be puzzling. Many of us are willing to think that animals such as dogs and horses have beliefs and desires like us and are equally capable of intentional action. And many of us are disposed to ascribe some brand of consciousness or self-consciousness to such creatures. But even if we have no inhibitions in these ways, few of us think that it is appropriate to use the language of freedom in describing the situation of non-human animals; we think of freedom as something that belongs only to us human beings and, if we have any, to our metaphysical betters (Bramhall 1962, 43). This general attitude is unsurprising, under the approach taken here. We do not hold animals responsible for the things they do, for we do not think that they make evaluations of their options such that we might hold them to the values involved. If freedom means fitness to be held responsible, then clearly we are not going to credit them with the enjoyment of freedom. We may say that one environment gives animals greater freedom than another, say in criticizing the arrangements in a zoo, but we will not think that freedom talk has any application to the mode of agency exercised by such animals.

The tenth and last advantage of equating freedom with fitness to be held responsible for action is that it makes sense of why we also hold people responsible for certain consequences of action, and of why we treat some of those consequences but not others as freely sustained by the agent. So far as the consequences of free action are foreseeable they will be within the control of the agent as securely as the actions themselves and it will naturally be appropriate to hold the agents responsible for them. That a consequence is foreseeable will mean, as in the case of the foreseeable aspect of an action, that under our criteria for holding people responsible there is nothing to excuse an authorized respondent for not having foreseen it; no one who aspires to be authorized as a participant in the practice of ascribing responsibility can avail themselves of the excuse that they did not foresee it.

The consequences of free action for which we hold people responsible are usually the consequences of past action. Thus we hold someone responsible for the possession or display of certain habits of character, as we may hold them responsible for the path beaten across their front lawn, because we presume that those things came about as the foreseeable result of their past pattern of free actions. We hold them responsible for acts of negligent omission, for example, that we see as produced by such past actions. And we hold them responsible too for acts of beneficent omission – as in the failure of most people even to contemplate criminal deeds (Tyler 1990) – that we put down to the effect of past choices.

With the consequences of such past action, we will not think of people sustaining the consequences freely, as there may be little or nothing that they can now do about them; thus we will not speak of people exercising certain habits of negligence freely, or of freely holding by those habits. But things are bound to be different in this respect with the foreseeable consequences of continuing as distinct from past action, since the consequences of continuing action will be subject to the agent's current influence. In this case we will have to think of the agent as freely sustaining the consequences. I shall be arguing in chapter 4 that the beliefs and desires we hold are often embraced as a continuing, foreseeable consequence of their receiving our implicit seal of approval, and that to the extent that we give that seal of approval freely, we will hold freely by the beliefs and desires in question (Pettit and Smith 1996).

Freedom as an objective, anthropocentric property

But though the responsibility perspective on freedom has these many advantages, it is striking that the literature on freedom has barely given it recognition up until recent decades. Why should it have been so long neglected, if the connection is as tight as I have suggested and if it has long been marked in the principle that 'ought' implies 'can'? One reason may be a suspicion that the approach compromises the status of freedom as an objective property of agents and I turn finally to that issue. Those who find the issue excessively metaphysical should go straightaway to the next chapter.

The question is whether the approach allows us to think that freedom — the freedom of a particular action or a particular agent — consists in a feature that belongs, uncontroversially, to the way that people are independently of our coming to know about them, or indeed their coming to know about themselves. I believe that the equation is consistent with a fundamentally objectivist approach, even if it does introduce a degree of anthropocentricity. I make three points by way of arguing for that objectivity.

The first point is that under the approach taken here, being free is equated with a feature of actions and agents that is true of them independently of their being actually held responsible. Freedom consists in the agent's being fit to be held responsible — specifically, in the capacities that resource that sort of fitness — not in their actually being held responsible. Thus there is no question of our making someone free, so far as we hold them responsible in a given choice. We discover that they are free — we discover that they are such as to merit being held responsible — we do not invent or create the freedom that we attribute to them.

The second point to make is that this approach does not commit us to thinking that freedom is an elusive reality. It does not mean that the question of whether someone is free can be answered in the affirmative if we happen to be dealing with them from within the practice of holding people responsible but that it must be answered in the negative otherwise. Even if we are actually dealing with them from another perspective — even if we are looking at them from a narrowly neuroscientific point of view — we can think that the person is free if and only if they are fit to be held responsible from within the responsibility perspective. Freedom need not be an elusive reality that comes and goes — as David Lewis (1996) argues that knowledge comes and goes — with the perspective adopted (O'Leary-Hawthorne and Pettit 1996). Freedom would be elusive in this way only if 'X is free' had to be paraphrased within perspectives other than that which is provided by the practice of holding people responsible as 'X is fit to be held responsible from here', where 'here' picks out the perspective currently adopted. But under our approach, of course, it should be paraphrased within those other perspectives as 'X is fit to be held responsible from there', where 'there' picks out the responsibility perspective.

The third point to make is that the equation of freedom with fitness to be held responsible does not mean that freedom is a value-dependent reality. It does not mean, say, that depending on how we ought in morality or prudence to treat other agents – depending on what values obtain and are relevant – they will count as free or unfree. Such value-dependence would be entailed by the claim that whether it is right or wrong to treat someone as fit to be held responsible and therefore free is itself an ethical matter of how it is right or fair to treat the person (for claims that suggest this view see Wallace 1996, Bilgrami 1998). But under the approach taken here, freedom remains a matter of how things are, as seen from a non-evaluative viewpoint. Someone who is fit to be held responsible, and who is therefore free, must be such that others would rightly hold them responsible, by the criteria implicit in the practice of holding people responsible. But I as a normatively detached outsider can still tell whether someone is fit to be held responsible according to those criteria. I do not myself have to make any normative judgement as to how they ought to be treated. I only have to see that by the criteria implicit in the practice of holding people responsible – which, in principle, I might not endorse – they ought to be treated thus and so.

What sort of value-independent feature might constitute an agent's freedom in doing something? Consistently with the approach taken here, the feature may be a wholly naturalistic form of organization and performance. It may be a mode of being that is fixed in place by the way the world is in naturalistic respects: say, by the way it is constituted, and the way it is organized by law, in the microphysical realm postulated in physics (Pettit 1993b; cf. Jackson 1998). The naturalistic idea is that if we were to replicate the way the actual world is in naturalistic respects, and do nothing else, we would still preserve the freedom of agents. There is nothing about the approach taken here that denies freedom a naturalistic status, then, requiring us to think that the world is not subject to natural law, deterministic or indeterministic, or that it involves entities that escape the rule of such law. This comment will be borne out by the discussion in chapter 4.

The three observations made so far all go to support the thesis that the equation of freedom with fitness to be held responsible does not compromise the possibility of taking their freedom to be an objective property of agents. But, that said, we should emphasize that the approach does have anthropocentric implications for the nature of freedom that give it a distinctive cast in relation to alternatives. There are two ways, in particular, in which this anthropocentricity is salient. First, the concept of freedom as elucidated here is a perspective-dependent or response-dependent notion; and second, the property of freedom as elucidated here is a concept-bound reality.

Under the approach taken, the phenomenon in which the freedom of an agent or action consists will be non-parasitically discernible only to someone who is party to the practice of holding people responsible and who has the evaluative and other concepts required for taking part in this practice. Observers who were not party to that practice – Martians, perhaps – might be able to identify the property of freedom as the property that leads those who are party to the practice to ascribe fitness to be held responsible; this parallels the way in which colour-blind people are able to identify the property of redness as the property that leads those who are not colour-blind to ascribe redness. But in order to be able to identify the property of freedom non-parasitically, it is going to be essential for those who do so to be immersed in the practice of holding agents responsible; it is going to be essential that they are prone to reactions like resentment and gratitude, indignation and approval, or are at least in a position to understand those reactions.

This is to say that the concept of freedom is perspective-dependent or response-dependent, as the concept of redness is often said to be response-dependent (Pettit 1991). In order to understand the meaning of 'free' – in order to grasp the concept involved – people must be in a position to see what the word connotes: to see which ties with other words, and which ties with observation, go without saying. Thus they must be able to see that 'free' connotes responsibility, ownership and underdetermination, to go back to our earlier examples, and they must be able to recognize both the sorts of situation and behaviour that are evidence for freedom, and the sorts that are evidence against. But the ability to recognize such connotations comes spontaneously only with the perspective associated with the practice of holding people responsible, as the ability to recognize the connotations of 'red' come only with having sensations of redness. If others can grasp the connotations, that will be by focusing on people involved in the practice and discerning what connotations they tend to find compelling: this, in the way the colour-blind discern the connotations of colour terms by focusing on people with normal sight.

The perspective-dependence of the concept of freedom is well worth marking but it does not compromise objectivity, because it means that the concept of freedom is perspective-dependent, not that the property picked out by the concept is perspective-dependent. It may be that we can only get to conceptualize freedom from the responsibility

Conceptualizing Freedom 29

perspective – it may be that freedom only becomes salient from that perspective – but there is no reason to think that freedom is called into existence by the adoption of the perspective or that there is nothing more to being free than being seen in a certain way from that perspective.

The second anthropocentricity that attaches to freedom under our account does involve the reality or property of freedom, not just the concept. It consists in the fact that not only does the responsibility perspective provide the standpoint required for non-parasitically mastering the concept of freedom, it also provides a standpoint such that only those who occupy it can be free. Only those who occupy that standpoint and are in a position to master the concept of freedom are able to instantiate the property of freedom. The property of freedom, as we can put it, is concept-bound.

That fact that freedom is concept-bound in this sense means that being free is on a par with being a friend or having money. It is a property such that we cannot credit anyone with instantiating it without supposing that they are in a position to recognize and conceptualize the sort of property involved (Searle 1995). In order to be free it is essential that one be in a position to conceptualize freedom. There is no access to the property without access to the concept.

This result, surprising though it may be, follows straightforwardly from the fact that in order to be fit to be held responsible, an agent must be in possession of concepts like those that bear on what ought to be done, what is justifiable or unjustifiable, what is worthy of blame or praise, and must be in a position to understand reactions like resentment and gratitude, indignation and approval. Someone who did not have access to such concepts or such reactions would, like the dog, be unfit to be held responsible for anything. But to have access to those concepts and reactions is just to occupy the perspective from which it is possible to form the concept of being fit to be held responsible and so of being free. Thus it follows that there is no access to the property of freedom without access to the concept of freedom. The reality is concept-bound.

That the property of freedom is concept-bound, however, does not mean that being free consists in being seen as responsible, in the way that idealists hold that the reality of observed objects consists in their being observed. It does not compromise the objectivity of freedom any more than the fact that the concept is perspective-dependent. That freedom is concept-bound simply means that among the conditions for instantiating freedom is a condition – occupation of the responsibility perspective – that guarantees access to the concept of freedom. We do not think that friendship or money is any the less real or objective for being concept-bound. And neither should we think anything of the kind about freedom.

Conclusion

The concept of freedom is applied in the first instance to agency, allowing us to speak of free actions, free selves and free persons and in the second instance to the environment of opportunities within which free agency is exercised. Our concern in this chapter has been to provide a single, unifying analysis of the concept of freedom as it applies on the side of agency and our concern in the three chapters following will be to provide a theory of freedom, so analysed; we will return to considerations of environment in the later chapters.

Any analysis of the concept of freedom will tend to take one or another connotation of talk of freedom and build an account of the concept around that connotation. One well-known analysis focuses on the fact that talk of freedom connotes that the agent was not predetermined to act as he or she did, while another gives centrality to the fact that talk of freedom connotes that the agent was truly the owner of what he or she did; it was not something imposed from outside. The analysis adopted here prioritizes the connotation of responsibility, as distinct from the connotations of ownership or underdetermination. It starts from the practice whereby people hold themselves and one another responsible and identifies freedom with fitness, under that practice, to be held responsible for what one does.

The analyses of freedom in terms, respectively, of underdetermination, ownership and responsibility put different conundrums at the centre of discussion. The first focuses on the problem of explaining how it is that the author of a free action could have done otherwise; the second on the problem of explaining how the agent necessarily has a first-personal presence in free action; and the third on how an agent can be held responsible for free action, given that the agent must also be responsible for any controlling factor in virtue of which the responsibility obtains in the first place: given that responsibility, as we put it, is recursive. The focus here, particularly in discussions of free action, will be on the recursive problem but the other problems will figure too.

The idea in the analysis adopted is that we live and think within the practice of holding one another responsible and that this makes the condition of being fit to be held responsible salient to us and available as the referent for our talk of freedom. The fitness to be held responsible with which freedom is equated under this approach has three features that we spent some time elaborating. It is fitness, prior to choice, to be held responsible for whatever one does. It is personalized fitness to be held responsible, not just fitness according to standardized criteria for ascribing responsibility. And it is fitness to be held properly responsible, not fitness to be treated — for developmental reasons — as if one were fit to be held responsible.

The main argument for the analysis of freedom as fitness to be held responsible is that it explains why it is *a priori* by our lights that if someone is free in making a certain choice then they are responsible for whatever they do there. The condition in question is not a vacuous ground for holding someone responsible; rather it involves the satisfaction of a variety of constraints. If one is fully fit to be held responsible for a choice then one must recognize the options available in the choice, for example, and one must be able to recognize standards of right and wrong and to apply them to oneself.

There are a variety of advantages attaching to the analysis of freedom as fitness to be held responsible that support this argument and we commented on ten of these. The analysis explains why freedom connotes underdetermination and ownership as well as responsibility; it represents freedom as something that engages intimately with emotional responses like resentment and gratitude; and it shows how freedom can be a feature of person, self and action. Equally, the analysis makes sense of the way freedom comes in degrees, is relative to the alternatives on offer, is symmetrically related to doing what is right and doing what is wrong, is more clearly diminished by threats than by offers, is something inherently desirable, and is not generally ascribed to non-human animals. And finally it allows us to recognize that while agents may be held responsible for the foreseeable consequences of their free actions, the consequences of past actions will not be freely sustained, the consequences of continuing actions will.

This analysis of freedom makes it into an objective but distinctively anthropocentric property. The freedom of an agent will consist in something — perhaps in something naturalistic — that is independent of how we look at the agent or treat them. But the concept of freedom will be perspective-dependent and the property of freedom concept-bound. The concept will be perspective-dependent in the sense that it is only from within the practice of holding people responsible that we can come to master the concept of freedom in a non-parasitic way. The property of freedom will be concept-bound in the sense that only those who have access to the concept of freedom will have access to the possibility of instantiating freedom in themselves.

2

Freedom as Rational Control

Towards a theory of freedom

The responsibility perspective adopted here suggests that we ordinary folk think of freedom in purely functional terms. We conceive of it as that capacity, whatever it involves in itself, in virtue of which an agent is fit to be held responsible, satisfying the various constraints that that involves. Freedom is identified for us, then, by reference to the function it plays in making agents fit to be held responsible and its essential character – what it is in itself – is left in the dark. This functional characterization immediately opens up the question as to what the capacity involves in itself. And that is the question that theories of freedom, as I think of them, should address.

On this picture, there are clear analogies between the theory of freedom and other intellectual pursuits. Colours are conceived in optics as properties that make a certain range of observational discriminations possible and then colour science tries to identify those properties in purely physical terms. Genes are functionally characterized in biology by reference to their role in inheritance and that functional characterization is complemented by biochemical attempts to characterize the mechanisms in which they consist. Various information-processing devices are postulated in psychology and then neuroscience is called on to give an account of how such functional entities are implemented. And so on.

But though the theory of freedom will have a standing analogous to the second pursuit mentioned in each of these cases, there is also an important disanalogy to be mentioned. The pursuit in each of the cases mentioned is an *a posteriori* endeavour that requires empirical experimentation and observation whereas the various theories of freedom to be considered here are not empirical in the same way. They each aspire to identify skills and accomplishments that are presupposed to fitness for being held responsible; in that sense they seek to give a substantive account of the capacity in which freedom consists. But they do not claim to identify the requisite skills and accomplishments by empirically probing agreed cases of free actions, free selves or free persons. They take a different, *a priori* line of argument.

Think of how we might go about articulating the sort of capacity that we expect to find in someone who counts as fit to be held responsible. The only plausible way to go will be to consider actual and possible cases where we would be intuitively disposed to treat an action, a self or a person as consistent with responsibility – as free – and to identify a pattern of capacities that we would require to be present in those cases. This will be a pattern such that in its absence – so we find as we consult our dispositions – we would not be inclined to posit responsibility, whereas in its presence we would. It will not be just the pattern that we happen to find in the examples considered; it will be a pattern that we find ourselves disposed to expect.

If the natural way to go in trying to give a substantive account of freedom is to follow this method of cases, as it has been called, then what it requires is *a priori* argument of just the kind that we followed in thinking about how freedom should be conceptualized. In thinking about how to conceptualize freedom, we reflected on what connotations are carried by talk of freedom and on how they can be best organized. In thinking about what pattern of capacities constitutes freedom in that sense we will reflect on the pattern that we are disposed to expect in cases where we are willing to predicate freedom of actions, selves and persons. This enterprise may well involve us in a revision of some of our pre-existing intuitions, of course. No revision will be required only in the unlikely event that our dispositions are entirely consistent among themselves and entirely consistent with the theoretical preferences or dispositions that will naturally guide the project: for example, the preference for finding a single, general capacity with which to equate freedom.

To say that the method employed in the search for a theory of freedom is *a priori* in this sense is to say that, extending the project of finding a suitable conceptualization of freedom, it continues to implement the strategy of reflective equilibrium (Rawls 1971). The idea will be to go back and forth between a general description of the freedom capacity and the intuitions that we have about whether there is freedom present in this or that imagined or actual case and, by revising now one, now the other, to find a stable equilibrium between the two. In describing his own use of reflective equilibrium, Rawls says that he begins with a concept of justice – roughly, giving everyone their due – and then uses the method in the theory of justice to derive a satisfactory, more specific conception of what people's dues are. We can say, in parallel, that we begin with the concept of freedom as fitness to be held responsible and that we seek in the theory of freedom to identify a satisfactory, more specific conception of what fitness to be held responsible involves.

This chapter and the two following look in turn at three theories of freedom in this sense. The first identifies freedom with rational control, the second with volitional control and the third with discursive control. These are the grand attractors, so I believe, in the turbulent debates to which the topic of freedom has given rise. I shall argue that each of the first two theories is inadequate as a theory of what makes for freedom in action, self and person and that the third is satisfactory on all counts. Then, with freedom identified as discursive control, I shall use the final three chapters of the book to explore its connection with collectivization, politicization and democratization.

From the free action to other freedoms

The theory of freedom as rational control takes its starting point from an account of free action, and then extends its analysis to the free self and the free person. It suggests that the first and basic question of freedom is what makes for a free action. And having identified the requirements of a free action, it then accounts for the free self and the free person on that basis. Someone will be a free self so far as they have the intrapersonal constitution that goes with free action, and someone will be a free person so far as they have the interpersonal status that free action requires.

The fact that it focuses on free action in the first place marks off the theory of freedom as rational control from the two main rivals that we shall be considering. The theory of freedom as volitional control starts from a focus on the notion of the free self, and later extends its analysis to the free action and the free person. And the theory of freedom as discursive control starts from a focus on the idea of the free person, extending its analysis later to the free action and the free self. More on those contrasts in the chapters that follow.

The theory of freedom as rational control says that an action is free just so far as it is an exercise of rational control or power on the part of the agent. In order to understand the theory, then, we need to have a sense of what such control or power involves.

Agents will enjoy rational control or power just so far as they operate properly as intentional subjects: that is, as subjects of intentional states like beliefs and desires. These states are intentional in the technical sense that they have an *intentio* or direction written into them: they are identified by reference to a state of affairs on which they are directed, as the belief or desire *that p*, *that q*, *that r* or whatever (Dennett 1987). What will it be, then, for people to operate properly as intentional subjects (Pettit 1993a, chapter 1)? I distinguish two aspects of the rational control involved.

The first aspect of rational control appears in the fact that depending on how his or her beliefs and desires go, the agent will act, now in this way, now in that. More specifically, the agent will do whatever it is rational to do in the light of the beliefs and desires that are present; they will act in a manner that, according to their beliefs, will tend to satisfy their desires (Stalnaker 1984). The agent will act, in other words, under the rational direction of their beliefs and desires. The agent will often produce responses like nervous tics and automatic reflexes, of course, that have nothing to do with rational action. But there will be a broad domain of behaviour over which their beliefs and desires will have dominion.

Not only will intentional agents act in a way that is rationally directed by their beliefs and desires. However they come to hold those beliefs and desires in the first place, they will be disposed to update them as new information requires. This is the second aspect of rational control. Let properly intentional agents be exposed to evidence that not-p and we will expect them to revise their belief that p. Let them be exposed to evidence of inconsistent desires and we will expect them to amend those desires. Let them be exposed to evidence that p, where they already believe that if p then q, and we will expect them to come to believe that q, or to revise one of their original beliefs. And so on.

The first aspect of rational control is action-related, the second evidence-related. The first requires the agent to act as their beliefs and desires rationally dictate and the second requires them to amend their beliefs and desires in the light of the evidence available, so that they do not embrace unsupported beliefs or unimplementable desires.

No one thinks that ordinary intentional subjects like you and me are going to be perfectly rational in these evidence-related and action-related ways. We all allow that there are unfavourable circumstances, however defined, in which the best of us don't do too well in these respects (Pettit 1999b). And we acknowledge that in any case there are limits to how rational a finite subject could ever be: say, to how far we can expect a finite subject to derive the implications of the things they already believe (Cherniak 1986). But it is pretty clear that, still, we regard rational control as something that we all want and that we all achieve in some measure.

The theory of freedom as rational control says that acting freely, and being a free self or a free person, amounts to nothing more or less than performing as a rational intentional subject in this way (Davidson 1980, Essay 4). However far rational control is achieved, to that extent – and only to that extent – freedom will be achieved also.

A theory of the free action

How does the theory of freedom as rational control do in elucidating its primary target, the notion of free action? The theory has determinate content in this area so far as it marks off the freely chosen action from a number of other possibilities. There are at least five salient contrasts.

The first and most obvious contrast is with the tic or the reflex – the blink or yawn or twitch – that has no claim at all to count as an action; it lacks the appropriate connection to beliefs and desires. This is not a case of the agent acting without rational control, and therefore unfreely, so much as a case of the agent doing something that is not a candidate for counting as free or unfree; it is a non-free response.

A second contrast is the response that is produced by beliefs and desires but not produced in the right way for action (Davidson 1980, Essay 4). Take the jabbing action with a putter that I produce by way of a nervous tic, as a result of coming to believe that the way to sink a desired putt is to jab at the ball. In such a case the beliefs and desires make jabbing rational, and produce the jabbing, but they do not do so in the right way for action. Roughly speaking, they do not produce the jabbing in virtue of being intentional states that make it rational; rather they produce it in virtue of being states that distract and unnerve me. This response, like the tic or the automatism, is not an action at all and counts as non-free rather than unfree.

A third contrast with the freely chosen action, under this theory, is the action that is produced non-intentionally. When I intentionally strike a ball with my tennis racquet, I may non-intentionally hit a bird in flight. Striking the ball and hitting the bird are one and the same action – so we may assume without begging any pertinent questions (Davidson 1980, Essays 6 and 8) – but the action is intentional under the first description and not under the second. It is clear from what we have said so far that such non-intentional actions will also contrast with free actions. They count as actions, unlike the other contrasts considered so far, but they do not count as freely chosen actions. The performance of such actions is not, as such, an exercise of rational control.

The fourth contrast with the free action, under this approach, is the action that is produced on the basis of attitudes that are irrationally held or that lead to action in an irrational way. It will have to be possible for an action to count as free, even if the agent is not perfectly rational; otherwise there would be no free actions at all. But at a certain level of shortfall, this theory will have to say that an action is too irrational to count as free. Thus it will tend to say that the compulsive or obsessive action, or the action that expresses a paranoid belief or pathological disposition, is not freely chosen.

The fifth and last contrast with the free action, on this theory of freedom as rational control, involves an action, A, that is produced on the basis of the agent's beliefs and desires, where there is no comparable alternative, B, such that had the agent's beliefs and desires rationalized it, they would have produced it instead. In this case the control of the agent's behaviour by his or her intentional states is not irrational, as in the previous case, but it is ineffective. The states have the capacity to lead to alternative A, if that is the one chosen; but they do not have the capacity to lead to any comparable alternative, B: their influence is suspended or frustrated in the event of the agent's not going for A.

This last contrast takes us back to the case where an agent is held responsible for doing A, even though he or she would have been forced or hypnotized or neuroscientifically induced to do A, had they not chosen to do it of their existing volition. In that case we said in the last chapter that the agent is fit to be held responsible, and is correspondingly free, only in relation to restricted possibilities: doing A of his or her existing volition or being manipulated into doing A; trying to do A or trying to do something else instead. That observation can be vindicated under the theory of freedom as rational control. The agent is not free to perform A rather than B, since the required rational control is lacking, but the agent is free to try to A rather than trying to B, having the lesser control required for this particular freedom.

The theory of freedom as rational control says that the free action, as distinct from any of these five sorts of antonyms, is an action that materializes under the rational control of the agent. It materializes in a rationally required way on the basis of rationally held beliefs and desires. But we now need to notice that in employing the notion of an action materializing under certain influences, this formulation is deliberately abstract and indeed ambiguous. There are two possible readings of what it is for a free action to materialize under the rational control of rationally held beliefs and desires. Under a narrower reading, the action must come about as an active causal result of the presence of those beliefs and desires. Under a broader reading, the action may also come about under the virtual influence of those states.

The narrower construal would say that free actions have got to be causally occasioned by the psychological states that come and go – rationally, as we suppose – in the agent's head. The idea is that if I act freely then it must be that I act as a causal result of what I am thinking: what I am believing and what I am desiring. And it must be that had I been thinking things that required a different response, then I would have been causally led by those beliefs and desires to perform a different action. The theory of the free action, construed in this narrow way, is relatively implausible, since it would mean that many of the actions I or anyone else performs are not free. For while I am certainly capable of forming beliefs and desires that cause me to do this or that, I very often act without engaging any such process. I act out of habit or inertia or impulse. I act, as we say, without thinking.

The broader construal of the theory of the free action avoids this problem and makes the theory that much more plausible. It begins from a distinction between active and virtual control and it argues that what free action requires is that rationally held beliefs and desires be in virtual control of the action, not necessarily in active control (Pettit 1995).

Let there be laws dictating what results should follow the appearance of certain controlling factors, C_1, C_2, and the like; call the results R_1, R_2, and so on. One way in which the C-factors may control the R-results is by each causing the required R-result to appear, when it itself is present. That is the standard or active mode of control. But another way in which the C-factors may control the R-results is this. The C-factors are generally followed by the corresponding R-results, on the basis of some independent or collateral causal order. But were a C-factor not to be followed by the corresponding result, or not to look likely to be followed by that result, then a corrective influence would put things right. This correction might come about, for example, through the C-factor itself becoming causally active in such a case, and triggering the result required by the relevant laws. Under any such scenario the C-factors will exercise control over the R-results, not just when they are activated in this exceptional way, but also when they remain in the background and have the status only of standby factors. The mode of control that they exercise from that background position is what I describe as virtual control.

Under the narrow construal of the rational control of free action the agent forms certain beliefs and desires and is causally led to act as they dictate; those psychological states control the free action in the active mode of control. But even in cases where there is no causal triggering of the action performed, the rationally held beliefs and desires of the agent may be in virtual control of what the agent does. And that is what the broad construal of the theory postulates.

The idea is that agents may often act out of habit or inertia or impulse, finding themselves in relatively familiar situations or exposed to relatively familiar prompts. The actions thereby performed may not be actively caused by any rationally held beliefs and desires. And yet it may be that they conform, and not just by accident, to such beliefs and desires. While the actions are performed under more or less automatic pilot, it may be that the agent would be alerted to any failure on the part of the spontaneously generated behaviour to satisfy the intentional states, and would be led by those states to adjust the behaviour appropriately. In such a case the rationally held beliefs and desires are not active causes that direct things this way or that, but standby causes that are ready to be activated in the event of things not going the way that they rationally require.

I shall assume in what follows that the theory according to which an action is free just so long as it is rationally controlled interprets control in the broad sense in which it may involve active or virtual control. The active–virtual distinction is not often drawn in explicit terms – it will be relevant to us again in a number of later discussions – but the point it encodes can occasionally be found in the relevant literature. A good example is provided by David Lewis (1983, 181).

> An action may be rational, and may be explained by the agent's beliefs and desires, even though that action was done by habit, and the agent gave no thought to the beliefs or desires which were his reasons for action. If that habit ever ceased to serve the agent's desires according to his beliefs, it would at once be overridden and corrected.

The problem with this theory of the free action

How plausible is it to say that free action should be equated with action that is rationally controlled in the way illustrated? Clearly, the presence of rational control, in the intended sense, ensures that suitable behaviours do indeed count as actions. But does such control ensure that suitable actions count as free or freely chosen?

By the concept of freedom developed in the last chapter, an action is free if and only if it is of a character that is consistent with the agent's being rightly held responsible for it; the action is responsibility-compatible. This means that an action is free if and only if it materializes in such a way that the agent is fit in that respect to be held fully responsible. But the fact that an action is rationally controlled does not ensure that that condition is fulfilled. And so an action may be rationally controlled without counting as free.

The executor of rationally controlled actions must hold beliefs and desires rationally, and must act in a way that they rationally require, at least in presumptively favourable conditions and within presumptively feasible limits. But this rational control is quite consistent with the agent's not having any beliefs to the effect, say, that this or that is what they ought to do and that they can be rightly held responsible for whether or not they conform to that evaluation. Thus it is quite consistent with the agent's being unfit to be held responsible for what is done. There may be no standards acknowledged or embraced by the agent and no standards to which they can be expected to answer.

Consider non-human animals, for example. They may well have beliefs and desires, and conform to certain standards of rationality, by the account of what rational control involves. But for all that rational control requires, these agents need not be capable of recognizing those standards of rationality, let alone capable of recognizing standards of any other kind: say, prudential or moral standards. The constraints of rationality that they must generally satisfy are articulated in philosophical theories of inferential rationality, evidence-related and action-related. But while being rationally controlled in the sense of the current theory, and conforming therefore to such standards, they may not be able to recognize the standards as such. They may rationally form beliefs and desires, and act rationally in the light of those beliefs and desires, and yet not have any beliefs about what it is to be rational, let alone any desire to be rational in that sense (Pettit 1993a, chapters 1 and 2; McGeer and Pettit 2001).

This line of thought shows that if an agent is fit to be held responsible then not only must their beliefs and desires constitute rational controls of what they do; the agent must also have evaluative beliefs to the effect that this or that is what is required of them, whether in rationality or in prudence or in morality, and they must have desires to live up to such evaluations. Only agents who are capable of recognizing and responding to standards in this way can be held responsible for what they do and can count as free or unfree. The controlling intentional states that operate in an agent who is fully fit to be held responsible in a given choice must be susceptible to the influence of the agent's recognizing – as the agent may be expected to be able to recognize – that one or another option accords or fails to accord with such standards.

I said earlier that the main conundrum of freedom, under its conceptualization in terms of fitness to be held responsible, is that responsibility is recursive. If an agent is responsible for a given action in virtue of its being controlled by certain beliefs or desires, then the agent must be responsible for those beliefs and desires in turn; and so on. The problem raised here is that we don't even get to first base in the recursion that responsibility appears to require. The beliefs and desires that are in control of action are not sufficient to ensure that the agent can be held responsible for the action, let alone for those states themselves. They need not include beliefs to do with standards of any kind or desires that such standards be satisfied. They need not constitute beliefs or desires in virtue of the presence of which the agent might count as fit to be held responsible.

How might the theory respond to this challenge? One of the most prominent defenders of freedom – certainly freedom in action – as intentional control is Donald Davidson, who sees himself as defending a line he associates with 'Hobbes, Locke, Hume, Moore, Schlick, Ayer, Stevenson, and a host of others' (Davidson 1980, Essay 4, 63). He would seem to offer a response to the challenge when he argues that believing and desiring are states such that to have any belief at all it is necessary to be able to have beliefs about beliefs, and about which beliefs are true, which false; it is necessary to have the concepts of belief and truth (Davidson 1984, Essay 11). Any subject with such beliefs and concepts would surely be able to form beliefs about rational constraints or standards and might be able to respond to the recognition that some action or proposed action is not what they ought in rationality – or ought in prudence or morality – to do. But the Davidsonian line on this issue amounts to dropping the theory of freedom as rational control – and departing from most of those in the long line with which he associates himself – in favour of the theory of freedom as discursive or ratiocinative control; the agent he imagines is capable, not just of being rational, but of reasoning. More on this in the fourth chapter.

Is there any other reply available to the theory of freedom as rational control? The only one I see is too rigged and artificial to have a lasting appeal. I am thinking of a response on these lines. Maybe the rationally controlled action is not actually susceptible to the influence of recognizing a relevant standard, since the subject cannot recognize any standards. But it is such that were the agent able to recognize standards of that kind – a remote hypothetical – then it would be suitably susceptible. This response says that maybe the free action is not responsibility-compatible, just as things are, but it is such that it would be responsibility-compatible in the fantastical event that the agent had certain extra capacities. I see little appeal, however, in this response. It suggests that an agent – say, a non-human animal – can be described as being able to respond to standards of a kind that it cannot even recognize. And the sense of 'able' presupposed in the suggestion is as silly as the sense presupposed in the old joke: 'Are you able to play the piano?'; 'I don't know, I've never tried'.

The theory as it applies to the free self

The theory of freedom as rational control starts with the question of freedom in action and, having provided an answer to that question, goes on to develop corresponding answers to the questions as to what makes for freedom in the self and freedom in the person. Someone may hold that freedom in action is indeed a matter of rational control, of course, without sticking by the theory of freedom as rational control in dealing with the free self and the free person. But I want to spell out the pure theory in all three areas – as I will do with the pure theories of freedom as volitional and freedom as discursive control – and I won't try to document the possibility of mixed approaches; in any case that exercise should prove fairly routine.

We have seen that the theory of freedom as rational control does not do well even in making sense of freedom in action, for it fails to ensure that the controllers of action are responsive to the agent's awareness – available awareness, as it must be – of the relevance of certain standards. But how does the theory do in making sense of the notion of the free self, as distinct from the free action?

It suggests that an agent will be a free self – a responsibility-compatible self – so far and only so far as they have the capacity for free action: that is, the capacity to exercise rational control in action. The presence of this capacity ensures that the agent's relationship to their own psychology – their intrapersonal constitution – will allow them to think in the first person of what they think and do and will allow us to hold them responsible for their actions. The self will not be cast in the role of a bystander who has to view the genesis of action as an alien process, welcome or unwelcome.

The theory of freedom as rational control scores well, at first sight, in securing the freedom of the self. Intuitively we all think that the worst enemies of a self's freedom is subjection to pathologies such as compulsion, obsession, paranoia, *idées fixes*, weakness of will, and the like. It is the presence of such factors that typically alienates a person from what they do and that leads us to question whether they are fit on this front to be held responsible. When the theory requires the free self to have the capacity to exercise rational control in action, it requires it to be rid of such forms of irrational fixation and fickleness. And if we equate the free self with a self that is rid of those particular pathologies then we may well conclude that the theory of freedom as rational control does very well indeed in making sense of freedom in the self.

The problem with the theory of the free self

But this is too hasty. The theory requires that beliefs and desires materialize and mutate according to certain rational constraints within the agent and issue in the actions that they rationalize. In other words, it requires that the process that unfolds in the agent's psychology will be of a certain type; in particular, it will not be marked by the influence of various pathologies. But why should the fact that the process is of one type rather than another mean that the self can identify with the process involved? For all that we have been told, the self may still have to see the process as something alien and imposed.

A theory of freedom in the self should not just identify the sort of control that we intuitively think of as friendly to such freedom. It should also make sense of why it is friendly in that way. It should explain why the agent who operates under such control will have little or no difficulty in identifying with what they think and do, assuming first-person responsibility for their actions. We intuitively equate the freedom of the self with the absence of rational pathologies and may be prematurely delighted to find that the theory of freedom as rational control secures that absence. But the theory should be expected to do more than this. It should also be able explain why that which it ensures — the absence of pathologies — can figure in our phenomenology as an experience of being free in ourselves: being in charge, in our own name.

Why should the agent whose beliefs and desires operate rationally and issue rationally in action be able to think of the process as one in which they are present as the author: as the self that can be held responsible for what is done? Pathologies are certainly phenomena that the agent can look on as impersonal events that do not involve them. But why shouldn't the same be true of the beliefs and desires that enjoy control in the rational agent? Why shouldn't the agent in whom beliefs and desires operate rationally still find themselves distanced from that process, and ill-equipped to assume responsibility for the actions to which it leads? The theory of freedom as rational control fails to address this question.

The failure of the theory is often hidden in the way in which its defenders choose to state it. A. J. Ayer (1982, 21) says that an agent is free in doing something when the action done is caused by beliefs and desires in the rational way but not when it is caused by 'constraining' factors such as the pathologies mentioned. But Ayer nowhere tries to explain what makes beliefs and desires unconstraining causes – causes, as we may put it, that are consistent with freedom in the self – while the pathologies mentioned are supposed to count as constraining causes that are inimical to such freedom. What is it about beliefs and desires which is supposed to ensure that their presence, unlike the presence of other influential factors, makes for freedom in the self? The theory of freedom as rational control has no answer.

The theory as it applies to the free person

The theory of freedom as rational control can be extended also to the free person. What it says in this area is that a person will be free so far, and only so far, as they relate to other persons in such a way that they retain rational control of their actions. The person is in rational charge of their actions, not anyone else. And having such control over one's behaviour is just what being a free person amounts to.

It is entirely plausible to say that the freedom of a person in relation to others involves nothing more or less than their retaining a certain basic sort of control. The freedom of the person requires that the crucial elements of control, whatever they are thought to be, are not lost to any other agent or collection of agents. It consists in the person being so related to their fellows that they can be held responsible for what they do. That responsibility is not removed in any measure from the agent by the role those others play in shaping what is done.

In this respect, the theory of freedom as rational control articulates the sort of thing that we ought indeed to expect a theory of freedom in the person to articulate. It says that a person will be free so far and only so far as their interpersonal relations allow them to retain a certain control of their actions. But, nevertheless, the theory is counter-intuitive. It may be right to associate the freedom of a person with their having a certain sort of control in relation to others but the control involved cannot be anything as simple as the rational control of action.

The problem with the theory of the free person

The failure of the theory becomes apparent when we ask about what freedom in the person requires of the way he or she is treated by others. For if it only requires that the person retain rational control over their actions, then it will be quite consistent with other people coercing them for their own ends, by threatening to impose certain costs on the choice of a particular option. Indeed it will be consistent with a range of intrusions – including various forms of manipulation and intimidation – that operate in the same way as a hostile threat.

The striking thing about hostile coercion – I shall concentrate here on coercion alone – is that it typically leaves the coerced individual with a choice, and with rational control over how that choice is to be made. It has the effect of raising the costs of taking the option which the intruder wants the person to avoid but it does not put that option altogether beyond the reach of the agent. Thus, when the robber says 'Your money or your life', you are still left with a decision; all that happens is that the option of keeping your money becomes extremely costly. And so under the theory of freedom as rational control, you will retain your freedom in such a case.

The environment for the exercise of rational control becomes less friendly in this situation, of course, since keeping your life and keeping your money are alternatives that are no longer available on easy terms. But the freedom of the agent as such, where this is understood as rational control, is not compromised by such a worsening in the options faced by the agent. It would only be compromised if the options disappeared altogether, as in suffering obstruction or force.

I take this tolerance of coercion to be so counter-intuitive that the theory of freedom as rational control has to be deemed an inadequate account of freedom in the person. In some cases coercion may seem to be consistent with freedom, as the obstruction practised by Ulysses' sailors in keeping him bound to the mast is consistent with his freedom; in keeping him bound, the sailors are guided by what they take to be his real, and indeed his avowed, interests. But in most cases coercion is hostile to the avowed interests of the coercees and is intuitively inconsistent with their freedom as persons.

This intuition of inconsistency is supported by the fact that in cases where people are coerced in this way we tend not to hold them fully responsible for what they did. We may think that they could have resisted the threat in question but we will not think that they were fully fit to be held responsible; how fit they were will depend on how credible and how challenging the threat in question was. We may think that responsibility for what was done rests as much with the coercer as with the coercee but we will in any case think that the coercee's responsibility is mitigated or reduced.

It may seem that in extending the theory of freedom as rational control from free action to freedom in the person, I am constructing a theory of the free person that no one endorses. But that is not so. A famous defence of the view is provided by Thomas Hobbes (1968, 146) when he equates freedom in the strict sense with 'corporall liberty' rather than 'civil liberty' and says that for any subject such liberty 'consisteth in this, that he finds no stop, in doing what he has the will, desire, or inclination to doe'. This view leads him to say that the coercive threat of punishment, while it may deprive a person of civil liberty, does not take away natural or corporal liberty; it does not put a stop to choice. Even if one is subject to the intense coercion experienced by a slave, one can still be free in the strict sense. 'I find no reason for a *slave* to complain on the ground that he lacks *liberty*' (Hobbes 1998, 111).

The Hobbesian view has recently attracted the support of a very ingenious group of defenders (Taylor 1982; Gorr 1989; Steiner 1994; Carter 1999). They argue that, strictly speaking, coercion and related intrusions do not take away a person's freedom. Stressing the fact that where I have rational control of a choice, I am free, they maintain that it is only the removal or prevention of options that can reduce my freedom and ultimately render me unfree. They hold that this is the most straightforward line to take and that it has the great advantage of facilitating the measurement of freedom across individuals and groups.

Whatever those advantages, however, I find it entirely counterintuitive to say that coercing someone in a choice between A and B leaves the freedom of that choice unaffected. Ian Carter (1999, 224–33) points out that faced with the threat 'Your money or your life' I lose out in freedom overall, even if my freedom to give or keep the money is unimpaired; I lose the freedom, if the threat is sincere, to keep my money and go on living. But this observation does not really help. As Carter himself mentions, I do not lose out in overall freedom when the threat is a bluff, or when the threat is to someone that I care about. Yet in such situations my freedom is reduced in intuitively the same manner as with a sincere threat to my own person.

The necessity of rational control

We have seen that the presence of rational control is not sufficient to ensure freedom of action, freedom of the self or freedom of the person. But that leaves the question as to whether a satisfactory degree of rational control is perhaps necessary for freedom. I shall assume that it is. Being fit to be held responsible may not consist just in being subject to rational control, as we have argued in this chapter. But being fit to be held responsible does seem to presuppose that there is a satisfactory measure of rational control in place. It is hard to see how we could regard an agent as fit to be held responsible in any choice, or fit in general to be held responsible for choices, if they were not possessed of such a measure of rational control.

The theories of freedom to be considered in the next two chapters both uphold this intuition. The volitional control and the discursive control with which they respectively associate freedom presuppose rational control in the sense explored here. Strictly speaking, then, the first is a theory of freedom as rational-cum-volitional control, and the second a theory of freedom as rational-cum-discursive control.

The fact that by all the accounts offered, rational control is an element in the capacity that makes for freedom means that the discussion of this chapter has not been entirely of negative significance. The chapter serves, not just to knock out a familiar theory of freedom, but also to put in place one important element that must be recognized by any plausible alternative.

Conclusion

If freedom is to be conceptualized as fitness to be held responsible, then that raises the question as to what sort of capacity can make an agent free in this sense. That is the question addressed by different theories of freedom and we look in this and in the next two chapters at the main contenders.

The theory addressed in this chapter says that freedom is essentially tied up with the exercise of rational control. It defines the free action as any action that is rationally controlled by rationally held beliefs and desires. It says that someone will be a free self so far as they have the intrapersonal capacity for free action. And it holds that someone will be a free person so far as they have the interpersonal status required for free action: their relations to other people leave them in rational control of what they do.

We criticized the theory as it applies in each of these areas, starting from the assumption that freedom is fitness to be held responsible. The rationally controlled action need not be one for which the agent can be held responsible, since the rationally controlling agent may lack the concepts presupposed to being held responsible; the agent may even be a simple, non-human animal. The agent with the intrapersonal capacity for rational control of their actions will not be bedevilled by the usual psychological blocks to responsibility but it is not clear why they will be enabled thereby to see themselves as the author of what occurs in their psychology: as the self responsible for it. And the agent with the interpersonal standing required for rational control of their choices will not, just on that account, meet the intuitive requirements for personal freedom and responsibility. Having such control is consistent with suffering hostile coercion and by almost all accounts such coercion reduces an agent's freedom as a person.

But however far the theory fails to show that rational control is sufficient for freedom of action, self or person, it does plausibly identify a necessary condition for such freedom. This necessity claim is built into the other two theories we shall be considering.

3

Freedom as Volitional Control

From the free self to other freedoms

The theory of freedom as rational control is in the first place a theory of the free action and it generalizes from there to become also a theory of the free self and the free person. The theory of freedom as volitional control is a theory of the free self in the first place and generalizes in similar fashion to become a theory of the free action and the free person. The same pattern is maintained, indeed, with the theory of freedom as discursive control, as we shall see in the next chapter. It begins as a theory of the free person and is developed later as a theory of the free action and the free self.

We saw in the last chapter that the theory of freedom as rational control fails to give us a persuasive sense of how a self comes to be free. A self will be free so far as there is nothing about the psychology of the agent in virtue of which they are distanced from what they want or think or do, and have to look on those attitudes and actions like a helpless bystander. The scenario in which the agent is a helpless bystander of his or her own psychology is precisely a scenario where we must think that it is inappropriate to hold them properly responsible. Bystanders are observers of what unfolds before them, not its authors, and it is inappropriate to hold observers responsible for the occurrences they observe. Yet the bystander scenario, so it appeared, is fully consistent with the presence of rational control.

The theory of freedom as volitional control begins with this problem. The idea is that if an agent enjoys volitional as well as rational control of what they do, then there is no question of that agent being alienated from their doings; there is no prospect of the agent's having to view the process and the product of their psychology as if it involved an impersonal sequence in which they had little or no part. This being so, the theory proposes that it is volitional control – strictly rational-cum-volitional control – that constitutes an agent's fitness to be held responsible and so an agent's freedom.

The philosopher who has done most in recent times to give currency to the notion of volitional control – freedom of the will, as he puts it – is Harry Frankfurt (1988; 1999) and it is only right that we focus in this chapter on his work. But it is important to remember that while Frankfurt constructs the notion of volitional control that we shall be discussing, he does not put it to the use we envisage for it here. For him, being free involves being able to own what one does, and he argues that volitional control gives an agent such ownership. For us, being free involves being fit to be held responsible for what one does, and the theory to be examined suggests that volitional control gives an agent such fitness. Thus the points we make in explication and evaluation of that theory do not necessarily engage with Frankfurt's own views, especially with his distinctive views on how far the ownership and freedom that volitional control ensures – as he thinks – connects with responsibility. The chapter should not be read as a dialogue with Frankfurt himself, but rather with a theory that his notion of volitional control helps us to construct.

A theory of the free self

The first step towards the theory of freedom as volitional control – in particular, towards this theory of the free self – is the observation that the bystander problem arises when the action taken by an agent fails, intuitively, to represent his or her free will. It may express the agent's desires, and it may even be subject to full rational control, but so long as it does not answer to the agent's free will it cannot count as fully free. Agents will be unable to identify with what occurs within them, or with what materializes by their hands. What takes place will materialize without the endorsement of their will or perhaps even against that will (Frankfurt 1988, 12).

This gloss is intuitive and plausible, since we often say that certain desires and responses occur against an agent's free will, without the agent's identifying with them. But the gloss is 'analytically puzzling', in Frankfurt's (1988, 18) own expression. For what does it mean to say that an agent does something without their free will being in it, or does something against their free will? What does it mean to say that the agent fails to identify with the desire or the action in question?

There are different views that might be developed in response to this challenge for clarification and they will generate different versions of the theory of freedom as volitional control. Some will go with traditional Aristotelian and Thomistic notions of deliberative control (Stump 1996; 1997), others with Kantian ideas of autonomous agency (Korsgaard 1996; 1999), others with existentialist images of the self-determining consciousness (Sartre 1958), and others still with the concept of agency-causation popularized by Roderick Chisholm (1982). In this chapter, however, we will consider only the version that is found in Frankfurt's own work, which is closely related to one developed independently by Gerald Dworkin (1970; 1988). It has the advantage of being well known, relatively unmysterious and not necessarily inconsistent with naturalism.

Frankfurt's idea is that agents will identify with an action, A, seeing it as representing their free will, to the extent that they have 'a second-order volition' to do A. And they will have such a volition to do A, he says, so far as they want to be controlled by the desire to A; they want it to be the desire that moves them effectively to act (Frankfurt 1988, 15).

In introducing this analysis of volitional control, Frankfurt deploys two distinct ideas. The first is that free agents are all capable of having, not just first-order desires to do this or that, but also second-order desires to have first-order desires of one kind or another. Second-order desires are desires which, as a matter of syntax, can only be specified by mention of other desires; first-order desires are desires of which this is not true. The second idea mobilized in the account is that among an agent's second-order desires may be a desire that he or she be effectively moved by a certain first-order desire: that that first-order desire, as Frankfurt also says, be their will. This distinguishes those second-order desires that count as second-order volitions from more idle second-order desires: from desires just to have and experience certain first-order desires, but not necessarily to be moved by them to action.

Frankfurt claims that so far as agents meet the condition of acting according to their second-order volitions, to that extent they can be said to will what happens and to identify fully with it; to that extent they will each avoid onlooker status and be a free self that is fully implicated in what they author. He sees a number of ways in which agents may fail, as I put it, to be a free self. One is by not having any capacity at all to form second-order desires; this is the way non-human animals will fail to be free selves. Another way is by having such a capacity but by not being able to form second-order volitions; such an agent will be a 'wanton', as Frankfurt puts it, not a person properly speaking. And yet another is by having a capacity for second-order volitions but by not succeeding in exercising that capacity in this or that situation.

There are two ways, in turn, in which people may not succeed in exercising this capacity for second-order volition in a particular situation. One is the case where one finds oneself unable to act in accordance with one's actual volition: this, as in the case of the unwilling drug-addict. And the other is the case where one acts in accordance with one's actual volition – say, in the fashion of the willing drug-addict – but one would not be able to act in accordance with one's volition, did one will otherwise: did one try to reject drug-taking, for example. Here the agent may act freely in taking the drug, as we would intuitively say, but he lacks volitional control or, as Frankfurt himself puts it, freedom of the will.

The fact that Frankfurt sees willing addicts as lacking volitional control shows that he thinks of volitional control on lines that parallel the notion of rational control explicated in the last chapter. Rational control requires that the agent is disposed to form beliefs and desires in a rational pattern and is disposed, whatever those beliefs and desires should be, to act as they rationally require. Volitional control requires that the agent is disposed to form certain higher-order volitions in regard to what they do and is disposed, whatever those volitions should be, to act as they require. Willing addicts are not in volitional control because the higher-order volition not to take drugs – a volition that they might form, even if they do not currently do so – would not be effective if it materialized; it would be blocked by the person's addiction. 'A person's will is free only if he is free to have the will he wants. This means that, with regard to any of his first-order desires, he is free either to make that desire his will or to make some other first-order desire his will instead' (Frankfurt 1988, 24).

Not only does Frankfurt model volitional control on lines that parallel our account of rational control. He thinks that freedom requires rational control – or at least something close to rational control – as well as volitional control: 'it is only in virtue of his rational capacities that a person is capable of becoming critically aware of his own will and of forming volitions of the second order. The structure of a person's will presupposes, accordingly, that he is a rational being' (Frankfurt 1988, 17; cf. 22–3). I propose to construe the theory of volitional control, in the spirit of this passage, as a theory of rational-cum-volitional control. Rational control may not be sufficient for freedom of the action, the self, or the person, as we saw in the last chapter, but it is intuitively necessary for responsibility and freedom, and the current theory honours that claim.

Adding the requirement of volitional control to rational control, as we are taking the theory to do, is neither a redundant nor a troublesome move. It is not redundant, because being in rational control does not entail being in volitional control: after all, non-human animals and human wantons may enjoy rational control without volitional control. It is not troublesome, because being in volitional control is quite consistent with being in rational control; it merely requires that a particular subset of the agent's desires – higher-order desires to be effectively moved by certain first-order desires – are stronger than others.

Frankfurt does not make the distinction drawn in the last chapter between active and virtual modes of control, though talk of being effectively moved by this or that desire certainly suggests that he often has active control in mind. It is possible to interpret the theory of freedom as volitional control, however, with control being understood in the broad sense in which it may be either active or virtual and while I shall not comment further on the matter, that is how I shall take it here. The criticisms I make of the theory apply even when we allow both that higher-order desires may control lower-order only in the virtual way and that they may be desires to be effectively moved by the lower-order desires only in the sense in which such movement can involve active or virtual control.

The problem with this theory of the free self

Does the addition of volitional to rational control see us beyond the problem of the free self? Does it ensure that the self of the agent will be able to identify with what transpires, recognizing its own signature in the things that the agent desires and does? Does it guarantee that those desires and those doings will implicate the will of the agent in such a way that there is no question about the agent's being their author, and there is no doubt on that score about the propriety of holding the agent responsible? I do not think so.

The problem with the theory, on which many commentators have remarked, is that it gives an arbitrary blessing to desires of the second order, in particular to those desires that count as second-order volitions (see for example Watson 1982; Velleman 1992). If my first-order desires, just as such, are phenomena that I can view as an onlooker or bystander, without being implicated as an author, why can't the same be true of my second-order volitions? Why can't I find myself in the same impasse in relation to them?[1]

Consider the difference between having a first-order desire to do something, A, and having a second-order desire to be effectively moved by the desire to do A. It is admitted with the desire to do A that I may have to look on it in the fashion of a bystander or onlooker as a force that operates within me but doesn't emanate from me. But why isn't the same possibility going to threaten the second-order desire to be effectively moved by the desire to do A?

Let the action of doing A be that of keeping my desk clean. And let it be admitted that I might have to treat this as an alien compulsion by which I find myself sometimes assailed; I might fail to identify with it and make it my will. But suppose now that I have a second-order desire to be effectively moved by this desire to clean my desk. Does that mean that I must thereby identify with the desire to clean the desk, and make it my will?

I think not. For imagine that I conceive of that second-order desire as a drive that comes to me from childhood drilling in the Victorian principle that cleanliness is next to godliness. And imagine that I distance myself from that second-order desire, recognizing it for what it is: an unwelcome inheritance from a past that I view with disapproval. The presence of such a second-order desire – such a second-order volition, as it is – cannot lead me to identify with the first-order

---

[1] This problem as to what is so special about second-order volition is not the problem as to why it isn't necessary to have higher-order identifications as well as a second-order identification. Frankfurt deals with that other problem when he argues that if I identify myself in a second-order desire with a first-order desire to do A, then that identification will echo up through any higher-order desires I may have: I will not only want to want to be moved effectively to do A; I will find myself disposed to want to want to want to be moved effectively to do A, and so on. 'When a person identifies himself *decisively* with one of his first-order desires, this commitment "resounds" throughout the potentially endless array of higher orders' (Frankfurt 1988, 21; 168–9). Nor does the problem raised amount to the question as to why I shouldn't fail to achieve identification at the second level, being pushed up to the third, and why I shouldn't then fail at every subsequent level, being always pushed to a further one. Frankfurt addresses that question in the following remark. 'There is no theoretical limit to the length of the series of desires of higher and higher orders; nothing except common sense and, perhaps, a saving fatigue prevents an individual from obsessively refusing to identify himself with any of his desires until he forms a desire of the next higher order. The tendency to generate such a series of acts of forming desires, which would be a case of humanization run wild, also leads towards the destruction of a person' (Frankfurt 1988, 21; cf. Frankfurt 1999, 104).

desire that it favours, treating that desire as my will. It will leave me at just the same distance from myself that the experience of the original compulsion may have left me.

In response to this line of thought, defenders of the theory of freedom as volitional control might observe that the very description of the case so far presupposes that there is a certain level at which I have desires that I do not treat as alien in the fashion of the desire to keep my desk clean, or the desire to be effectively moved by that desire. In the scenario described I am distanced from those desires in virtue of disapproving of compulsiveness and puritanism. And that must mean, they might point out, that there is a still higher level of desire from which I view those lower-level ones with disapproval. But if I view those lower-level desires with disapproval from the perspective of that still higher level, then presumably that higher level is the level where identification potentially begins. It is on the basis of the desires at that level that I can identify myself with certain lower-level desires – distancing myself from others – and thereby hope to make them my will.

Following on this observation, defenders of the theory of freedom as volitional control will deny that volitional control begins at the first level where the agent forms desires to be effectively moved by lower-level desires. They will say that it begins rather at the first level where the volitional desires formed are not themselves viewed with detachment from any higher level. The level from which identification begins, then, will be taken to satisfy a dual condition: first, that the agent forms desires there to be effectively moved by lower-level desires; and second, that the agent does not form any higher-level desires not to be moved by those desires.

Frankfurt himself seems to have moved towards this sort of view in recent writing. 'On hierarchical accounts, a person identifies with one rather than with another of his own desires by virtue of wanting to be moved to action by the first desire rather than by the second . . . But what determines whether he identifies with this second-order preference? . . . The mere fact that it is a second-order desire surely gives it no particular authority . . . The endorsing higher-order desire must be, in addition, a desire with which the person is *satisfied*' (Frankfurt 1999, 105). Such satisfaction with a higher-order desire, it transpires, is to be understood in a wholly negative way. 'Satisfaction is a state of the entire psychic system – a state constituted just by the absence of any tendency or inclination to alter its condition' (Frankfurt 1999, 104).

Does the theory, as amended on these lines, point us to a good account of when an agent is a free self: that is, someone whose psychology ensures that he or she identifies with what they do, making it their will, and someone who is fit on that account to be held responsible for their doings? I do not think so. Imagine that the desire to be effectively moved by a desire to keep my desk clean is present in me, without my having any higher-level desires in virtue of which I disapprove of that volition. That does not yet mean, intuitively, that I identify with the desire to keep my desk clean, and make it my will. For consistently with not disapproving of the volition – that is, consistently with not disapproving of the second-order desire to be effectively moved by the desire to keep my desk clean – I might not approve of it either. I might look on it, precisely, as an indifferent bystander.

The fact is that I may adopt any of three positions, not just two, in relation to a second-order volition. I may approve of it, I may disapprove of it, and I may fail either to approve or disapprove. The original theory suggested that no matter what position I adopt, the second-order desire will initiate identification and that seems clearly wrong. The amended theory suggests that if I fail to approve or disapprove then in that case the second-order desire will initiate identification. But that also seems wrong, since a failure to approve of the second-order desire in question would suggest that I will view the first-order desire that it endorses as an indifferent bystander. I will not think of it as a desire that counters my free will, but neither will I think of it as a desire that answers to my free will. It will present itself as a more or less impersonal event, not as something that I properly own.

Can defenders amend the theory of freedom as volitional control in the direction that this critique suggests? Can they say that identification begins at the first level where there is a desire to be effectively moved by lower-level desires and where that desire enjoys the active approval of the agent? Alas, no. For such a theory will explain identification with desire only on the basis of assuming that there is a prior, unexplained sort of identification with the approval postulated. It will explain why I identify with the desire to A, whatever that is, by saying that there is a desire to be effectively moved by the desire to A present in me and that I approve of the presence of that desire. But if there is a problem about what is involved in identifying with a desire, making it into my will, there is a similar problem about what is involved in identifying with an act of approval, making it into my point of view on the world. For why should I not find an act of approval occurring within me, without being able to identify with it? Why should I not have to look on that act of approval in a bystander mode?

I conclude that while the theory of freedom as volitional control starts from a serious problem in the account of the free self that is given by the theory of freedom as rational control, it fails ultimately to resolve that problem. We need to be able to explain what is required for an agent to have a free self: what is required for the agent to be implicated as author in the things he or she desires and does. Otherwise we will not be able to specify the conditions under which an agent is fit, on this account, to be held responsible. But the theory of freedom as volitional control, at least in the versions that start from Frankfurt's pioneering observation, does not promise us any satisfactory resolution.

The theory as it applies to the free action

Although it starts out as a theory of the free self, the theory of freedom as volitional control also points us towards a view of what makes for the freedom of a free action and the freedom of a free person. Or at least that is the comprehensive way in which I take it here.

As a theory of action, it requires that the free action should be subject, not just to rational control, but also to volitional. The action that is controlled by the agent's beliefs and desires, but without the volitional blessing of the agent, cannot be regarded as properly free on this account. What is required in addition is that the desires that control it are desires with which the agent identifies in the appropriate sense; desires that the agent wants to be effective in producing that action.

This theory is similar to the theory of free action described in the last section. It takes the free action to be free in virtue of the sort of control exercised by certain antecedents. The action must be rationally controlled by rationally held beliefs and desires, as in the earlier theory. Specifically, it must be rationally controlled by rationally held beliefs and desires that conform to the volitional requirement, the desires being ones that the agent wants to be effective.

The idea behind both approaches is that there are certain controlling factors such that if they are in control of an action, then the action is free; and if they are not in control of the action, then it is not free. The freedom-favouring antecedents are unconstraining factors, as Ayer (1982, 21) would put it; the freedom-removing antecedents are constraining ones. While the first theory suggests that their being rational controls is enough to make certain antecedents unconstraining, this second theory says that they must be both rational and volitional controls.

The problem with this theory of the free action

Apart from the problem with explicating the notion of volitional control, which we have discussed in relation to the free self, this theory of free action faces a problem that is continuous with the problem raised for the theory of freedom as rational control. The problem is that in order for the controllers of an action to make it intuitively free, they must be responsive to standards that the agent endorses: they must be responsive to the agent's sense of what he or she ought to do. Or at least this must be so within presumptively feasible limits and under presumptively favourable circumstances.

Neither rational nor rational-cum-volitional controllers look capable of satisfying this condition. The problem with the theory of freedom as rational control was that it does not require that the agents of free acts be capable of endorsing any standards, let alone capable of applying them and responding to them. The non-human animal may act in a way that is rationally controlled, for example, yet such an animal need not be capable of forming beliefs about matters as abstract as standards that bear on what it does; it need not be capable of forming beliefs as to what it ought to do, whether in rationality or prudence or morality.

The theory of freedom as volitional control avoids this problem to the extent that the higher-order volitions of agents can be treated as giving standards to which they hold themselves, and to which we might hold them at a second remove. Such higher-order volitions are self-addressed prescriptions of a kind that non-human animals almost certainly do not display (Frankfurt 1988, 16). Let us favour the theory by assuming that to be fit to be held responsible involves, at base, being fit to be held to such higher-order volitions. The question to be raised, then, is whether the theory thereby allows the controllers of action to be suitably responsive to standards that the agent endorses.

At one level it does seem that the theory meets this constraint satisfactorily. Taking the immediate controllers of action to be the agent's lower-level beliefs and desires, it postulates that they make an action free only so far as they are themselves responsive to higher-order volitions. The action would have been different had the volitions been suitably different and a variation of volitions is indeed within the agent's reach: 'with regard to any of his first-order desires, he is free either to make that desire his will or to make some other first-order desire his will instead' (Frankfurt 1988, 24). In that sense the beliefs and desires that the theory sees in control of free action are themselves subject to the control of higher-order volitions. We can think of the agent as being fit to be held responsible for what they ought to do, by the lights of those higher-order states.

But, unfortunately for the theory, things do not stop there. Responsibility is recursive, as we saw earlier, in the sense that if you are fit to be held responsible for a given choice, say between doing A and doing B, in virtue of holding by certain beliefs and desires, then you must be fit to be held responsible for those beliefs and desires in turn; and so on. You cannot be responsible for something in virtue of the operation of a factor for which you are not also responsible. Responsibility is inherently recursive in nature.

According to the current theory a person will be fit to be held responsible for certain actions in virtue of having higher-order volitions – if you like, self-prescriptions – that play a controlling role in shaping their behaviour. The recursive character of responsibility means, then, that they must be fit to be held responsible in turn for those higher-order volitions. And the problem is that nothing in the theory explains how that is going to be ensured. Nothing in the theory of freedom as volitional control suggests that you must be fit to be held responsible for higher-order volitions.

You will be fit to be held responsible for such volitions, only so far as there are further standards available to which you are responsive: only so far as you recognize and respond to a sense of ought that bears in turn on the volitions. But no such further standards need to be available under the theory we are considering. For all that the theory says, higher-order volitions may represent brute givens about which you, as an agent, can do nothing. They may be the unmoved movers of the system; or at least they may not be moveable in the manner that we might expect a responsible agent to be able to move them. It may be that the standards associated with the volitions are standards to which you are a slave, being incapable of finding a standpoint from which to assess or try to alter them.

This shows, I think, that volitional control as it is conceptualized by Frankfurt cannot possibly claim to realize all that is necessary for an agent to be fit to be held responsible in a choice. The presence of rational control would be insufficient for such fitness, because it would be consistent with the agent's having no sense of ought whatsoever. The presence of volitional control would be insufficient, because it would be consistent with the agent's having no sense of ought in relation to their volition or will. Volitions might serve to shape the controllers of action – ground-level beliefs and desires – but they would not themselves be subject to the sort of control required for fitness to be held responsible.

It is worth noting, in concluding this discussion, that the failure of volitional control to vindicate the connotation of responsibility does not mean that it will fail to vindicate the connotation of ownership, however that is construed. This is important because, in fairness to Frankfurt, he thinks of freedom as ownership and uses the idea of volitional control to explicate what ownership requires. I have nothing to say here on how far his project succeeds. The argument of the first chapter, which should be supported by the larger appeal of the position maintained in this book – if indeed it is appealing – is that freedom should be conceptualized as fitness to be held responsible. My focus in this chapter has been on how far the theory of freedom as volitional control can make sense of freedom in that sense, not on how far it can make sense of freedom in the sense of ownership.

The theory as it applies to the free person

Although it is developed in the first place as a theory of the free self, the theory of freedom as volitional control extends to give us a theory of the free person, as it extends to give us a theory of the free action.

Under the responsibility perspective, we conceive of free persons as agents whose relations to others are compatible with our generally holding them responsible for the things they do. What makes someone's status in relation to others compatible in this way with responsibility? The theory of freedom as volitional control has a simple answer. It says that agents will be free persons so far as their relations with others are consistent with their being free selves: that is, are consistent with their enjoying rational-cum-volitional control of what they do.

This view of the free person is directly analogous to that which is yielded by the theory of freedom as rational control. Under that theory, as we saw in the last chapter, agents are said to be free persons so far as their interpersonal standing is consistent with their exercising rational control over what they do. Under the present theory they are said to be free persons so far as their interpersonal standing is consistent with their exercising rational-cum-volitional control.

We said in defence of the earlier theory that at least it seems to get things on the right general lines. We may say the same thing in support of this. Intuitively, we think of persons as free so far as they enjoy a certain control in relation to one another. And that intuition is borne out in both approaches.

The problem with the theory of the free person

But that is where praise must end. For this theory of the free person, like its predecessor, is subject to a salient line of objection. It has the deeply counter-intuitive implication that even hostile coercion should not count as an offence against the freedom of the person. Hostile coercion is consistent with the agent's retaining rational-cum-volitional control of what they do and so, by the lights of the current theory, it does not take freedom away.

People are coerced, roughly speaking, when they are subject to threats of penalty in the event of taking or not taking something that is currently available as an option. People are coerced in a hostile way, when the threats are not dictated by the avowed or at least the avowable – the ready-to-be-avowed – interests of the coercee: say, the sorts of interests that dictate how his sailors treat Ulysses. Such coercion is distinguished from downright obstruction by the fact that the people coerced, unlike those obstructed, do still retain their original choice, say between doing A or doing B. All that has changed is the array of costs that they face; the threat means that one or other option is likely to be more costly than it would otherwise have been.

Because they retain the original choice, people who are coerced are still in a position to exercise rational and also volitional control. They are in a position where they can act in a way that answers to the beliefs and desires relevant to the situation and, in particular, where they can act in fidelity to their higher-order desires as to what lower-order desires should effectively move them there. Thus my higher-order volition in regard to a situation where I am threatened with a physical beating unless I hand over my money may be that I do not get angry and defiant but rather give up my cash. And I will act under volitional control so far as I manage to bring my lower-level motivation, and my behaviour, in line with that volition.

The fact that the theory of freedom as volitional control can find no fault with coercion and the like, even when it is of a hostile complexion, is a telling objection. It leaves adherents of the theory in a position where they have to defend something close, intuitively, to the indefensible. What, then, are they likely to say in reply?

Frankfurt (1988, 39) speculates at one point that the sort of coercion that reduces freedom has to make compliance psychologically irresistible, as in triggering a morbid fear. This suggests that he may want to take the view – adopted, as we saw, by some defenders of freedom as rational control – that the coercive threat that merely raises the expected costs of doing something does not reduce freedom, properly speaking. But what he says later shows that that is not so, for he goes on to offer an argument for why coercion reduces freedom as volitional control that would apply even in the case of ordinary cost-raising coercion. He proves himself keen on being able to resist the criticism made here and to hold that volitional control – and so, freedom as volitional control – is reduced by regular, hostile coercion.

Frankfurt (1988, 44) argues, to be specific, that the successful act of coercion in which the victim submits to a threat does indeed reduce the agent's volitional control. He maintains that 'a person who submits to (and who does not merely comply with) a threat necessarily does so in order to avoid a penalty'. And he argues, on that basis, that 'a person's motive when he submits to a threat is one by which he would prefer not to be moved': 'he would prefer to have a different motive for acting'. It appears, then, that the person who submits to a threat necessarily acts against the higher-order volition not to be moved by a desire to avoid such threats and that the coercion involved in the imposition of that threat takes away their volitional control.

This argument does not work, however, because it slides between two senses in which it may be true that a person does not want to be moved by a certain first-order desire or motive. If I am coerced into giving a robber my money by the threat of being beaten up, then there is a sense in which I would prefer not to be moved by the motive in question. I would prefer not to be in the situation that triggers the desire to avoid the threatened penalty; I would prefer not to have to be moved by that motive. But that this is so is consistent with another sense in which I may prefer to be moved by the motive. I may well prefer, being in the situation in question, to be moved by the desire to avoid the penalty and not to let myself be physically assaulted.

It should be clear that volitional control requires, not that the situations in which I find myself answer to my higher-order desires – that would amount to fortune, not freedom – but rather that the things I do in the situations in which I find myself answer to those desires. In arguing that the theory of freedom as volitional control rules out certain forms of coercion, Frankfurt takes volitional control in the inappropriate fortune-related way, not in the way he ought to have taken it. We can understand the wish to be able to say that coercion of a certain kind diminishes the freedom of the person, under his theory. But we can hardly endorse this attempt to argue that it does.

The necessity of volitional control, properly understood

We saw in the discussion of the free self that we can think of certain higher-order desires as volitions proper only so far as two conditions are fulfilled. First, they are desires to be effectively moved by lower-level desires, as in Frankfurt's original formulation. And second, they are desires that bear the agent's active stamp of approval. We complained that the theory of freedom as volitional control fails to explain what is involved in an agent's approving of certain higher-order desires and that it is in this way a failure.

Assuming that such an explanation can be provided, however – and the assumption will be defended in the next chapter – we can retain the notion of volitional control in its amended form. And to the extent that we do that, the question arises as to whether volitional control is necessary for freedom of action, self and person. I said in the first chapter that while rational control was not sufficient for freedom of action, self or person, it did have a good claim to be necessary. I think that something similar holds of volitional control, properly understood.

The claim of volitional control in this regard rests squarely on intuition. We could hardly think that an action, self or person was fit to be held responsible if the things that the agent did flouted some volitions that they had formed. Assume that an agent has higher-order volitions in regard to certain desires or doings. If those desires or doings went counter to such volitions, then it would be hard to think of the agent as anything other than an arena where certain responses are centred. This intuition does not suggest that an agent's desires and doings must all be controlled by higher-order volitions, only that when there are higher-order volitions in place then they must play a controlling role. And that intuition is very hard to resist.

Conclusion

The results of this and the last chapter are remarkably convergent. We have seen in each case that the sort of control under discussion is intuitively necessary for freedom. And we have argued that for almost exactly parallel reasons it is not sufficient.

Rational control is not sufficient to make an action free, because it is consistent with agents recognizing no standards to which they can be held responsible in action. Volitional control is not sufficient to make an action free, because it is consistent with agents recognizing no standards to which they can be held responsible in volition. We may be able to hold them to the sense of ought provided by their higher-order volitions but the agents need have no sense of ought that bears in turn on those volitions. The volitions may lie beyond their control and beyond the sphere in which they can be held responsible.

Rational control is not sufficient for freedom of the self, because it is consistent with the self looking on its desires and actions as a bystander, not as an author. Volitional control is not sufficient for freedom of the self because, nothwithstanding the higher-order volitions that it introduces in control of desires and actions, it ultimately fails to ensure against these volitions being themselves matters that the self has to look on as a bystander; they may be desires that attract only the disapproval or indifference of the agent.

Rational control is not sufficient for freedom of the person, because it is consistent with the agent's submitting to coercive threats from others. Volitional control is not sufficient for freedom of the person for exactly the same reason, and notwithstanding the argument in Frankfurt that would seem to prove otherwise. In submitting to the coercive threats of another, agents may be acting out of a desire that they desire to be moved by in that situation – say, a desire to pay the robber and avoid a beating. And that can be true, even if they would prefer not to find themselves in such situations.

4

Freedom as Discursive Control

From the free person to other freedoms

The aim of a theory of freedom, as we have been taking it, is to identify those skills and accomplishments in virtue of which agents are fit to be held responsible in their actions, in their self and in their person. We conceive of freedom as fitness to be held responsible – this conception was defended in the first chapter – and different theories of freedom give different accounts of what constitutes such fitness. Each theory tries to identify what is needed in an agent's actions, in the constitution of his or her self, and in their position as a person for that agent to be fit to be held responsible.

The theory of freedom as discursive control is a theory, in the first place, of the free person, and a theory of the free self and the free action only by way of extension. In this respect it complements the two theories that we have just considered and rejected. The theory of freedom as rational control is primarily a theory of the free action and only by extension a theory of the free self and the free person. The theory of freedom as volitional control is primarily a theory of the free self and only by extension a theory of the free action and the free person.

When we describe persons as free, we often have two things in mind. First, we say that in their agency as persons – in the agency allowed to them by their standing relative to others – they are fit to be held responsible; they do not act under pressure or duress or coercion or whatever. And second, we may suggest that they are fit to be held responsible relative to an environment of choice that makes significantly numerous and distinct options available. If their options were restricted to few or only trivially different alternatives, whether by natural limitation or as a side-effect of social arrangements, then we might be loath to say that they were free persons.

It is important to remember, however, that we have abstracted from the nature of environment in discussing the theory of the free person up to this point and that we will continue to do so in the present chapter. We lift that abstraction later, assuming for the moment that the environment makes available at least the minimum of options required for choice. We take the theory of the free person to be the theory of the standing that an agent – in particular, an individual agent – must have among persons if he or she is to be regarded as free in the choices they make.

A theory of the free person

We stand in a variety of relationships to others, each of them characterized by its own distinctive pattern of power and vulnerability, authority and liability, and by the reflection of this pattern in the assumptions shared in common among the parties. The question with which the theory of freedom as discursive control begins bears on whether any sort of relationship is particularly suited to the freedom of the person.

It is clear from the criticisms made in previous chapters that being in rational or volitional control of one's actions is consistent with a variety of possible relationships with others, ranging from the friendly to the hostile, the facilitating to the coercive. All that rational or volitional control strictly requires is that others do not make choice unavailable by downright obstruction or force. If one's standing among persons is to make one free, therefore – if it is to leave one fit to be held properly responsible for things – then it must be richer than that. It must rule out, not just the obstruction of choice, but also a myriad of other coercive and quasi-coercive ways in which people may intrude upon a person or inhibit them.

Can we identify any particular sort of relationship or standing, then, that would give an agent the status of a free person in relation to others? Is there any sort of relationship such that the mode of influence that people have on one another within it leaves fully in place their fitness to be held responsible for what they do? Does any relationship mean that those involved, the influenced as much as the influential, retain a full and equal title to be held responsible?

Discursive interaction

There is one sort of interaction, and one sort of influence, that paradigmatically meets the requirement expressed. That is the interaction that occurs when people attempt to resolve a common, discursive problem – to come to a common mind – by common, discursive means.

The word 'discourse' derives, etymologically, from the idea of running to and fro, or back and forth, and thereby connotes a social exercise in which different parties take turns in exchange with one another. In this respect it has the same connotations as 'conversation', which derives from the idea of turning things around. But discourse does not refer to just any form of turn-taking between people. Specifically, it refers to the sort of turn-taking involved in the attempt to resolve a problem by reference to what all parties regard as inferentially relevant considerations or reasons. To discourse is to reason and, in particular, to reason together with others (Scanlon 1998). One may discourse with oneself, of course, but this should be thought of on the model of talking to oneself: that is, as a social activity that one replicates in relation to oneself.

The paradigm discursive problem is the purely theoretical sort of issue, bearing on what perceptual or inductive evidence suggests about a given question, or on how an abstract puzzle is to be deductively resolved. But discursive problems may be practical as well as theoretical, having to do with what action or response is best in view of a range of prudential or moral or political considerations. There are different theories of practical reason and while they disagree about the reach of practical discourse – some will limit it to means–end reasoning, others extend it to reasoning about ends – they all admit that many practical problems are discursively resoluble; the problems are susceptible to reasoning, in particular to reasoning together, and need not be determined by the vagaries of taste or power.

When we discourse, or reason together, about a theoretical or practical problem we recognize it as a common problem: that is to say, we all recognize the problem, we all recognize that we all recognize it, and so on in the usual hierarchy (Lewis 1969). Recognizing it as a common problem, then, we search for considerations that we can recognize in common as relevant to its resolution, and we look for a resolution that we can agree in common is supported by those considerations. We may do this in twos or threes or in larger numbers. We may do it in any of a variety of contexts, ranging from dinner-table and seminar discussions to debates on matters of practical, sometimes pressing significance. And we may do it on matters that concern us all equally or on matters that concern one or two in particular and that involve the rest of us only in the role of advisers.

When we reason together in this way we will typically have a decision-making influence on one another, and some may have a greater influence than others. The more influential may have an impact on the rest of us in any of a number of ways. By drawing attention to a neglected but relevant consideration, for example. Or by putting such a consideration on the table, in the form of a contractual offer. Or by presenting a reason why further relevant considerations should be actively sought out in empirical research or mutual negotiation. Or by challenging the relevance of considerations already in play. Or by revealing an unnoticed implication of those considerations, say on the basis of analogies from elsewhere. The possibilities are endless.

The influence achieved in such moves may or may not lead to greater insight, and may or may not support an eventual consensus. But whether or not it has such features, it is the influence of a co-reasoner. And so none of us can have any objection to it, for the influence achieved will advance the discursive task on hand, according to criteria that all of us who are party to that task endorse. That we can have no objection shows up in the fact that, intuitively, an agent will be just as fit to be held responsible for what they do under this sort of influence as the person who exercises the influence.

I said above that by all accounts there is some possibility of practical discourse between people but that theories differ about the reach of practical considerations, be they considerations of inferential rationality, of prudence or of morality. The difference between these theories bears on what is required in any domain for questions there to be discursively resoluble, and how far different domains satisfy the requirements. The issue is of the greatest importance, since the answer is going to determine the range of discursive interaction and influence available to people (Smith 1997).

My own view is that discursive resolubility requires that the issues raised are or boil down to matters of truth and falsity, probability and improbability, but that this is not a severe restraint: questions of evaluation and practice generally constitute or turn on questions that are just as factual as those raised in descriptive and explanatory contexts (Pettit 2001d; 2001e). But I will not be defending that position here. I assume that whatever view is taken on the requirements for discursive resolubility, most people will agree that they are satisfied across a wide range of contexts, including discussions of inferential, prudential and moral matters. In every generation there are sceptics who see discussion as war by other means but the very notoriety that such views procure for their defenders – say, the notoriety enjoyed by today's postmodernists – testifies to the fact that few give the views serious credence. They may serve well as theses for idle dialectic but they are not assumptions by which people are willing to conduct their lives.

Discourse-friendly relationships

With the notion of discursive interaction in place, we can distinguish between discourse-friendly and discourse-unfriendly relationships, and we can go on to introduce the notion of discursive control.

Relationships will be discourse-friendly so far as they do not obstruct or jeopardize or restrict discursive influence between the parties and do not raise the costs of achieving it. They will have to be relationships that allow people to exercise discursive influence on one another. And they will have to be relationships such that while they may also allow other forms of influence – say, the influences of style and charm – they do not allow influences of the kind that would undermine or warp discursive influence. The resort to the latter forms of influence – more on these later – would run counter to the spirit of the relationships.

The relationships that involve most of us most of the time are perfectly capable of being discourse-friendly in the sense required. In normal dealings with my family or my friends, my colleagues or my acquaintances, we are each in a position to resort at any moment to discursive interaction; without challenging that relationship, we may each address another in a reason-giving, reason-taking way. And that this is so is a matter of common or shared understanding; to do anything hostile to such discursive influence would be to break the frame within which we usually operate (Goffman 1975).

We may not spend a lot of time, of course, discoursing with family or friends, colleagues or acquaintances. We may devote most of our energies in such relationships to routine activities that serve to signal and reinforce our feelings for one another, and to the more or less pedestrian enjoyment of doing things together. And even when we do explicitly converse with one other, most of our talk may consist in gossip or banter, telling jokes or playing games. But it remains a permanent possibility in the relationships envisaged that you or I can have recourse to reasoning together, as when one of us asks for the advice of the other, or two or more of us find that we have a common problem, practical or theoretical, on hand. The non-discursive activities in which we routinely involve ourselves do nothing to obstruct or jeopardize, restrict or raise the costs of discoursing together in that way. In that sense, the relationships are discourse-friendly.

The claim that discourse-friendly relationships preserve people's freedom as persons is not a casual observation about a happy accident of human and social life. We conceive of ourselves and one another, not just as intentional systems with beliefs and desires, but as subjects who can conduct discourse with one another, and with ourselves, in the attempt to shape our beliefs and desires. And this self-conception naturally has important implications for our attitude to discourse-friendly relationships.

It means that we cannot help but give salience and importance to such relationships. We see them, more or less uniquely, as relationships in which we each undergo the influence of others but not in a way that compromises our fitness to be held responsible and our freedom among persons (Rovane 1997). In the conversation that figures within the context of the relationships, we will each change some of the beliefs that we hold, and perhaps some of our dispositions to action, under the influence of others. But that influence will only be exercised on the basis of discursive considerations that we ourselves take to be relevant. The considerations whereby others move us will all be reasons by which we would want, as discursive subjects, to be moved. If we are moved by others, then, we will only be moved in a way that we would want to be moved; we will ourselves retain discursive determination of where those movements take us.

Discursive control

And so to the denouement. An agent's freedom as a person will naturally be identified, according to the line of thought we have been following, with the form of control that people enjoy within discourse-friendly relationships. An agent will be a free person so far as they have the ability to discourse and they have the access to discourse that is provided within such relationships. That someone is free in this sense will be consistent with their undergoing the discursive influence of others. But that, of course, is no problem. For the discursive influence to which a person may be subject, consistently with retaining discursive control, will leave them fully fit to be held responsible for what they decide and do; it will be consistent with their counting as a fully free person.

Under this account discursive control has a dual aspect, ratiocinative and relational. It involves the ratiocinative capacity to take part in discourse, and the relational capacity that goes with enjoying relationships that are discourse-friendly. We might describe the capacity as a discursive power or even a discursive status, since these words emphasize the relational as well as the ratiocinative aspect of what is involved. Indeed we shall see a special reason in the next section of the chapter for why it is appropriate to speak of the capacity as a power or status of this kind.

With any characterization of freedom in terms of a capacity, there is going to be a question as to whether freedom requires the existence or the exercise of the capacity. So does discursive control involve just the existence of the ratiocinative and relational capacity involved? Or does it also require the exercise of that capacity?

Like the theories of freedom as rational and volitional control, the current theory says that the existence of the capacity is enough for freedom as a person. So long as an agent has the ratiocinative and relational capacity in question – and independently of how far they actually exercise it – they will be free. But it would be misleading to leave matters at that, for relational capacities involve two complexities that are worth noting in this connection.

The first complexity is that a relational capacity cannot exist without the occurrence of some interactions with others. The capacity or power or status that someone has so far as their relationships with others are entirely discourse-friendly presupposes that those relationships are actually in place. And no relationships can be put in place without actual interactions. I can have no social connections with family or friends, colleagues or acquaintances, short of engaging with them and establishing a common understanding. It is possible in principle that the interactions required to establish discourse-friendly relationships do not involve the exercise of discourse – reasoning together – and so it is possible to envisage someone's having discursive control without ever having exercised it. But it is not possible to envisage someone's having discursive control without being actively related to others in some manner, discursive or non-discursive.

The second complexity with a relational capacity of the kind that discursive control involves bears on the way in which it strengthens with exercise. The ratiocinative capacity for discourse is bound to strengthen with exercise, for reasons to do with learning and habituation; in this respect it will resemble the capacities associated with rational and volitional control. But the relational capacity involved in discursive control will strengthen with exercise for rather different, and more interesting reasons. The more that a person is involved in the exercise of discourse with others, the more will the relational capacity in question be recognized as a matter of common awareness. And the more it is recognized as a matter of common awareness, the stronger and surer it will become.

If someone is incorporated with others in a discursively active group, it must be a matter of common assumption among members of the group that he or she satisfies the conditions that make it possible to incorporate them discursively (Pettit and Smith 1996). And it must equally be a matter of common assumption that, satisfying such conditions, the person can be given discursive control and is actually given such control in the group in question. The person has a voice that has some claim to be given a hearing, and an ear that can give an effective hearing to the voices of others. And these are things that each registers, that each registers that others register, and so on. The person is authorized as a discursive partner and is publicly recognized as a locus of discursive authority (Honneth 1996). This is someone, others acknowledge, with whom one can do discursive business; this is someone, in Stephen Darwall's (1999) phrase, whom one can address in conversational mode.

No one will be incorporated in every discursive group that operates in a society, of course; no one would be competent to join every group, since the knowledge required for many groups will be quite specialized. But incorporation in any group will be sufficient in principle for recognition by all. It will be a common assumption among the members of that group that the agent in question satisfies the sorts of conditions given. And it will be a common assumption among the members of the society as a whole that anyone incorporated successfully in such a group must satisfy those conditions.

To the extent that these are matters of common assumption, incorporation in a group will establish the person in sure and secure possession of the relational capacity associated with discursive control. There will be no question of people's thinking that the person is discursively incompetent. And there will be no question of their thinking that the person is not appropriately incorporated in discourse: that they are a second-class citizen in that respect. There will be a presumption in place that as the person is treated in those groups where they gain recognition as a discursive subject, so they ought in general to be treated; the failure to accord such treatment will call for special explanation.

Beyond the previous problem for the free person

Hostile coercion is inconsistent with discursive control

To sum up the line of thought so far, then, agents will be free persons to the extent that they have the ratiocinative capacity for discourse and the relational capacity that goes with enjoying discourse-friendly linkages with others; that capacity, with its dual aspect, is what constitutes discursive control. Agents will exercise such freedom as persons so far as they are engaged in discourse by others, being authorized as someone worthy of address, and they will be reinforced in that freedom so far as they are publicly recognized as having the discursive control it involves.

In dealing with the theories of freedom as rational and volitional control, we saw that a common problem bedevilled the line they take on what it is to be a free person. The problem was that agents retain rational and volitional control of what they do, even in the case where others coerce them by threatening some penalty if they go a certain way; even indeed when others do so for hostile reasons and not, say, because this answers to the avowable interests – that is, the ready-to-be-avowed interests – of the coercee. When I am threatened by a mugger with physical violence unless I hand over my money, I am given a choice – I am not simply obstructed or forced – and I can exercise rational and volitional control in making that choice. Thus it seems that I can retain my freedom as rational control and my freedom as volitional control. Yet my relationship with the coercer is inconsistent with my being held fully responsible in such a case; and so it ought to mean that I count as less than properly free.

The main challenge for the theory of freedom as discursive control, as it applies to the freedom of the person, is to avoid this and related problems. The challenge is to show that coercion and other ways in which a person's freedom may be compromised – judging by ordinary intuition – remain ways in which it may be compromised under this theory.

The challenge is readily met. The notion of rational and volitional control is wholly privatized in the sense that whatever costs others may impose on various choices, people retain this sort of control in relation to the options involved; the control is constituted by purely psychological factors within their own person. But the notion of discursive control has a social as well as a psychological dimension. It requires, not just that the person have a certain sort of psychological capacity – ratiocinative power – but also that others relate to them in a certain way. In particular, it requires that others not try to influence them in a discourse-unfriendly manner. This requirement rules out all interventions by others that restrict or undermine or jeopardize discourse, and hostile coercion will certainly figure in any list of such interventions.

Hostile coercion is unfriendly to discourse, because it inevitably transforms the relationship between those involved – the coercer and the coercee – in a way that restricts the range of discursive interaction between them. If I make a threat of exercising violence against you unless you do something, I may go on to discourse with you about why you should take that threat seriously and perform the action required. But I will no longer be discoursing with you from the baseline of all the considerations that were relevant prior to the threat; I will have pre-empted such unfettered discussion. By making the coercive threat, I will have put limits on how far discourse is to rule in our interaction. I will have restricted discourse, at best, to the issue of why you should take the threat seriously and act accordingly.

How distinctive is hostile coercion in restricting discourse in this way, and in compromising the agent's freedom as a person, without actually removing the possibility of choice? We shall see in the next subsection that there is an important contrast to be drawn with what I describe as friendly coercion. But it is worth observing that there are a number of other contrasts to be drawn too. I shall mention three, which I describe as the plea, the bid and the offer.

'Give me some money or I will make you suffer' is a threat. 'Give me some money or I will be made to suffer' is a plea. The threat rigs the reasons by which I, a coercer, want you to be moved and shows that I am not content just to discourse with you about what the pre-existing considerations require. Short of representing emotional or moral blackmail of some kind, however, the plea does nothing of the kind. It merely puts on the table a discursive consideration that you might otherwise have overlooked. Strictly speaking, it may be on a par with my drawing attention, not to the fact that I will suffer unless you help, but to the fact that someone else is in that situation. Thus the plea can be perfectly consistent with the rule of discourse between us, where the hostile threat is designed to restrict that rule.

A second contrast with the hostile threat is provided by the bid, in particular the contractual bid that I make in discoursing with you about the terms on which some arrangement ought to be set up between us. In the course of our exchange I say that I am willing to contribute such and such to a joint enterprise or willing to pay you such and such for a contribution of yours. In making this bid I do change the reasons relevant to what you should do – I go beyond what I do in making a plea – but there is still a salient contrast with the coercive threat. The discourse in which we are involved requires me to make a bid of this kind, and perhaps to debate the adequacy or fairness of different bids. And so my making a bid does nothing to restrict discourse between us; on the contrary, it is precisely what the discourse on hand demands.

The third contrast with the coercive threat is provided by the offer. This involves my promising you a reward for doing something, where the offer is not required in the manner of a bid – it has the aspect of a bribe – and where it is not made out of consideration for your avowable interests. At the extreme where I make you an offer that activates irrelevant passions and may even mesmerize you, the offer will be just about as unfriendly to discourse as the hostile threat. But at the level where it merely involves facilitating or warming you to a particular option – at the level, say, where I make clear that you will win my lasting affection or esteem by choosing the option – the offer is bound to have a very different profile.

It is always possible that by coercively threatening you, I will have deprived you of the capacity to be moved as the pre-existing reasons require; we drew attention to this in the first chapter. But it is highly unlikely that I will have done this just by offering you a modest reward. That offer will make the choice of the rewarded option easier than it would otherwise have been. And while it may have made the choice of other options harder – it will have raised the opportunity cost of choosing any of them – this may not make a serious impact and may not even be registered among the parties involved: the concept of opportunity cost belongs to economic theory, not – or at least, not yet – to common sense. It may well be possible for me to make you an offer, then, and to claim at the same time that I want to reason with you about what the pre-existing considerations require; this will certainly be the case where I make an offer that supports what I think those considerations require. But nothing similar will be possible with the hostile threat. I will not be able to present myself at once as your coercer and your co-reasoner; the two profiles will be at war with one another.

Friendly coercion is consistent with discursive control

Hostile coercion, as we have been understanding it here, is coercion that is not guided by the coercee's avowable interests and it is entirely intuitive that such coercion reduces a person's freedom; it is generally taken to diminish someone's fitness to be held responsible for anything it leads them to do. But what of friendly coercion, as we might call it, in which the coercer is guided by the coercee's avowable interests: guided in the way Ulysses' sailors are guided by his avowed interest in remaining bound to the mast? Is this also inconsistent with discursive control? I do not believe that it is and I think that that is an intuitive result.

Friendly coercion may occur in a context where the coercee gives another person the right to coerce them at a certain point to do something, fearing that at that point they will lose sight of their own best interests. But it may also occur in other contexts too. You and I may think that it is in our best interests overall to combine with one another in a certain enterprise and, recognizing that we are each capable of backsliding, we may be willing to set up a coercive agency that will force each of us to keep in line with the agreement if ever we are tempted to defect. Of course it is always possible that our avowable interests will change – this, as distinct from our experiencing momentary temptation – and were the coercion envisaged to be insensitive to that possibility then it would no longer be friendly. In order to be genuinely friendly it must be guided, not just by what my avowable interests now happen to be, but by whatever they might come to be.

Is friendly coercion consistent with discursive control? It will be to the extent that what happens between coercer and coercee is controlled by the coercee's avowable interests and those interests are the discursive considerations that are intuitively relevant to what should happen. The coercee may not act so as to determine what happens – the determinative action, in the nature of the case, is performed by the coercer – but what happens is designed to happen so as to match the discursive sensibilities of the coercee. Did the coercee cease to think that his or her avowable interests were the crucial factors, or did the interests in question shift, then that would also induce a change in what transpires between coercer and coercee. The coercee is not denied discursive control by the coercion exercised. On the contrary, the coercion represents a means of implementing that control. The coercee is the principal figure in the relationship, the coercer is the deputy or agent.

What occurs in the case of friendly coercion can be conceptualized in terms of the notion of virtual control that we used earlier (Pettit 1995). The coercee is in virtual control of what happens so far as two things hold. First, the happenings in question normally materialize under the influence of the coercive agent, as when that agent puts penalties in place that shape what the coercee does. Second, if what happens is not in line with the avowable interests of the coercee, then that influence is suspended and redirected so as to ensure that those interests are served. As the avowable interests change, then, so will any coerced outcome, though the change in the outcome will be directly brought about by the coercer, not the coercee.

It is entirely intuitive that friendly coercion, in this sense, is consistent with freedom. The reason is that the coercee remains fully responsible for what happens under a regime of friendly coercion. Whatever transpires is controlled by the coercee's avowable interests, albeit in a virtual fashion, and so responsibility for it must rest squarely with the agent in question. Given that the coercion is required to track the coercee's avowable interests, it is the coercee who is ultimately in charge.

What is true of friendly coercion is going to be true, more generally, of any form of friendly interference: say, any form of friendly obstruction or force. And what is true of friendly interference is going to be true, more generally still, of any form of friendly service that one party may render to another: say, any service in ensuring that the other's preferences are satisfied. If one person acts in a way that is virtually controlled by the avowable interests of another, then far from the service depriving that other of freedom, it expands the domain in which freedom is enjoyed. It increases what Amartya Sen describes as their indirect liberty (Sen 1983, 19; Pettit 2001a).

Forms of influence that are inconsistent with discursive control

So much by way of showing that the theory of freedom as discursive control entails that hostile but not friendly coercion is inconsistent with freedom of the person. So much by way of vindicating the theory in these respects. But can we say, more generally, what the theory requires for freedom of the person? Can we use it to identify those interactions with others, and more generally those connections with others, that are inconsistent with a person's having discursive control? And are its implications in these respects intuitive? Does the occurrence of such interactions mean that the person is less than fully fit to be held responsible and less than fully free?

When one is actively treated in a discursive manner by others, and thereby recognized as a free person, one enjoys discursive authorization or address. One is taken to be able to entertain and offer reasons that are relevant to the task in hand; and one is effectively treated in the manner appropriate for a fellow reason-taker and a fellow reason-giver. There are a number of interactions and connections with others that are clearly inconsistent with the enjoyment of discursive address in this sense – and ultimately with the enjoyment of discursive control – and these connections must all be seen as ways in which one's freedom as a person is more or less deeply compromised.

The connections in question divide into those of a more or less standing or stable kind and those passing initiatives that people assume, now on this occasion, now on that. The passing initiatives that most obviously flout address are those intentional actions whereby others obstruct what an agent does, try to coerce him or her into doing something, or just punish them for having done it. Such initiatives are certainly inconsistent with freedom when they are hostile: when they are not guided by the agent's avowable interests in the way in which Ulysses' sailors were guided by his express interests in keeping him tied to the mast.

The passing initiatives just mentioned announce the fact that they reject address in favour of a non-discursive sort of influence. Other initiatives that are hostile to discursive control masquerade as forms of address but are really something different. These are the overtures involved in deception and manipulation and the like. They enable a person to mislead others and thereby to deny them discursive control. While they are not always indicted as assaults on the freedom of the agent, there is nothing surprising about seeing them in that light. And the theory of freedom as discursive control certainly gives us reason to view them so.

But certain stable connections, including connections that involve no occurrent initiatives, may also be inconsistent with a person's enjoying conversational address. Suppose that a person is manifestly vulnerable to obstruction or coercion or manipulation at the hands of another – in particular, to forms of interference that are not guided by the person's avowable interests – because of having a lesser degree of relational or social power. Suppose that in that sense they relate to the other as to a *dominus* or master. They are 'dominated' in the way in which an employee may be dominated by an employer in a tough labour market, a wife by a husband in a sexist culture, or an illegal immigrant by the citizen who gives them a job and a living. It is a commonplace of received lore that such a person will not be able to speak out in a forthright and free way – or act on a basis that such speech might justify – but must always have an eye out for what will please the powerful and keep them sweet (Pettit 1997a; Skinner 1997). The powerful may adopt a posture of conversational address in relation to such a person, and perhaps even do so sincerely, but the realities of the connection will undermine the posture and jeopardize the agent's discursive control as effectively as any act of outright coercion or manipulation.

The fact that subjection to others reduces a person's discursive control means that in ascribing such control to someone – in ruling out such subjection – we are ascribing relational power in a very distinctive sense. Not only are we saying, as we said earlier, that the person has the capacity that goes with enjoying discourse-friendly relations with others. We are saying that the person is in a position where no one can interfere with them at will – more generally, in neglect of their avowable interests – or certainly that no one can do so with impunity. The person not only receives from others the gift of being treated as a discursive subject, they have an effectively implemented claim to such treatment. They not only receive recognition and respect; they command the recognition and respect that they receive.

We return in the next chapter to a politically more pointed consideration of what it is about the occurrent and stable connections mentioned that reduces or removes an agent's freedom as a person. All that we need to notice here is that they are intuitively the sorts of connections that we would expect to indict as more or less deeply inconsistent with the enjoyment of such freedom. In particular, they are all connections that diminish in some measure the agent's fitness to be held responsible. Let someone be subject to hostile coercion or deception or manipulation, or let them live in subjection to another, and their responsibility for various of the things they do becomes more problematic. And that observation serves to support the theory of the free person offered by the approach that privileges discursive control.

The theory as it applies to the free self

That an agent is a self means that he can think of himself, or she can think of herself, in the first person as the bearer of certain beliefs and desires and other attitudes and as the author of the actions, and perhaps other effects, to which they give rise. And that an agent is a free self means that the way attitudes are formed, and lead to action, is consistent with holding the agent responsible. There is nothing about the psychology of the agent in virtue of which they are distanced from what they want or think or do, for example, and have to look on those attitudes and actions like a more or less helpless bystander. They must be able to see their own signature in those attitudes and actions. They must be able to think: *I* want or think or do that; this is *me*, and not just the work of an alien mechanism within me.

Where does the theory of freedom as discursive control – freedom as discursive power, ratiocinative and relational – lead us in thinking about what might make for such freedom in the self? It will say that the free self is the sort of self that a person is bound to be, so far as being that sort of self is consistent with their enjoying discursive control in relation to others. But what sort of a self is that?

I will elaborate the implications of the theory for our account of the free self in three stages. First I will argue that discursive control presupposes that the agent enjoying such control satisfies certain conceptions of what it is to be a person and a self; second, that they must satisfy related criteria for being the same person and the same self over time; and third, that they must be a sort of self that meets certain conditions. This sort of self will be the free self, according to the theory of freedom as discursive control, and I will argue that this theory of the free self gets over the bystander problem that arises for the theories associated with the views of freedom as rational and as volitional control.

Person and self

The word 'person' derives from the Latin *persona*, which refers etymologically to the mask through which actors would present a character or play a part on stage. The word 'self' derives from the pronominal *se-* whereby we indicate that an attitude or action bears on the agent himself or herself: it is something that the agent can only describe, in their own words, as a case of what 'I' do to 'me' or think about 'me' or whatever.

These etymologies strongly suggest that it is natural to reserve the use of the words 'person' and 'self' for those agents who can in principle speak for themselves and think of themselves under the aspect of the first-person indexicals 'I' and 'me', 'my' and 'mine' (cf. Hobbes 1968, chapter 26). Babies and some other human beings may not actually have this ability but they can count as persons and selves in the extended sense that they share a common nature – our nature as humans – with those who can. Not only do persons and selves in the strict sense have beliefs and desires, then, like any intentional subjects. They can give expression to those states in words – or in signs of some sort – and they can be held to those words; they can be expected, so far as they are sincere, to live up to the words in the things they believe and desire and do. Moreover, being able to express the contents of their own intentional states, and to live up to them in this way, they can equally be expected to be able to mark off those states – say, from the states ascribed to others – as, in their own words, what *I* believe or *I* desire or *I* intend or whatever.

These quick remarks should help to justify the first claim I want to make, that discursive control presupposes that the agent exercising such control is a person and a self. Specifically, the agent is a person and a self according to intuitive conceptions that etymology supports. It is going to be possible for agents to enter discourse, and enjoy discursive control, only so far as they can speak for themselves and think of their own contributions in the first person. And so, by our etymologically derived conceptions, it is going to be possible for agents to enjoy discursive control only if they count as persons and selves.

Might it be possible for an agent to exercise discursive control and yet think of himself or herself, not in the first person as 'I' or 'me', but rather by name: say, as PP? No, for reasons related to a fairly well-known observation (Perry 1979; Burge 1998). Were I to think of myself under a name in this way, then I could reason about what to think or do only by reasoning about what PP should think or do. But there would always be a deliberative gap between my thinking that PP believes that p and that the truth of 'p' entails the truth of 'q' and my actually adjusting beliefs by coming to believe that q or by giving up one of the other beliefs. For why should my beliefs about PP's beliefs have any discursively mediated effect on what I believe and assert, short of my believing that *I* am PP? And if I can think that *I* am PP, of course, then I do think of myself in the first person, not just under a name.

What distinguishes those beliefs and desires and other states that I express or ascribe in the first person is precisely that they may lead me, the agent in question, to respond as they require without the intervention of any other belief: say, any other belief to the effect that the agent in question is the one who should fulfil the requirement attached to holding by those states. If I am deliberatively moved to assert and believe that q – moved in a way that involves no gap – then I must be moved by the thought that *I* believe that p and that if p, then q; or, expressing rather than ascribing what I believe, by the thought that p and that if p, then q. I will not provide myself with a similar, gap-free reason for concluding that q by saying that PP came to believe that p and that if p, then q. Beliefs may be describable by me as PP's without its being the case that they must lead me automatically to respond as they require; I may have forgotten or never have known who 'PP' refers to.

Not only is this true, of course, at the level of my thought. It is also going to hold at the level of speech, when I utter words to which others will wish to hold me. Discursive partners must find me capable of first-person thought, and ready to acknowledge in first-person mode the deliberative implications of the things that I say and do. I must be able to see and respond to the implications for *me*, as I will have to be willing to put it, of acknowledging that p and that if p, then q or that I believe those things. If I prove capable only of speaking about what PP believes and desires, and of what PP should conclude and do, then that will put me beyond the reach of discourse. It will leave no room for the idea of my being held to my words or of my living up to my words, for such third-person observations will support no implications by which I can be judged.

Personal identity and self-identity

My first claim, to return to the main line, is that anyone who enjoys discursive control must count as a person and a self, by intuitive criteria. My second claim is that any such agent will deserve to be regarded as the same person and the same self over various stretches of time according to equally intuitive criteria. No person without personal identity, we might say, and no self without self-identity. And so it is just as well that discursive control engages with suitable criteria for these forms of identity at the same time that it engages with suitable conceptions of what it is to be a person and a self.

What makes someone in middle age the same person as a teenager of some forty years previously? If being a person is just a matter of being capable of discursive control, then there is an answer ready to hand. Being capable of discursive control involves being expected over time to be able to square what one does or claims or feels on any occasion with what one did or claimed or felt at earlier times. That is to say, being capable of discursive control involves being situated on an intertemporal trajectory such that one is expected to bring the doings and sayings and thoughts that occur earlier on that trajectory to every discursive tribunal. One's current claims can be questioned for their consistency with earlier claims on the trajectory, for example, in a way that they cannot be questioned for their consistency with any other claims: with anyone else's claims, as we will say. One's current actions can be questioned for their consistency with earlier intentions on the trajectory, in a way that they cannot be questioned for their consistency with any other intentions: that is, with anyone else's intentions. And so on. But if this is so, then we can say that someone at a later time is the same person as someone at an earlier, just so far as they are bound under discursive practice to answer for, or answer to, the earlier person in this distinctive fashion. The later agent is the same person as the earlier just so far as they are related in the manner – whatever this is – that makes such intertemporal answerability possible.

The line I am taking here is close to one defended recently by Carol Rovane (1997) and, as she argues, it can be traced back to John Locke's *Essay Concerning Human Understanding*. Locke (1975, s. 26) suggests the approach in a famous passage. 'Where-ever a Man finds, what he calls *himself*, there I think that another may say is the same *Person*. It is a Forensick Term appropriating Actions and their

Merit; and so belongs only to intelligent Agents capable of a Law, and Happiness and Misery. This personality extends it *self* beyond present Existence to what is past, . . . it becomes concerned and accountable, owns and imputes to it *self* past Actions, just upon the same ground, and for the same reason, that it does the present.' The idea is that 'person' is a forensic concept that is tied up with questions of who is responsible for what and that personal identity is nothing more or less than that relationship, whatever it is, that propagates responsibility across time.

But though the line I am defending can be traced back to Locke, it is not often pursued in the literature on personal identity. The usual approach to the question of how personal identity over time is established is to look for a natural connection over time, psychological or physical, such that if people at different times have that connection with one another then it will follow that the later can be held responsible for or to the earlier. That approach was also prompted by Locke, for he suggests in other comments that continuity of consciousness is what makes two agents at different times into the same person. That suggestion has dominated the discussion of personal identity, channelling it into a debate on whether it is indeed continuity of consciousness or some more physical sort of continuity that makes for personal identity.

The approach taken here is very different from the theories developed within the confines of that debate. What is said to make two people at different times the same person is that they are connected in such a way – whatever that is – that under existing discursive practice the later can be held responsible for and to the earlier. I argued in the first chapter, with the practice of holding people responsible in place, that we conceptualize freedom in an agent as whatever it is – we know not what – that makes the agent fit to be held responsible for what they do under that practice. I argue here, with the practice of discourse in place, that we conceptualize personal identity over time as consisting in whatever it is – we know not what – that connects people at different times in such a way that under that practice the later can be held responsible for or to the earlier. I connect personal identity conceptually with the relationship that propagates responsibility across time, whatever its nature should prove to be, and I abstract from the task of analysing the nature of the relationship in more substantive terms, though the topic will come up briefly in the next chapter.

The account of personal identity in terms of intertemporal responsibility is not a conventional, more or less arbitrary criterion of personal identity. It does not lend itself to the conjecture, for example, that I might be held to very different trajectories in different cultures. Thus it would not support any fantastical notions such as that in another culture I, the current person we identify under our rules, might be identified in childhood with my oldest brother, in teenage years with my second oldest, and in the periods after that with me. The practice whereby a person is held responsible along one trajectory rather than another is going to work effectively – is going to generate a successful pattern of discourse – only so far as there is a deep-running, causally grounded continuity between the current states of that person and the states that occurred earlier on the trajectory. It is nature, not culture, that dictates that my earlier experiences show up as memories of a certain kind, for example, whereas the experiences of my brothers do not. Any practice of discursive authorization, and discursive identification over time, has got to respect such natural limitations.

We might say that so far as there is personal identity, to that extent there is self-identity also. But it is useful, following many contemporary precedents (Parfit 1984), to think of self-identity in such a way that one and the same person may change their self: may be one self over one period, and a different self over another. And it turns out that the approach sponsored by the theory that persons and selves are marked off by discursive control allows us to identify a richer criterion for self-identity over time than the criterion for personal identity.

The possibility of the richer criterion becomes visible, once we recognize that there are two ways in which I at a later time may respond to the challenge to square current claims with claims that I made earlier, or to square current actions with intentions expressed earlier, or whatever. First, I may own the earlier claims or intentions and try to establish their consistency with my current dispositions or allow their inconsistency to force a change in those dispositions. I may admit that yes, for example, I did say such and such and remain committed to it, so that I am well rebuked for now maintaining something inconsistent. Or, second, I may disown the earlier claims or intentions, admitting that they are mine as a person, but rejecting the expectation that my current dispositions should answer to them. I may say that yes, I did say such and such but that I am no longer committed to it – I think the claim was mistaken – so that it is not a fault in me that I now maintain something inconsistent. In this second case I marginalize the claims or intentions or whatever in question, allowing them only an inert presence in the trajectory with which I am identified: a presence that does not provide a legacy that actively interacts with my current discursive performance.

With these observations to hand, we can offer a criterion of self-identity that fits nicely with our criterion of personal identity. The fact that an agent has to answer to earlier agents on a certain trajectory – to agents who bequeath a mixed and incoherent legacy of commitments – makes someone the same person as those earlier agents. But the fact that an agent owns only a presumptively coherent part of that legacy, and embraces his or her answerability only to some aspects of those earlier agents, means that there is more involved in being the same self. The agent will be the same self as the person they were at an earlier time just so far – and this will be a matter of degree – as they actively own or endorse the claims and attitudes and actions of that earlier agent.

This criterion of self-identity means that the self carries less freight, as it were, than the person. As a person I can never be rid of anything done by agents – strictly, agent-slices – on my trajectory in time. As a self I can. But it is worth noticing that if I am to maintain discursive interactions with others, then the self in question cannot recede to the point of being a purely formal 'I', with a thin, commitment-free identity (Sandel 1982). In order to maintain discursive interactions with others, I must continue to stand by certain claims and intentions; I cannot change minute by minute, interaction by interaction. And that means that I must give my self a substantive specification; I must assume a substantive character. The substantive self I am at any time will be specified in the past commitments that I own. If you want to know who I am in that sense, you will only have to look at the intentions and claims by which I stand, in particular at the rich intentions and claims that are encoded in my patterns of allegiance and affiliation.

The specification of self that I authorize in this way is not a conscious, intentional construction of the kind imagined by those who talk of people telling a narrative about who they are. It is an inevitable side-product – and in the ordinary case an unintended side-product – of my being a discursive subject who has to own some of the commitments to which I can be held as a person, even if it is possible for me to disown others. It will be true, as narrative theorists say, that each of us constructs the self that he or she is in the course of their development and engagement with others. But it will not be true that this construction will evolve in a narcissistic way. Self-construction or self-specification will be an inevitable precipitate of living the discursive life, not something that I need espouse as a conscious goal.

The free self

So much for the first two of the three claims I promised to defend in this discussion. The first claim was that anyone who enjoys discursive control will count in an intuitive sense as a person and a self; the second that any such agent will enjoy personal and self-identity over time in an equally intuitive sense. The third claim I now want to make is that any such agent will be a free self: a self that is to be held responsible.

In order to enjoy discursive control, people must satisfy two conditions that bear on the nature of the self. They must own or endorse a rich part of the legacy they inherit from their accumulating personal history, and they must succeed in living up to this legacy. On the one hand, they must not continually alienate themselves from the things they did and thought and felt in the past, allowing no record of licensed commitments to materialize. And on the other, they must live up to those commitments that they do license in discourse with others. According to the theory of freedom as discursive control, the free self is the self that discursive control presupposes. And so, according to that theory, the free self is the self that meets such conditions.

There are two ways, then, in which a person will not be a free self under this approach. The person will not be a free self to the extent that they keep changing their minds and hearts, holding themselves aloof from what they have done and been and continually seeking comfort in a fresh, unfreighted identity. And the person will not be a free self so far as they fail to live up to the legacy of commitments that they own, the self-identity that they endorse. In the first case the self is elusive, in the second it is weak, and both failures are sufficient for the self to count as unfree.

This theory of the free self is both inherently attractive, I believe, and reassuringly intuitive. It is attractive, because it builds so naturally on the independently appealing theory of the free person. And it is intuitive, because it lets us see how anyone who fails to have such a free self will prove unfit on that account to be held straightforwardly responsible.

Take the person who fails in any significant measure to own the legacy that he or she inherits as a person from their past thoughts and feelings and doings. Such a person will not be fit to be held responsible, so far as they are permanently alienated from themselves. They will be subject to a malaise that leaves them effectively without a self, forcing them to see everything in their past like the work of another agent. We may hold such a person responsible for having allowed this to happen, but to the extent that it does happen we will think that they are not fit in the ordinary way to be held responsible for the past that is disowned. The person will be something like the wanton imagined by Harry Frankfurt. They will be so systematically estranged from their past that we will not be able to regard them as anything other than an impersonal arena where actions materialize in no particular order, and with no unified sense.

Or take the person who does own or endorse a rich legacy from their personal past but who fails to be a free self, through continually failing to live up to this legacy. Such a person, we must suppose, will be bedevilled by obsession, or compulsion, or chronic weakness of will, or something of the kind. And with anyone subject to such pathologies we will naturally say that, just like the person who is unable to own anything, they are not fully fit to be held responsible. The theory of the free self proves to be as intuitive in this implication as it is in the other.

Beyond the previous problem for the free self

We saw in earlier chapters that the theories of freedom as rational control and as volitional control fail to deal effectively with the bystander problem, as we might call it. Rational control and volitional control each require that the self is not subject to weakness of will or compulsion or any such malaise but they are consistent, it appears, with the possibility that agents do not look on their desires and actions as something with which they are identified.

I said in criticism of the theory of freedom as rational control that such control requires merely that the intentional system be rationally well-behaved and that this is consistent with an elusive, bystander self. It allows for the possibility that the agent does not identify with the beliefs and desires that rationally materialize within them and that rationally generate such and such actions. I said in criticism of the theory of freedom as volitional control that such control avoids the bystander problem, only so far as the higher-order volitions which are in charge of an agent's desires and actions are volitions of which the agent approves, and approves without being a bystander on that act of approval. That is a problem for the theory, because it has no account to offer of what it is for the agent to identify with an act of approval as distinct from being a bystander who finds an act of approval occurring within them.

The current theory enables us to get beyond this sort of problem. It says that an agent will identify with an act of judgement or approval, or indeed a state of belief or desire, so far as it is avowed and honoured in discursive exchange: that is, so far as the agent owns the act or state involved and succeeds in living up to it. What is it to be a free self, then? It is to be ready to endorse past commitments that make certain responses appropriate, be those responses actions or adjustments in matters of belief and desire. And it is to be disposed, by the very fact of that endorsement, to display the responses required. In short it is to be a discursive party who avoids the twin problems of elusiveness and weakness.

Although rational and volitional control are consistent with agents having just bystander status, then, this is not true of discursive control. To be in discursive control in one's own psychology, it is essential that one not have a weak self – a self that leaves one systematically failing to live up to the legacy of past commitments – but also, crucially, that one not have an elusive self: a self that leaves one systematically deprived of a legacy to live up to. That the self is not weak means that the problem of pathologies of the spirit are avoided, as they are avoided under the other theories. That the self is not elusive means that the central, bystander problem is also avoided.

The bystander problem arises when agents use words like 'I' and 'me' only in connection with perceptions and beliefs and desires that are impotent in generating action. Such agents have to look with detachment at the states that actually produce action and at what they find themselves doing. They have to say that while such and such states are present in their psychology, and produce such and such actions, they do not carry the imprimatur of the first-person signature. The only states within those agents that do carry that imprimatur are the purely onlooker states in which they are trapped. Recast in the terms we have been using, the bystander problem is that while these agents may describe the desires and intentions that are effective within them as 'mine' in the broad sense in which that acknowledges personal identity, they do not claim them as 'mine' in the richer sense in which that expresses self-identity. They do not claim them as states to which they may be expected to remain faithful in their ongoing discursive performance. They disown them.

The bystander problem, understood in this way, is nothing more or less than the problem of the elusive self: the self that always distances itself from everything on its personal trajectory, receding to a point of the thinnest possible identity. But if discursive control is inconsistent with the self's being elusive in this way, then it is equally inconsistent with the self's being trapped in a bystander position. The problem, therefore, is avoided.

The conception of discursive control is not rigged to ensure that such control is inconsistent with the self's being a bystander. Agents will be in discursive control of their lives, as we argued in the last section, so far as they enjoy a certain power in relation to other persons. But no one whose self was elusive could be granted this power. Such a person would quickly prove unconversable, being incapable of being successfully held to discursive standards. They would constantly elude other persons, finding themselves at a distance from any commitment that is more than a minute old. How could others talk to the person and make plans in common with them? They might as well be talking to the wall.

It is quite consistent with an agent's being in rational or volitional control of their behaviour, so we argued, that the self remain consistently elusive in the way that gives rise to the bystander problem. And so we say that freedom of the self cannot consist simply in the presence of such control. But it is not consistent with the agent's being in discursive control that the self be elusive in this way, any more than it is consistent that the self be weak. And so it remains plausible that the freedom of the self – the fitness of the self to be held responsible – does consist in the presence of discursive control.

Is it really intuitive and compelling, someone may ask, that people will be strongly identified with any commitments that they happen to own and enfranchise in discourse? I will own and enfranchise a past belief that p so far as I take it as a fair challenge to anything I currently believe that it entails that not p. I will own and enfranchise a past intention to X so far as I take it as a fair challenge to a current plan that it is inconsistent with my X-ing. In the one case the fact that p, as I believe it to be, is licensed by me as a reason for not believing something inconsistent. In the other case the fact that I will X, as I intend to do, is a reason licensed by me for not planning anything inconsistent. Is it a plausible claim that where my reasons in that sense go, there go I: there go I, in a strong and significant sense?

I say that it is, because it is hard to see any ulterior point of view to which the self might migrate, consistently with the licensing envisaged. How can I practise that licensing in my relations with discursive partners – and indeed in my own discursive thoughts – and yet claim to occupy a position from which I must view the beliefs and desires and intentions in question as not bearing my signature? I see no space that can open up here and leave the self still isolated in a bystander perspective.

It is consistent with licensing certain intentional states, of course, that they not matter greatly in one's life. The beliefs and desires and intentions from which one starts in this or that context may be much less important in the larger framing of one's life than those that one licenses elsewhere. But this feature has little or nothing to do with whether they are intentional states in which the self is present. The self may be as fully present in states that are unimportant in this sense as in states that are important. While all of the states licensed and enfranchised go into the agent's self-specification – their not necessarily intended self-specification – some may be at the very centre of that specification, by an independent criterion, while others are at the periphery. Some may be such that the agent can easily imagine giving them up, for example, while others are such that for the agent to imagine giving them up is like imagining that he or she is replaced by someone else.

One last comment. While the theory of freedom as discursive control avoids the bystander problem that arises under the other theories, it does still presuppose the presence of the sort of control postulated in those other theories. Thus it vindicates the plausible claim that both rational control and volitional control are necessary for freedom.

The theory presupposes rational control, so far as it presupposes the absence of the sorts of pathologies and disruptions that would make the self weak. The theory presupposes volitional control, because it gives us an acceptable account of higher-order volitions and it entails, if not that such volitions always have to be explicitly present and controlling, at least that they cannot run against the grain of what the agent desires and does.

We saw in the last chapter that higher-order volitions have to fulfil two conditions. First, they are desires to be effectively moved by lower-level desires, as in Frankfurt's formulation. And second, they are desires that bear the agent's first-person stamp of approval. We can make sense of higher-order volitions – as the theory of freedom as volitional control itself could not – because we can explain what it is for an agent to approve of certain desires in the first person. And we can see that if a free agent has certain higher-order volitions in regard to lower-level desires or doings, then the volitions must dictate those responses. Did they not dictate the responses, then the agent's approving of the volitions would not have its expected effects and we would have to say that the self in question was too weak to support discursive control.

The theory as it applies to the free action

The theory of freedom as discursive control says that a person is free so far as they enjoy discursive power, ratiocinative and relational, in their dealings with other persons; and that the free self is the sort of self that such power presupposes: a discursively specified self that proves neither weak nor elusive. But what does the theory say about the free action? It says that, as the free self is the self presupposed by the free person, the free action is the action that is consistent with the authorship of the free person and the free self; the action that materializes under discursive control. And what sort of action is that? There are two answers. One construes discursively controlled actions in a narrow way, the other in a broad.

The narrow construal would say that free actions have got to be controlled by the explicit discursive reflections, private or public, of the agent. The idea is that if I act freely then I must act ratiocinatively. I must do so on the basis of a practical inference in which certain considerations are endorsed and are taken as grounds for adopting the course of action in question. And it must be that had I endorsed different considerations, and had they supported a different course of action, then I would have adopted it instead. The considerations endorsed in any instance may prove to be false, of course, or the principle of inference faulty, but they have to be discursively defensible in at least a *prima facie* way; they cannot be such as to impugn my discursive status.

The theory of the free action, construed in this narrow way, is completely implausible, since it would mean that most of the actions I or anyone else performs are not free. The reason is that while I am able to have ready access to discourse about what I should do, public or private, I mostly act without activating such access. I act out of habit or inclination or impulse in a manner that is not subjected to explicit discursive reflection.

The second, broad construal of the theory of the free action avoids this problem. It begins from the distinction between active and virtual control that we introduced earlier and it argues that what free action requires is that discursive considerations be in virtual control of the action, not necessarily in active. Under the narrow construal of the discursive control of free action the agent entertains certain discursive considerations and is led to act as they dictate; the discursive considerations control the free action in the active mode of control. But even in cases where there is no active discursive reflection of this type, still the discursive considerations may remain in virtual control. And that is what the broad construal postulates.

Let us suppose that for many contexts it is determined by the nature of that context, and by the agent's history, that the discursive considerations relevant to determining what the agent does are of this or that kind. Imagine now that whenever certain considerations are relevant in such a context, the agent acts as they require on the basis of what is habitual or salient or spontaneously attractive there, not on the basis of discursive reflection. Imagine, furthermore, that were such a collateral causal order to fail to produce the required action, then that would generally trigger discursive reflection and lead the agent to correct his or her response. Such a scenario would put the agent in virtual discursive control of their actions, though not in active, causally generative control.

With many of the things we do, and do intuitively of our free choice, it is clearly the case that we do them on the basis of explicit discursive reflection. But with perhaps the bulk of the things we do in day-to-day living, it is equally clear that we do them without discursive reflection, explicit or even implicit. We act out of habit, in a more or less unthinking way; we register the sort of situation on hand and we respond on automatic pilot to the cues that it provides. In most of these cases, however, we are not wholly beyond the reach of the relevant discursive considerations. Let anything go wrong – let the situation prove not so routine, or the response forthcoming from us not so obviously suitable – and the red lights go on, causing us to go into discursive alert and to take discursive charge of our doings. In these cases there was no active discursive control prior to the alarm but there was always virtual discursive control. Discursive reflection played no causal role, however unconscious, in generating the behaviour but it was there as a standby cause, ready to be activated in the event of proving to be needed.

It is not difficult to envisage cases where such virtual discursive control is in charge of the way we behave. Think of a ticket-seller at a railway station, or of a police officer dealing with inquiries from the public, or of a person walking on a familiar route to work. Or think of an attorney handling a humdrum case in court, or of a teacher taking pupils through an elementary lesson, or of the members of a committee going through a smooth agenda. In all of these cases it is easy to envisage people being ruled by habit and routine, achieving their goals with minimal attention and effort. But equally it is compelling that in most of these cases the people in question will immediately go over to conscious discursive reflection as to what they should do, in the event of the routine being broken, and will let such reflection determine their response. Think of the ticket-seller faced with a potentially violent traveller, of the police officer confronted with someone clearly on the brink of a breakdown, or of the person walking to work who suddenly finds that the landmarks have changed. We cannot but expect that they will respond to such alarms by taking back control from the automatic pilot and assuming discursive charge of what they do.

To return now to the main line of argument, we have seen that under the theory of freedom as discursive control, the free action is the sort of action that is discursively controlled in a manner that is consistent with freedom of the person and the self. This theory would be quite implausible, if control were understood in the narrow, active sense. But it begins to look natural and intuitive, once we recognize that the discursive control postulated may often be virtual, not active, in character.[1]

Beyond the previous problem for the free action

Under the concept of freedom developed in the first chapter, an action will be free if and only if it materializes in such a way that the agent is fit to be held responsible for it. The theory of freedom as discursive control gives us an intuitive categorization of free action, so far as it is natural to think that actions in the category are such that the agent is fit to be held responsible for them. If an agent does something that is under the control of discursive considerations then, whether that control is exercised in active or virtual mode, the action is guided by the agent's values. It materializes in the context of active or virtual evaluation, to the effect that this is or is not consistent with relevant discursive considerations, and it is subject to the control of that evaluation; the action goes through in the normal case, only when the evaluation is supportive. It is precisely action of that

---

[1] As a view of free action, the theory of freedom as discursive control coincides with a different theory that I am not considering here: the theory of freedom, so we might describe it, as ratiocinative control. This theory would say that freedom is constituted, not by the full relational-cum-ratiocinative capacity involved in discursive control, but merely by the ratiocinative capacity involved in being able to make up one's mind on the basis of reasons. Such a theory would be built on the theory of freedom as rational control, stipulating that freedom requires two things: first, that rationally maintained beliefs and desires should be in rational control of what the agent does; and, second, that the rational maintenance and rational control involved should reflect the agent's ability to reason: it is not enough that it should come about, as it apparently does with many non-human animals, in the absence of a ratiocinative capacity. Many defenders of the theory of freedom as rational control may actually have this ratiocinative theory in mind when they discuss freedom (Davidson 1980, Essay 4). I have not considered the theory separately because, while it coincides with freedom as discursive control in the view it would offer of free action, it holds out no prospect of doing any better than earlier theories in the views it would support of freedom in the self and the person. The reason is that it lacks any relational dimension. Lacking such a dimension, it would not enable us to find fault with coercion, since the coerced agent may retain his or her ability to reason. And lacking such a dimension, it would not have a basis for explaining what makes an agent a self and what ensures the presence of the self in the ratiocinative process leading to action.

evaluatively controlled type that we think of as action for which the agent can be held responsible.

But this observation, of course, does not take us out of the woods. Agents will be fit to be held responsible for an action, so we saw, only if they are also fit to be held responsible for any acts or states in virtue of which they are fit to be held responsible. Responsibility, in that sense, is recursive. What we have to show in conclusion is that the theory of freedom as discursive control gets us over this problem and scores better in that way than the rival theories of freedom as rational and volitional control.

The problem with the theory of freedom as rational control was that rationally controlled agents might be rationally controlled and not endorse any standards in respect of which they could be held responsible, let alone held recursively responsible; the beliefs and desires that serve as rational controllers of their actions might not be responsive to their sense of how they ought to perform. Non-human animals are often more or less rationally controlled in what they think and do, for example, yet they do not have any beliefs about the standards that they ought to meet.

The problem with the theory of free action as volitional control was that while volitionally controlled agents can be taken to treat the higher-order volitions as standards, no reason is provided by the theory for why they should be fit to be held responsible for those volitions. The recursive character of responsibility means that since the agents are responsible for actions in virtue of holding by the higher-order volitions, then they must also be fit to be held responsible for the volitions. But the theory gives no reason to think that that condition is fulfilled.

The problem that these two earlier theories raise for the responsibility connotation of freedom are closely related to a problem that they also raise for the connotation of underdetermined choice: the connotation whereby we assume with any free action that the agent could have done otherwise. Just as rational and volitional control fail to ensure that the agent is fit to be held responsible for an act, so they fail to ensure that there is any significant sense – or at least any significant and naturalistically unmysterious sense – in which the agent could have done otherwise. Perhaps the agent would have done otherwise if they had had different desires, or different higher-order volitions. But what is to ensure that they could have had different desires or volitions? It may be, as we mentioned in the first chapter, that in order to instantiate such different states they would have to have had a different childhood or background.

Back now to the theory of freedom as discursive control and the task of showing how it overcomes the recursive problem. The best way to appreciate how it does so is to see first how it deals with the modal problem raised by the connotation of underdetermined choice. The theory directs us to a distinctive sense in which it must be true of a discursively controlled action that the agent – assuming they are a free person and a free self – could have done otherwise. And in resolving the modal problem in this way, it also points us to a resolution of the recursive.

The modal problem

Suppose that I authorize you discursively in the sense of treating you as someone I can talk to, someone I can do discursive business with. You are not out of your mind, so I assume, and you are not operating under pressures or constraints or limitations that inhibit in any way your responsiveness to the discursive considerations – the reasons – that can come up between us for endorsement and that can sometimes call for action. You are not someone, for example, whom I treat as a discursive partner only for developmental purposes: only because this is necessary in order to induct you into the practice of discursive authorization. From my point of view, you are already fully enfranchised in discursive community. You are someone with an ear attuned to reasons, a voice capable of enunciating where reasons lead, and an ability to form your responses as reasons in the ultimate judgement required.

What might it mean for me, as I authorize and address you in this way, to hold in respect of an action you perform that you could have done otherwise? There are two salient cases to consider. In one you do as reason requires according to a common view of those requirements; and in the other you fail to do this.[2]

Suppose that you act as reason requires, then, by our common lights. What can I mean in that case by saying that you could have done otherwise? There is only one plausible candidate: that had the reasons required some other response, then that is what you would have done instead. Consistently with what I assume in discursively

---

[2] Why ignore cases where we do not achieve a common view of what reason requires you to do? In such a case, I will have to take you – as, presumably, you will have to take me – to form your beliefs about what reason requires in a way that is wrong and contrary to what reason requires; and, at some level, I will have to take your beliefs to be wrong and contrary to what reason requires, according to a shared view of those requirements: otherwise I could hardly authorize you as a discursive partner. Thus the case can be treated on the same lines as the case where you fail to act as reason requires according to a common view of those requirements. For, as I go on to argue, holding such beliefs can be treated in the same manner as free action.

authorizing you, I must mean that you are committed to the service of the reasons and that where the reasons go, there too you can be expected to go. It is no accident, I suggest, that in the case on hand you acted as reason required. That you so acted manifests a general disposition; it shows you to be a faithful servant of reason.

Suppose however that you acted contrary to what reason, by our common lights, required. What can I mean, then, by saying that you could have done otherwise? Here again there is only one plausible candidate. I must mean that this was an accident and not something that reveals your general disposition in respect of reasons. I suggest that a freak malfunction blinded or inured you to the claim of the reasons, or an untypical visitation of impulse or passion, oversight or illogic. I say that your performance in this instance reveals little about how you can generally be expected to perform. I imply that the possible world in which the malfunction or visitation did not occur, and you acted faithfully to reason, is very close indeed; it was a fluke that it did not materialize instead.

When I say in this sort of case that it was a mere accident, untypical of the general rule, that you acted contrary to reason, I do not put myself forward as someone with a clairvoyant's insight into metaphysical possibility. The judgement I express is likely to be grounded in two beliefs that my discursive experience of dealing with you will normally have supported. First, that had I been able to discourse with you at the moment of action, making reason's claims more salient and compelling, then I might well have nudged you towards the right action. And second, that it is possible to make you aware of having acted contrary to reason and that this awareness will tend to elicit an apology and to reduce the likelihood of your doing that sort of thing again. I have to believe such things so far as I continue to authorize you discursively and those beliefs will support the judgement that in the sense explained you could indeed have done otherwise.

We will ascribe the capacity to have done otherwise, interpreted in this way, whenever we ascribe free action. Thus, I will think that you could have done otherwise, not just when I believe that your action was actively controlled by discursive reasons, but also when I believe that it was only controlled in a virtual manner by such considerations. In both cases I will take you to be the sort of agent who is generally the servant of discursive reasons and that is all that is required to make it true that, whether you did well or ill, you could always have done otherwise.

We will also ascribe the capacity to have done otherwise whenever we ascribe states that we see as the result of continuing free action. Take the beliefs and desires that you maintain as a result of freely acting so as to determine whether they are supported by reasons; or as a result of choosing not to act in that way but to let the beliefs and desires evolve naturally, subject only to virtual checking and control. In any such case you will be responsible for your beliefs and desires, so far as they materialize as a consequence of free action, and you will maintain those beliefs and desires freely so far as they are the consequence of continuing action. Thus I will be able to think that in any case where you form a belief or desire, you could have done otherwise (Pettit and Smith 1996). If you respect the demands of reason in forming it, then I will think that this was no accident; you would have formed a different belief or desire, had that been what reason required. If you do not respect reason's demands in forming it, then I will think that this was an accident; you would normally respect those requirements in forming beliefs and desires.

We have been discussing how the theory of freedom as discursive control makes sense of the connotation of underdetermined choice, resolving the associated modal problem. The key to the resolution is that the theory forces us to interpret the notion that an agent could have done otherwise so that it bears, not on the process leading to what was done, but on the nature of the subject involved. Sure, the agent who acted in this or that manner may have done so as a result of a causal sequence – perhaps a sequence only visible from a scientific point of view – that made the action inevitable. But the important point, from the perspective of the theory of freedom as discursive control, is that the agent is of a type or character such that he or she generally serves reason (see Pettit 2001f).

You aspire to being of that type when you put yourself forward as a partner in discourse and I authorize your claim to being of that type when I recognize you as a discursive partner. When I say that you could have done otherwise, and regardless of whether you do well or do ill, I give expression to my maintaining that authorization and to my reinforcing you in your aspiration. I say nothing on the genesis of the action or response in question – I abstract entirely from the process that gives rise to it – and comment only on the sort of agent that I find you to be and intend to treat you as being.

The recursive problem

With this observation in hand, we can return to the question of how the theory of freedom as discursive control enables us to deal with the recursive problem raised by the responsibility connotation: that is, by the connotation that we prioritized in our conceptualization of freedom. The problem, spelled out in some detail, is this. If you are fit to be held responsible for doing something, then that is presumably because your action was controlled in a certain way: not by hypnotic suggestion, say, but by your ordinary beliefs and desires. But if you are fit to be held responsible for the action in virtue of its having been controlled by such beliefs and desires, then you must be fit to be held responsible for those states in turn. You will be fit to be held responsible for the beliefs and desires, presumably, because they are controlled by normal habits of belief and desire formation, not induced in you by any sinister means. But if you are fit to be held responsible for those beliefs and desires in virtue of their being controlled by such habits, then you must be fit to be held responsible for those habits too. And so on, it seems, indefinitely.

Our discussion of the modal problem directs us to an unwarranted assumption made in the generation of the recursive problem. The assumption is that whenever an agent is fit to be held responsible for something, then that is in virtue of that response being controlled by a separate state or event: a certain belief or desire, a certain habit of belief and desire formation, or whatever. It is only because of that assumption that a challenge can always be raised, to the effect that the agent must then be responsible for the state or event in question. And it is only because of the permanent availability of that challenge that there is an indefinite regress in prospect.

But the lesson of our resolution of the modal problem is that an agent can be fit to be held responsible for something, be it an action or belief or whatever, in virtue of being of a certain type – the reason-responsive type ascribed in discursive authorization – and not in virtue of any preceding event or state. When an agent performs an action under the active control of certain beliefs and desires, then it may be fair to say that he or she is fit to be held responsible for the action in virtue of the controlling role played by those states, and therefore that the agent must equally be fit to be held responsible for the beliefs and desires involved. But if the agent performs the action or forms those beliefs and desires under just the virtual control of discursive reasons, then there is no separable event or state in virtue of which they are fit to be held responsible. They are fit to be held responsible for the action or the intentional profile involved in virtue of being a reason-responsive type of agent, not in virtue of anything in a sequence of controlling events or states.

The response that we should make to the recursive problem, then, is fairly straightforward. We said that it is natural to think that discursively controlled actions, and indeed discursively controlled intentional states, are such that the agent is fit to be held responsible for them. They materialize in the presence of active or virtual evaluations to the effect that they are supported by relevant discursive considerations and they go through in general if and only if those evaluations are supportive. We can think that actions and intentional states are of this kind, and are such that the agent is fit to be held responsible for them, without thinking that an indefinite regress of responsibility opens up before us. We can think that the regress bottoms out with the type of agent that we take the person to be: the reason-responsive type to which we assign the person in discursively authorizing them.

But there is a question that may be raised in objection to this account of how things stand. If I think you are fit to be held responsible for something in virtue of your being a reason-responsive type of agent, then do I have to think that you are fit to be held responsible for being that type of agent? And if I do, does that raise a problem for the approach taken? I do not think that the answer to the first question is necessarily affirmative but even if it is affirmative, that does not present a serious problem for our approach.

The reason is that there is an obvious sense in which I may think you are fit to be held responsible for being a reason-responsive type of agent. I take you to be reason-responsive so far as you are generally disposed to act in accordance with reason. But I do not think that this responsiveness means that you will never act contrary to reason; and I do not think that the responsiveness will last, if you fall into the habit of acting contrary to reason. Thus I can think that so far as you are fit to be held responsible for acting in accordance with reason over a series of instances, you are fit to be held responsible for something that that pattern of action helps to ensure: viz., your remaining a reason-responsive type of agent.

Under this line of thought, the indefinite regress with which the recursive problem threatens us is replaced by a harmless circle or, better, spiral. You are fit to be held responsible for acting with or against reason so far as you are disposed to respond to reason. Yet you are fit to be held responsible for being disposed to respond to reason – strictly, for continuing to be disposed to respond to reason – so far as you are fit to be held responsible for routinely succeeding in acting with reason. The pattern of mutual dependence is complex but in no way incoherent.

The approach taken in this resolution of the modal and recursive problems is attractively straightforward. Moreover it promises to raise few naturalistic problems. Suppose I take you to be responsive to reasons, authorizing you as a partner in discourse. And now imagine that I am confronted by an agent who is naturalistically indiscernible from you, being an atom-for-atom replica and, if you like, being the product of a naturalistically identical history. If I am aware of the facts, then it is hard to see how I could think that there is reason to authorize you, casting you in the relevant type, but no reason to authorize this replica. And that is just to say that it is hard to see how the type in virtue of which you count as the author of free actions could fail to be naturalistically determined. There may be a big problem about explaining in naturalistic terms how you or anyone else can get to be discursive, and in particular discursively controlled. But there is little or no problem in believing that however you do manage this, the discursive status that you achieve is going to be supervenient on your naturalistic constitution and organization.

A bonus

We have seen that the theory of freedom as discursive control enables us to resolve not just the problems that arise with the free person and the free self, but also the problem that arises with free action. It makes the recursion of responsibility unproblematic, as indeed it makes the capacity of a free agent to have done otherwise unproblematic. But there is one further benefit that the theory yields in the area of free action and I turn finally to it.

An agent will be fit to be held reponsible for an action, by the account given in the first chapter, just so far as it is appropriate under existing practice to hold them responsible for what they did. It will only be appropriate to hold them responsible in this way if they could have done otherwise in some sense and if they can also be held responsible for factors involved in the control of what they did, and our discussion has just shown how those conditions can be fulfilled: how the modal and recursive problems can be resolved. But there is also another condition that must be fulfilled, so many will argue, if it is going to be appropriate under existing practice to hold an agent responsible. This, in a phrase, is that holding the agent responsible must be permissible under that practice: it must be unobjectionable under the norms associated with the practice. What I now want to point out is that the theory of freedom as discursive control can also make sense of how such permissibility is ensured.

Some may say that it will be permissible to hold a discursively controlled agent responsible, so far as doing this serves to shape their behaviour appropriately; and that it will serve in this way, so far as people care about being praised or blamed for meeting relevant standards: that is, pursue the good opinion expressed in praise and flee the bad opinion expressed in blame. The idea is that the susceptibility to praise and blame of the person who tracks discursive standards will make it useful and therefore permissible to hold them responsible for the different things they do.

This response makes the activity of holding someone responsible counter-intuitively strategic or manipulative (Strawson 1982). The posture of holding someone responsible for action will be of a kind with our disposition towards the dog – or perhaps the young child – when we expose it to rewards and penalties that are designed to shape its behaviour. Did we praise or blame an agent only because of hoping to reinforce or alter their behaviour in such a manner – and were this a matter of common knowledge, as it inevitably would be – then praising or blaming someone would be a highly disrespectful act and would be a reasonable ground for resentment. Praising or blaming a person is intuitively respectful in character, involving an acknowledgement of their agency and autonomy, and whatever makes the activity permissible, it cannot just be people's susceptibility to the shaping effects of praise and blame. The basis of permissibility must be more subject-friendly than that.

This observation provides the cue for what I think is the right answer to the permissibility problem. For the uniquely subject-friendly basis on which it might be permissible to praise or blame an agent is that the agent gave his or her permission for this to happen. And it turns out that we can identify such a basis of permissibility under the theory of freedom as discursive control.

If people enjoy discursive status *vis-à-vis* one another, being incorporated in discourse-friendly relations, then by the account given earlier it has to be a matter of common recognition among them that each is capable of entering discourse as a full and equal partner; each has all the ratiocinative and relational resources required. Let any one of them act as someone presumptively possessed of such control, therefore, making suitable discursive overtures to others, and they have to represent themselves overtly – that is, as a matter of common awareness – as someone who enjoys such resources. They have to represent themselves as being able to track the demands of reason, undisturbed by psychological or social pressures.

If people represent themselves in this way as a matter of common assumption, then it is bound to be equally a matter of common assumption that others will expect them to meet the relevant demands of reason and may act out of reliance on their doing so; such expectations and actions will be supported by the belief that the people involved are worthy of being authorized as discursive partners. But if people represent themselves as able to track such demands of reason despite its being a matter of common assumption that others will react in that manner, then they presumably acquiesce as a matter of common assumption in others forming and acting on such expectations; in effect, they give others a licence or permission to react in that way. And if that is so, then they must equally permit others to blame them for any failure to satisfy expectations, treating that failure as an act of betrayal; and they must permit others to praise them for success, treating success as a token of interpersonal fidelity. They must permit others to react as they would react to behaviour that breaks or keeps a promise.

Such reactions will not make sense, of course, except so far as it is a matter of common assumption in turn that they can have an effect on the agents involved: praise can reinforce the agents in acting according to reason, and blame can elicit an apology for any failure to do so, inducing an improvement in future behaviour. That is the observation that may have led some philosophers to think that it is permissible to hold agents responsible just so far as it is regulatively useful to do so. But the observation is equally consistent with the rather different view emerging here. On that view it is permissible to hold agents responsible just so far as those agents permit it, and those agents will permit it just so far as they act as subjects presumptively possessed of discursive control.

This view is intuitive and not too idealistic. Thus it allows us to acknowledge that many agents will act as agents possessed only of a measure of discursive control – or that it will become clear after the fact that that is all the control they had – and to accept that it will be permissible in that event only to hold them responsible in diminished measure or in a manner mitigated by circumstance. They may act under the sort of coercion or pressure from others that rigs the demands of reason, say by putting a hostile threat in place. Or they may act in the presence of psychological factors – compulsion, fatigue, or whatever – that reduce their capacity to track reason.

The perspective which the theory of freedom as discursive control gives us on the permissibility of holding agents responsible for what they do is an added bonus. The theories of freedom as rational and volitional control give us no plausible means of explaining that permissibility and it argues strongly in favour of the theory adopted here that it remedies that defect as well as resolving the other problems discussed.

Conclusion

Where earlier theories associated freedom respectively with rational control and volitional control, this last theory associates it with discursive control. Because it begins with the freedom of the person in relation to others, however, it is markedly different from those theories in taking the control in question to involve a relational as well as a ratiocinative capacity. People enjoy freedom as discursive control so far as they have the ratiocinative capacity to enter discourse and so far as they have the relational capacity that goes with having only discourse-friendly linkages with others.

A person is free, under this theory, to the extent that they have discursive status in relation to others. A self is free to the extent that it avoids the weakness and the elusiveness that would undermine discursive ownership and the possibility of discursive relations with others. And an action is free to the extent that it is discursively controlled, whether in active or virtual mode, and is consistent with the freedom of the person and the freedom of the self.

The shift to discursive control – and in an important sense it presupposes both rational and volitional control – makes it possible to surmount the problems raised for earlier theories in relation to the free person, the free self and the free action. It means that hostile coercion and other such intrusions are inconsistent with the freedom of the person, friendly coercion or not. It means that the free self not only escapes pathologies like weakness of will and compulsion but is present in active endorsement of much of its psychology. And it means that the free action is such that we can avoid the problem raised by the recursive character of responsibility that proved so difficult for other theories. Not only that indeed: it also means that we can make good sense of the intuition that if someone performed an action freely then they must have been able to do otherwise; and it enables us to explain why it is permissible under ordinary norms to hold such an agent responsible for what they did.

5

Freedom and Collectivization

From individual to collective agents

In speaking of freedom up to this point, our focus has been on the individual subject. The concept of freedom has been presented as the concept of what it is for an individual to be fit to be held responsible. And the theory of freedom as discursive control has been defended as a theory of what makes for such fitness in a particular human being. Discursive control, so it has been suggested, enables the individual subject to perform free actions, to be a free self and to relate to other such subjects as a free person.

This focus on the individual may suggest that the sorts of questions raised in connection with freedom arise only with individual subjects. And that suggestion, as it happens, has been tacitly supported by the approach to those questions that has dominated the literature for many generations. But the suggestion is mistaken. It turns out that everything we have said in connection with the freedom of the individual applies in a parallel way to the collective agents that individuals often constitute.

I argue two main points in support of this claim. First, that there are collective as well as individual subjects, in particular collective subjects that are capable of being held responsible and of holding others responsible in turn. And second, that the theory of freedom as discursive control applies to them just as much as it does to individual subjects; collective subjects are fit to be held responsible so far and only so far as they enjoy discursive control.

There are a number of reasons for introducing a discussion of the freedom of collective subjects at this point. One is that it puts right a sustained omission in the literature. Another is that it helps to bring to light some further implications of the theory of freedom as discursive control. And a final consideration is that it gives us a nice modulation to the discussion of the next chapter. We turn there to consider how a particular collective body – the polity or state – should conceive of the demands of freedom if it sets itself the task, as most philosophies would say it should, of furthering the enjoyment of freedom among its citizens. The chapter is not absolutely essential to the development of the argument, however, and those who are averse to the topic can go directly to chapter 6 without serious loss.

Are there collective subjects?

In a well-known discussion, Anthony Quinton (1975, 17) argues that to ascribe judgements, intentions and the like to social groups is just a way of ascribing them, in a summative and metaphorical way, to individuals in those groups.

> We do, of course, speak freely of the mental properties and acts of a group in the way we do of individual people. Groups are said to have beliefs, emotions, and attitudes and to take decisions and make promises. But these ways of speaking are plainly metaphorical. To ascribe mental predicates to a group is always an indirect way of ascribing such predicates to its members. With such mental states as beliefs and attitudes, the ascriptions are of what I have called a summative kind. To say that the industrial working class is determined to resist anti-trade union laws is to say that all or most industrial workers are so minded.

Quinton's position amounts to an eliminativism about collective subjects. There may be social sets of individuals, in the sense of set that is used in mathematics. There may be social wholes composed out of individuals, in the sense of whole that is regimented in mereology and approximated in some ordinary usage (Ruben 1985). But there are no collective subjects or agents in the sense in which subjectivity and agency imply the possession of mental properties. Groups and groupings of individuals only have mental properties in a summative and metaphorical sense, and can constitute subjects only in a summative and metaphorical way. Asked to count the subjects present in any domain, it will be a serious mistake to count any collective agencies alongside individual subjects; it will involve an egregious form of double-counting.

Such an eliminativism about collective subjects has occasionally been called into question in recent work (see Gilbert 1989, 306; Tuomela 1995, 331; cf. James 1984; Meijers 1994; Searle 1995). But the general tendency is to support an analysis of collective intention that may make it difficult to avoid eliminativism (Bratman 1999). I resist that tendency, providing an argument that offers fairly decisive support for realism about collective subjects, and I try to show that the collective subjects to which the argument directs us can enjoy freedom in the same sense in which individuals can enjoy it. My argument for the reality of collective subjects starts from a dilemma – a discursive dilemma – that collectivities often face. There are two possible responses to that dilemma, each illustrated in common practice – one involves individualizing reason, the other collectivizing it – and those collectivities that take the second option clearly constitute collective subjects. So at any rate I argue.

The discursive dilemma

The discursive dilemma is a generalized version of the doctrinal paradox that has recently been identified in jurisprudential circles (Kornhauser and Sager 1986; Kornhauser 1992a; Kornhauser 1992b; Kornhauser and Sager 1993. See too Chapman 1998a; Chapman 1998b; Brennan 1999). This paradox arises when a multi-member court has to make a decision on the basis of received, legal doctrine as to the considerations that ought to determine the resolution of a case: that is, on the basis of a conceptual sequencing of the matters to be decided (Chapman 1998a). It consists in the fact that the standard practice whereby judges make their individual decisions on the case, and then aggregate their votes, can lead to a different result from that which would have ensued had they voted instead on whether the relevant considerations obtained, and let those votes dictate how the case should be resolved.

I describe the problem, in its general form, as a discursive dilemma. I prefer the word 'discursive', because the problem in question is not tied to the acceptance of common doctrine, only to the enterprise of making group judgements on the basis of reasons. I prefer the word 'dilemma', because the paradox in question generates a choice in which each option has its difficulties. My analysis of the discursive dilemma is supported directly by that jurisprudential literature, though many of the points I want to make do not appear there; where they do appear, I explicitly acknowledge them (List and Pettit 2000; Pettit 2000c; Pettit 2001b).

The best way to introduce the dilemma will be to illustrate it. A good example is provided by this simple case where a three-judge court has to decide on whether a defendant is liable under a charge of breach of contract (Kornhauser and Sager 1993, 11). According to legal doctrine, the court should find against the defendant if and only if it finds, first that a valid contract was in place, and second that the defendant's behaviour was such as to breach a contract of that kind. Now imagine that the three judges, A, B and C, vote as follows on those issues and on the doctrinally related matter of whether the defendant is indeed liable.

	Contract?	Breach?	Liable?
A.	Yes	No	No
B.	No	Yes	No
C.	Yes	Yes	Yes

Matrix 1

There are two salient ways in which the court might in principle make its decision in a case like this. It might have the judges do their individual reasoning and then aggregate their votes about the conclusion – the liability issue – on, say, a majority basis. In this case, the defendant would go free. Or it might have the judges aggregate their votes on the individual premises – the contract and breach issues – and let the resulting, collective judgements on those premises determine what the court rules on the conclusion. Since each premise commands majority support, the result in this case is that the defendant would be found liable. The doctrinal paradox, as presented in the jurisprudential literature, consists in the fact that the two procedures described yield different outcomes.

The paradox described will arise, not just when legal doctrine dictates that certain considerations are conceptually or epistemically prior to a certain issue – an issue on which a conclusion has to be reached – and that judgements on those considerations ought to dictate the judgement on the conclusion. It arises more generally whenever a group of people discourse together with a view to forming an opinion on a certain matter that rationally connects, by the lights of all concerned, with other issues.

For an example that is close to the case just discussed, consider an issue that might arise in a workplace, among the employees of a company: say, for simplicity, a company owned by the employees

(Pettit 2000c; 2001b). The issue is whether to forgo a pay-rise in order to spend the money thereby saved on introducing a workplace safety measure: perhaps a guard against electrocution. Let us suppose for convenience that the employees are to make the decision – perhaps because of prior resolution – on the basis of considering three separable issues: first, whether there is a serious danger of electrocution, by some agreed benchmark; second, whether the safety measure that a pay-sacrifice would buy is likely to be effective, by an agreed benchmark, in the event of there being a serious danger; and third, whether the pay-sacrifice involves an intuitively bearable loss for individual members. If an employee thinks that the danger is sufficiently serious, the safety measure sufficiently effective, and the pay-sacrifice sufficiently bearable, he or she will vote for the sacrifice; otherwise they will vote against. And so each will have to consider the three issues and then look to what should be concluded about the pay-sacrifice.

Imagine now that after appropriate dialogue and deliberation the employees are disposed to vote on the relevant premises and conclusion in the pattern illustrated by the following matrix for a group of three workers. The letters A, B and C represent the three employees and the 'Yes' or 'No' on any row represents the disposition of the relevant employee to admit or reject the corresponding premise or conclusion.

	Serious danger?	Effective measure?	Bearable loss?	Pay-sacrifice?
A.	Yes	No	Yes	No
B.	No	Yes	Yes	No
C.	Yes	Yes	No	No

Matrix 2

If this is the pattern in which the employees are inclined to vote, then a different decision will be made, depending on whether the group judgement is driven by how members judge on the premises or by how they judge on the conclusion. Looking at the matrix, we can see that though everyone individually rejects the pay-sacrifice, a majority supports each of the premises. If we think that the views of the employees on the conclusion should determine the group-decision, then we will say that the group-conclusion should be to reject the pay-sacrifice: there are only 'Noes' in the final column. But if we think that the views of the employees on the premises should determine the group-decision, then we will say that the group-conclusion should be to accept the pay-sacrifice: there are more 'Yeses' than 'Noes' in each of the premise columns.

There are familiar practices of group deliberation and decision-making corresponding to these different approaches. Thus the group would go the conclusion-driven way if members entered into deliberation and dialogue and then each cast their personal vote on whether to endorse the pay-sacrifice or not; in that case the decision would be against the pay-sacrifice. The group would go the premise-driven way, on the other hand, if there was a chairperson who took a vote on each of the premises – say, a show of hands – and then let logic decide the outcome; in this case the decision would be in favour of the pay-sacrifice.

The discursive dilemma generalizes in many different ways. It will arise with disjunctive as well as conjunctive reasoning, since a disjunctive set of premises, p or q, will support a conclusion r just in case the conjunctive set of premises not- (not-p and not-q) supports that conclusion. It will arise whenever there are three or more propositions at issue. And it will arise whenever there are three or more persons involved.

The options for the group in each of the discursive dilemmas illustrated are to form a collective conclusion-judgement directly, relying on a voting procedure of some kind; or to form collective premise-judgements on such a basis and let those judgements determine the conclusion to be endorsed. If the group goes the first way, then it leaves all matters of reasoning to individuals – it individualizes reason – and allows voting to determine the collective view on any issue, whether that be the issue raised in the conclusion or the issues associated with the premises. The problem here, of course, is that as a result the group itself will not satisfy reason; it will reject a conclusion that is supported by premises that it endorses. If the group goes the second way, then it does not canonize voting in the same way and it does not leave all matters of reasoning to individuals. Rather, it allows only a pattern of voting that is constrained in such a way that reason is instantiated at the collective level: the group will not get into the situation of rejecting a conclusion that is supported by premises it collectively endorses.

Stated in its most general way, the dilemma illustrated in these cases is that a collectivity of individuals which is required to judge on certain rationally connected issues has to make a hard choice as to whether or not to ensure that the collectivity displays reason in the pattern of judgements it makes. It may let collective decision-making be responsive to the votes of individuals on every issue, thereby allowing collective unreason. Or it may enforce collective reason by reducing the extent to which collective decision-making is responsive to individual voting. In short, it may individualize reason or it may collectivize reason and it cannot have it both ways. It cannot have it both ways, at any rate, so far as it follows certain natural procedures: it sticks with a form of voting, like the majoritarian practice, that is bound to yield a determinate view on any issue voted on, for example; and it does not allow collectivities to refuse to draw the conclusions of views already adopted.[1]

The collectivization of reason

Any groups that seek to make deliberative, reasoned judgements, then, face a dilemma. They may impose the discipline of reason only at the individual level, running the risk of collectively endorsing inconsistent or incoherent sets of propositions. Or they may impose the discipline of reason at the collective level, running the risk of collectively endorsing a proposition – the conclusion, in our examples – that a majority of them, perhaps even all of them, individually reject.

But how many groups will face the discursive dilemma? And of those which do face it, how will they generally be disposed to go? I want to argue that any collectivity that embraces a common purpose will face this sort of dilemma. And I want to show that such a collectivity will almost inevitably be forced to collectivize reason.

Groups and groupings come in many different varieties (French 1984; Stoljar 1973). Some are organized, others unorganized. Of those that are organized some are merely networks of interacting individuals, others are committed to the pursuit of common goals. And of those that are committed to the pursuit of common goals some are agreed on the quite specific considerations that should guide them in pursuit of those goals – they agree on how to make up their mind on any issue that arises – while others are happy to have issues resolved in such a way that different people may vote on the basis of different

---

[1] Christian List and I have argued elsewhere for a general impossibility result that obtains here (List and Pettit 2000). Suppose that certain individuals each have rationally satisfactory views on a rationally connected set of issues: they do not fail to have a view on any issue, they do not fail to draw the conclusions of their views, and they do not have inconsistent views. There is no aggregation procedure that is guaranteed to yield a collective set of views that is rationally satisfactory in the same way if it is supposed to work for any profile of individual views, and if it treats all the individuals and all the issues on an equal footing: it does not give any individual dictatorial status, for example, and it does not suggest that the collective views on some issues should dictate the collective view on any another.

considerations: such people only theorize their decisions incompletely (Sunstein 1997). An example of a purposive group that agrees on how to make up its mind is provided by the workers who want to decide about whether to forgo a pay-rise. Such a group can certainly confront a discursive dilemma, as our discussion shows, but this may not be thought very significant since most purposive groups will not be of this kind; most will be incapable of agreeing on the sorts of considerations that ought to dictate their decision on any issue. I now want to argue, however, that all purposive groups and groupings will inevitably face such a dilemma and, moreover, that they will face a powerful pressure to impose the discipline of reason at the collective level.

My argument for the claim that purposive groups will inevitably face discursive dilemmas can be summarized in these steps.

1   So far as the pursuit of an assumed purpose requires reasoning and judgement – so far as it is not like the goal of a tug-of-war team – any group is going to generate a history of judgements which it is on record as making; these will be judgements that shape how it acts in pursuit of the purpose.
2   Those past judgements will inevitably constrain the judgement that the group ought to make in various new cases; only one particular judgement in this or that case will be consistent or coherent with the past judgements.
3   And so the group will find itself confronted with the spectre of the discursive dilemma; it will be faced across time with a set of rationally connected issues such that there may be a choice between individualizing and collectivizing reason.

This argument can be extended to yield the conclusion that the group will be pressurized to impose the discipline of reason at the collective level.

4   The group will not be an effective or credible promoter of its assumed purpose if it tolerates inconsistency or incoherence in its judgements across time; not all the actions shaped by those discordant judgements can advance, or be represented as advancing, the same purpose.
5   Every such group will need to be an effective promoter of its assumed purpose and will need to be able to present itself as an effective promoter of that purpose; it will lose any hold on members, or any respect among outsiders, if it cannot do this.
6   And so every purposive group is bound to try to collectivize reason, achieving and acting on collective judgements that pass reason-related tests like consistency.

How will a purposive group be disposed to collectivize reason? We do not need to answer this question for purposes of the present argument. But it is worth noting that while there are many different strategies available (List and Pettit 2000), two plausible, further steps argue that such a group will generally, if not inevitably, have to follow something like the premise-driven procedure illustrated in our earlier examples.

7   The group will be unable to present itself as an effective promoter of its purpose if it routinely seeks to establish consistency and coherence in the cases envisaged by renouncing one or other of its past commitments; if it never allows its present judgement to be dictated by past judgements, there will be no possibility of taking the pronouncements of such an inconstant entity seriously.

8   Thus, any such purposive collectivity must avoid automatic recourse to the revision of past commitments and must generally make those judgements that are required in consistency or coherence – in consistency and coherence at the collective level – by its past judgements.

The force of this line of argument can be readily illustrated. Suppose that a political party announces in January, say on the basis of majority vote among its members, that it will not increase taxes if it gets into government. Suppose that it announces in June, again on the basis of majority vote, that it will increase defence spending. And now imagine that it faces the issue in September as to whether it will increase government spending in other areas of policy or organization. Should it allow a majority vote on that issue too?

If the party does allow a majority vote, then we know that even in the event of individual members being perfectly consistent across time, the vote may favour increased spending in other areas. The members may vote in the pattern of members A to C in the following matrix.

	Increase taxes?	Increase defence spending?	Increase other spending?
A.	No	Yes	No (reduce)
B.	No	No (reduce)	Yes
C.	Yes	Yes	Yes

Matrix 3

But the party cannot tolerate collective inconsistency of this kind, since that would make it a laughing-stock among its followers and in the electorate at large; it could no longer claim to be seriously committed to its alleged purpose. This means that it must not allow its judgements to be made in such a way that the discipline of reason is imposed only at the individual level. It has to ensure that that discipline is imposed at the collective level. And that means that in the ordinary run of things it must make its judgements in cases like the one illustrated after a premise-driven pattern. It may occasionally revoke earlier judgements in order to sustain an inconsistent judgement that is later supported by a majority. But it cannot make a general practice of this, on pain of again becoming a laughing-stock. It must routinely allow past judgements to serve as endorsed premises that dictate later commitments.

This argument with the political party is going to apply, quite obviously, to a large range of enduring and episodic collectivities. The argument does not rule out the possibility that those groups or groupings will occasionally reject the premise-driven procedure. They may choose to reject an earlier commitment in this or that case, for example, rather than revise their spontaneous judgement on the issue currently before them. Or they may sometimes choose to live, overtly or covertly, with an inconsistency. But it is hard to see how they could fail in the general run to take their past commitments as authoritative and to force their current judgements and decisions to fall in line.

Groups or groupings that collectivize reason may be usefully described as integrations of people, or integrated collectivities, or perhaps social integrates. This way of speaking emphasizes the fact that the collectivity involved integrates members into collective patterns of judgement and decision that respect the demands of reason at the collective level. It sounds a contrast with those groups and groupings that do not reason at all or that individualize the use of reason. These we naturally describe as aggregations of people, or as aggregated collectivities, or just as aggregates.

Integrations of people may be as small as the small number of individuals involved in a collaboration of some kind or as large as a multinational corporation. Integrations of people may endure across long periods of time, maintaining the rule of collective reason across changes of membership, or they may be more or less episodic. And integrations of people may conduct their decision-making in any of a variety of patterns. Thus they may involve all of their members in deliberation on every decision; or they may stage their decisions so that the full assembly only votes on general matters, delegating others to smaller bodies and to officers of the group; or they may involve a membership that is largely passive, with most being involved in official decisions only to the extent of needing to be pacified; or they may be articulated into subunits that are each passive in relation to one another; or whatever. I abstract from such issues of detail here, being mainly interested in the claim of integrated groups and groupings to be regarded as collective subjects proper.

The reality of collective subjects

We have seen that groups and groupings often face a hard choice between individualizing and collectivizing reason – that is the choice presented by the discursive dilemma – and that those collectivities that have a purpose to promote are bound to opt for the collectivization of reason; in particular, that they will usually opt for the sort of collectivization that involves treating existing commitments as premises from which conclusions on new issues are to be derived. What we should now register is that the collectivities that do this, integrating their members into patterns of judgement and decision that respect the demands of reason, will constitute genuine collective subjects.

Collectivities will constitute genuine subjects or agents so far and only so far as they are subject to mental predications of a non-metaphorical, non-summative kind. So at any rate I shall assume they have (see Pettit 2000c for a fuller treatment). They must display mental properties in their own right, not just by projection from the mental properties displayed by their members. Any collection of individuals may be held to judge that p, so far as the members individually judge that p; any collection may display the property of judging that p in the metaphorical, summative fashion mentioned by Quinton. A collection of individuals will constitute a collective subject just so far as it does significantly better in this respect: just so far as it displays mental properties that cannot be seen as merely the summative shadows of the properties displayed by its members.

Social integrates that collectivize reason display mental properties that are not mere reflections – in a summative, metaphorical way – of the properties of individual members. For the judgements and intentions of integrated collectivities, so far as they are rationally unified, can be dramatically discontinuous with those of their members. Integrated groups and groupings can make judgements that are rejected by each of their individual members and they can form intentions to do something such that at the moment when the intention is formed, no one member intends that the group should act that way.

Consider the workers in our earlier example and imagine that they submit themselves to the rule of reason at the collective level, thereby constituting a social integrate. Imagine in particular that they face the issue of whether or not to forgo a pay-rise, and that they cast their votes after the pattern illustrated in the second matrix. In the scenario envisaged, the integrated collectivity will form one judgement in respect of that issue, while the individual members will all support a contradictory opinion. The example shows, beyond all possibility of controversy, that the collective judgement of a social integrate may be discontinuous with the individual judgements made by members of the collectivity.

As the point applies to judgement, so it naturally extends to intention. For the collectivity that makes the judgement involved in each case can be said thereby to form the intention to act accordingly. The chairperson who has conducted the voting on the premises is authorized by the procedure of collectivizing reason to announce: 'Colleagues, our intention is fixed: we will forgo the pay-rise.' At the moment where the intention of the integrated group is fixed by this sort of declaration, no one individual intends that the group act in that way, or that he or she play their part in the group's acting in that way. Such individual intentions will follow on the formation of the group intention, of course, since the group can only act through the actions of its members. But they are not the stuff out of which the group intention is constructed; on the contrary, they are effects that the group intention plays a role in bringing about. They are like the intention to adopt suitable means that an individual's intention to pursue a given end naturally engenders.

The claim that collective intentions may be discontinuous from the intentions of individuals runs counter to the intuition defended by Anthony Quinton, that collectivities are only ever subjects in a metaphorical, summative sense. The discontinuity claim vindicates in the most compelling way possible the claim that there really are collective subjects and agents. It shows that if we are to count the subjects present in any domain then we may well have to take into account centres of collective as well as centres of individual agency. To miss out on the presence of collective subjects would be to overlook a level of social reality that may be of the utmost significance in the evolution of collective affairs.

Collective subjects are candidates for freedom

By the account given in the first chapter, the concept of a free agent is just the concept of an agent that is fit to be held responsible; specifically, fit to be held responsible because of the way their actions materialize, their self or psychology operates and their person relates to others. The question to which we now turn is whether collective subjects are agents of whom freedom in this sense can be predicated or denied.

A collective agent will be a candidate for freedom only if it is a centre of personhood, selfhood and action. It is because we do not regard non-human animals as persons or selves, even if we do take them to be sources of intentional action, that we think it inappropriate in most contexts to raise questions of freedom about them. Collective agents are certainly sources of intentional action, since they form intentions discontinuously from the intentions of their members, as we have just seen, and they act in fulfilment of such intentions. But do collective agents score over non-human animals in the other two respects? Do they count, not just as sources of action, but also as persons and selves?

There is a long tradition of ascribing personality – personhood and selfhood – to certain collectives, though it has recently fallen out of favour (Runciman 1997). I believe that the tradition is fundamentally sound and that it is perfectly proper to ascribe personality to integrated groups and groupings.

We argued earlier, starting from etymology, that it is natural to reserve the use of the words 'person' and 'self' for those agents who can speak for themselves in some sense and think of themselves under the aspect of first-person indexicals such as 'I' and 'me', 'my' and 'mine'. Not only do they have beliefs and desires and intentions, like any intentional subjects. They can give expression to those states in words – or in signs of some sort – and they can be held to those words; they can be expected, so far as they are sincere, to live up to the words in the things they believe and desire and do. Moreover, being able to express the contents of their own intentional states, and to live up to them in this way, they can equally be expected to be able to mark off those states – say, from the states ascribed to others – as, in their own words, what *I* believe or *I* desire or *I* intend or whatever.

If we think of persons as conversable interlocutors, then it is clear that integrated groups should count as persons too (Rovane 1997). To the extent that integrated collectivities bind themselves to the discipline of reason at the collective level – to the extent that they endorse a norm of living up to reason – they must be expected to live up to the words they authorize, and the deeds they perform, in the other things that they say and do. They must count as conversable interlocutors, and as subjects who can be held responsible for the things they accept and bring about.

Integrated collectivities will contrast in this respect with any groups that impose the discipline of reason only at the individual level.

Collectivities of this aggregate kind will not be answerable in the same way to words previously authorized or deeds previously performed. It will always be possible for such an aggregate to vote in favour of a judgement or an intention that is out of kilter with earlier commitments, and to do so without recognizing any embarrassment.

So far as integrated collectivities constitute conversable interlocutors, on a par with individual persons, they will have a personal point of view. From the standpoint of those in an integrated collectivity, the words defended in the past – and the judgements or intentions expressed in those words – will stand out from any words emanating from elsewhere as words that bind and commit them. Specifically, they will stand out for those of us in the collectivity as words that 'we' as a plural subject maintain. The argument in the singular case for why I as a person must conceive of my attitudes as matters of what *I* think applies in the plural case too, showing that we, the members of an integrated collectivity, must think of the group's attitudes as matters of what *we* think.

We saw earlier that if I think of myself under a proper name, say as PP, then I may believe that PP judges both that p and that the truth of 'p' entails the truth of 'q', and yet see no reason why I should judge that q: not, at any rate, unless I believe that I am PP, in which case I will already think of myself under the indexical 'I', not just under the name 'PP'. The same line of argument goes through in the plural case. Suppose that we in a socially integrated group, SI, recognize that SI judges both that p and that the truth of 'p' entails the truth of 'q'. That will not lead us as a group to judge that q, unless we make the extra judgement that we are SI. And if we do make that judgement then of course we will be thinking of ourselves already in the first, plural person, not just under the name 'SI'. As members of the integrated group, then, we must be possessed of a personal point of view and we must be able to think in 'we' terms.

The emphasis on the importance of 'we' connects with the insistence by writers like Margaret Gilbert (1989), John Searle (1995) and Annette Baier (1997) that there is no possibility of analysing we-talk in I-talk (see too Tuomela 1995, 183). The obstacle to reducing talk of 'we' to talk of 'I' will be just the obstacle that stands in the way of reducing indexical talk of what I think and do to non-indexical talk of what PP thinks and does. As there is a personal perspective that is available only with talk of 'I', so there is a personal perspective that becomes available only with talk of 'we'.

It appears, then, that integrated collectivities are persons in their own right, with the first-person point of view that is characteristic of selfhood. They are subjects that can enter into dialogue with individuals and with one another, being capable of being held to a growing record of commitments, both in the judgements they make and in the intentions they form and enact. And they are subjects such that those who compose them are forced, *qua* members of a collectivity, to think of it in the first person plural. From the point of view of those of us in any such collectivity, the things that the social integrate judges and intends are things that we judge and intend; they are not matters of merely impersonal record.

So far as collective subjects can count as persons and selves in this way, we should notice that corresponding criteria of personal identity and self-identity apply to them. We argued that someone at a later time is the same person as someone at an earlier time if and only if they relate across time in such a way that the later can be called upon, under discursive practice, to answer for or to the earlier. And we pointed out that a person at a later time can be regarded as the same self as that person at an earlier to the degree to which the later does not disown the attitudes and actions of the earlier. These conceptions of personal identity and self-identity apply in the collective as well as in the individual case.

An integrated collectivity at one time will be the same institutional person as a collectivity at an earlier just so far as the later collectivity can be held answerable, under standard discursive practice, for the judgements and intentions and actions of the earlier. What underlies this identity across time will be very different, of course, from what underlies the identity of an individual person across time: it will be a matter of interpersonal organization, not neuronal or psychological architecture. But the relationship itself will be of just the same kind as in the individual case.

As the same criterion of personal identity applies in the institutional as in the individual case, so too will the same criterion of self-identity apply in both cases. An integrated collectivity will be the same self as that collectivity at an earlier time just to the degree that it still owns or endorses the judgements, intentions and actions of the earlier. It may sound strange to speak of collective subjects as having or being selves but this is due to the powerful association of the notion of self with a breathing, sensate individual, not to any incoherence in the idea. Those who baulk at the usage may prefer to speak of the psychology or mind of an integrated collectivity but I shall stick to talking of its self.

Although social integrates have to be ascribed personality in the same way as individual human beings, it is worth emphasizing that such collective subjects differ from individuals in as many ways as they resemble them. They are not centres of perception or memory or sentience. They form their collective minds only on a restricted range of matters, to do with whatever purpose they are organized to advance. And they are artificial creatures whose responses may be governed by reason, not in the spontaneous manner that is characteristic of individual human beings, but only in a painstaking fashion. Their reasoning may be as tortuous as that of the impaired human being who has to work out reflectively, case by case, that in virtue of believing that p and that if p then q, he or she ought also to believe that q.

While integrated collectivities are persons and selves in virtue of being conversable and responsible centres of judgement, intention and action, then, they are persons and selves of a bloodless, bounded and crudely robotic variety. The most natural way to think of them is as agents to which individuals give life by suspending their own projects, now on this occasion, now on that, in order to serve the collective point of view. Those individuals retain their own points of view, at least in a virtual way, as they constitute social integrates in that manner. The integrates may take on a life of their own but it is an entirely artificial form of life and it remains always dependent on the continuing compliance – in the normal case the voluntary compliance – of the individuals who constitute them. (For a more radical point of view see Rovane 1997.)

Collective subjects can enjoy freedom

It remains to show that the collective subjects that socially integrated collectivities constitute can be free or unfree in ways that parallel the possibilities for individual subjects. We argued in the last chapter that what makes for freedom on the three fronts of action, self and person is always the presence of discursive control. This is true of collective subjects as well as of individual. They are capable of enjoying discursive control, just as individual subjects are capable of enjoying it, and they will be free just to the extent that they do indeed achieve such control.

The primary locus of freedom, under the discursive control theory, is in the relationship of a person to other persons. Agents will be free persons just to the extent that their relationships with other persons enable them to enjoy discursive control. And they will have free selves or perform free actions to the extent that the selves and actions in question are the sort that discursive control presupposes.

There is no problem in applying the theory of the free person to the collective subjects that we have in mind. Integrated collectivities, by our account of them, are precisely the sorts of collective subjects that can enter relationships with other persons, individual or collective, and that can grant and be granted discursive control in those relationships. They may themselves exercise force or coercion or manipulation in relation to other persons, and they may themselves experience the effects of force or coercion or manipulation. But equally they may avoid the practice of such hostile overtures, acknowledging the discursive control of those they deal with; and they may be lucky enough not to experience overtures of that kind, being dealt with in a discourse-friendly manner.

A collective subject will be a free institutional person, then, to the extent that it enjoys discourse-friendly relationships with other persons, individual or institutional. And it will be a person which itself respects the freedom of other persons, individual or institutional, to the extent that it grants those agents the enjoyment of discourse-friendly relationships. We will be raising later the question of how important it is that collective subjects enjoy freedom, especially when this is not correlated with an enjoyment of freedom on the part of members. And we will be looking equally at the question of how far collective subjects may represent a particularly important threat to the freedom of individual persons. But for the moment we put such issues aside.

A person will be a free self, we argued earlier, just so far as their self or psychology is the sort that discursive control presupposes. They do not have the elusive self of the person who routinely disowns past commitments, seeing the things they do from a bystander perspective. And they do not have the weak self that is incapable of sustaining the person in fidelity to those commitments that they do continue to own.

Collective subjects are capable of being free selves in this sense, as they are capable of being free persons. The social integrate that continually slips the noose of responsibility, claiming a fresh start with every challenge to answer for or to its past, will be an elusive self. The integrate that proves incapable of living up to the past commitments that it endorses, due to whatever flaw of internal organization, will be a weak self. But it should be clear that many social integrates are neither of these things. And to the extent that that is so, they will count as having a free self or psychology.

The distinction in view here between the free and the unfree collectivity marks the difference between the regular, robust sort of institutional entity that recognizes a past and effectively lives up to it and the entity that vacillates in the recognition or fidelity that it gives the past. If this vacillation becomes chronic, then the entity in question will begin to seem less and less like a properly integrated collectivity: a proper institutional person. But that should be no surprise, for equally the permanently vacillating human being will look less and less like a person in the proper, individual sense of the term; they will begin to look like what Harry Frankfurt (1988) calls a 'wanton'.

Finally, to free action. An action will be free, so we argued in the last chapter, to the extent that it materializes under discursive control. The free action will typically materialize under virtual discursive control, not active. It may be the product of routine or inertia or whatever but if there is ever a question about whether it is justified from the point of view of the agent, then the action will be maintained or defended only so far as it is supported by relevant discursive considerations.

This theory of free action, like the theories of the free self and the free person, applies as readily to collective subjects as it does to individual agents. The actions of a social integrate may materialize in any of a variety of ways, depending on such variables as how far there is delegation to officials and how far joint decision-making is conducted according to blind routine. But it is obvious that however they materialize, they may be subject to discursive control, active or virtual. And to the extent that such control is ensured, so too will the fitness of the group to be held responsible.

It may be that the actions come about under the pressure of myopic or self-serving responses on the part of the officials involved, of course, and that they are more or less insulated from discursive interrogation and revision at the collective level. In this case, the actions will not reflect the mind of the social integrate, only the minds of factions within it, and will not properly count as things it freely does. But equally it may be that whatever the pressures at work in their genesis, discursive interrogation remains always so likely and so effective that we can think of the actions as discursively controlled at that level. In this case the actions will reflect that controlling, collective mind and we will be able to speak of them as things the social integrate freely does.

Responsibility, individual and collective

One of the things that our discussion makes clear is that we can distinguish between the actions of individuals when they perform in group roles – say, when they represent the group or cast a vote in group deliberations – and the actions of the collectivity itself. We should note in conclusion that this has an important implication for the distinction between individual and collective levels of responsibility. It means that it will often be appropriate to hold a group responsible for what is done by the agency of an individual or individuals, and yet not appropriate to hold those individuals themselves responsible; they will be fit to be held responsible only for their individual contributions.

Consider the case of the workers who collectivize reason and, voting as in Matrix 2, adopt the pay-sacrifice. In this case all the individual members vote, and the individual who happens to be chairing the meeting determines the votes on each premise and the conclusion that those votes support. And in virtue of those actions of the individuals involved the group as a whole adopts the pay-sacrifice. It is possible and essential in this case to distinguish between individual and group action, and individual and group responsibility. The group can be praised for making the pay-sacrifice, say on the grounds of this being a far-seeing initiative. But the individuals involved cannot be held responsible and praised for that result, only for their individual contributions in voting as they did. The result came about, after all, without the support of a single individual in the group; each individual came to the conclusion that the group should not forgo the pay-rise.

Still, this may be thought too quick. The individual members are fit to be held responsible for going along with the procedure – the premise-driven procedure – that ensures, given the views on the premises for which they are also fit to be held responsible, that the group votes in favour of the pay-sacrifice. And doesn't that mean that they are fit to be held responsible for the particular decision taken? Not necessarily, for the individuals involved may not have been in a position to foresee such a result. Given that the individuals involved may have been far more numerous than the three represented in the matrix, it may even have been a consequence no one could reasonably have predicted.

In exploring matters of responsibility, then, we need to allow for a possible bifurcation between individual and collective responsibility. We need to be ready to admit that there are two streams of action along which to trace lines of responsibility, one at the collective level, the other at the individual. The group may be fit to be held responsible for a given action, the individuals fit to be held responsible for their particular contributions, and yet it may make no sense to parcel out responsibility for the group action among those individuals. The bifurcation of individual and collective responsibility is only one of many complexities that arise in this area but it has a particular salience from our perspective (see Kutz 2001). It comes into view only when we recognize, as we have done here, that collective subjects are not the shadows projected by their individual members but have the capacity to function in their own right as free and responsible agents.

Conclusion

Having argued in previous chapters that what makes for freedom in the individual human being is the enjoyment of discursive control, we raised the question in this chapter as to whether collectivities of human beings might not enjoy a corresponding sort of free agency. I argued for two main propositions. First, that we have to countenance the reality of many collective subjects as agents which are discontinuous with the individuals who make them up. And second that we have to recognize that those subjects can enjoy freedom as discursive control in a manner that exactly parallels the ways in which individual subjects may enjoy it.

The argument for the reality of collective subjects began from the discursive dilemma exemplified in the doctrinal paradox that has recently attracted attention in jurisprudence. The dilemma is that when individuals have to form collective views on rationally connected issues, then they face a hard choice between being sensitive to individual reason and thereby allowing collective irrationality, or enforcing collective rationality and thereby reducing sensitivity to individual reason. I argued that any collectivity that pursues or avows a purpose will confront this dilemma and that it will have to impose the discipline of reason at the collective level. And I then showed that such a group or grouping will form intentions and make judgements that are discontinuous with the intentions and judgements of their members, sometimes even the unanimously supported intentions and judgements of their members. This illustrates in a particularly dramatic way the reality of collective subjects as entities that are discontinuous with the individual agents who make them up.

Having showed that such collective subjects – such social integrates – can have this sort of discontinuous reality, I went on to demonstrate that they will be persons and selves in a sense that makes them candidates for freedom. They will be persons and selves so far as they are capable of entering discourse with others as conversable interlocutors: in particular, capable of giving their word on various matters and then living up to those words. I argued that any such collective subject can enjoy freedom in person, self and action. It will be a free person so far as it enjoys discursive control in its relations to other persons, individual and institutional. It will be a free self to the extent that it does not systematically elude past commitments and is not so weak that it cannot live up to those commitments. And its actions will be free so far as they are controlled, virtually or actively, by relevant discursive considerations.

The chapter concluded with a brief observation on individual and collective responsibility. Under the account offered here, it is possible for groups and groupings to do things in such a way that while the collectivities are responsible for those things, the individuals who act on their behalf are not. The individuals in question will be responsible for the things that they do as individuals in enacting their group-roles, of course, together with the foreseeable results of those actions. But the foreseeable results may not extend to what the group does in consequence of their behaviour.

6

Freedom and Politicization

Towards a political ideal of freedom

Much of the discussion up to this point has been indirectly relevant to political matters. While questions to do with freedom of action and freedom of the self may be primarily of psychological interest, the psychology involved may be the collective psychology presupposed to group agency, not just the psychology of the individual. And in any case questions to do with freedom of the person connect up directly with political concerns. This is particularly true once we take the freedom of the person, as under the theory of freedom as discursive control, to involve a social power in relation to others, not just a psychological capacity.

But we now shift focus and give a more central place to the political perspective. Drawing on the theory of freedom as discursive control, we turn to the conception of freedom as a political ideal. This is the ideal of freedom that we ought to have in mind when we say, as most political theories say, that the polity or state ought to do what it can to enable its members to enjoy freedom. I shall argue that the ideal that we ought to have in mind when we say this is not discursive control as such but rather something more specific.

The polity or state is a collective subject of the kind discussed in the last chapter. Specifically it is a collective subject to which we give a special status within the boundaries of its operation. We take it to include all permanent residents – broadly, citizens – in its membership;

we take it to have a uniquely legitimate claim on the use of force on behalf of the members as a whole, even when that force is deployed against individual members; and we take it to be obliged to further various ideals, such as the ideal of freedom for its members or citizens. We shall be discussing the conditions under which the state is legitimate in the next chapter; in this, we take its existence and legitimacy for granted.

The question I want to discuss arises for anyone who thinks that the state should indeed be concerned with freedom or liberty. If we say that it should have this concern, then we must have some particular ideal of liberty in mind. And the question is, which ideal ought we to have in mind? In particular, which ideal ought we to have in mind, starting from a conception of freedom as discursive control?

The obvious suggestion to make in response is that discursive control is the ideal that the state ought to foster. But there are three respects in which the conception of freedom as discursive control does not give us, in itself, an attractive political ideal. First of all, the conception of freedom as discursive control applies as much to collective subjects as it does to individual; secondly, it is dependent on variables in individual psychology that are better insulated from the concerns of the state; and thirdly, it abstracts from how far individuals have rich opportunity sets in regard to which they can exercise discursive control. I comment on each of these points in turn.

It would be highly counter-intuitive to say that the state had the task of furthering discursive contol in respect of collective as well as individual agents. For there are many cases where the demands of individual freedom and the demands of collective are likely to clash and it scarcely seems right to say the freedom of certain individuals should be sacrificed for the sake of an increase in the freedom of a collectivity, taken as such. Of course increasing the freedom of a collectivity will often mean increasing the freedom of individuals involved in that collectivity, in which case a sacrifice may be easy enough to justify. But the justification would not then be grounded in the increase of collective freedom as such, only in the corresponding increase in the freedom of the individuals involved.

I propose that only the discursive control of individual human subjects ought to be of concern for a state, even a state committed to freedom. The state should take an interest in the discursive control of collectivities, so I suggest, only so far as that is associated with a corresponding level of discursive control on the part of the individuals involved. Collective subjects come into existence in order to serve the interests of individuals, or they are justified in their existence by the way they serve individuals. It would represent a bizarre normative position to think that their freedom as discursive control mattered in itself, and not just in virtue of the correlated freedom that individuals may enjoy. This option in favour of concentrating on people's personal freedom represents a sort of moral or ethical humanism but not one that is likely to prompt serious misgivings (Kukathas and Pettit 1990, chapter 1; cf. Raz 1986).

Should we restrict discursive control a little, then, and say that the state ought to be concerned with the discursive control enjoyed by individual subjects but not by collective subjects? Not quite. A second problem is that among the variables that affect people's enjoyment of discursive control are psychological or intrapersonal factors to do with the nature of their selves, their strength of will, and the like, and it would be reckless to put these within the purview of a coercive state. There is only so much that such a state can be usefully expected to do and by the lights of most of us, it is unlikely that the state can do anything useful on the intrapersonal front. On the contrary, it seems all too likely that were the state to embrace the ambition of improving people's psychology in the respects required then it might well degenerate into an intrusive and oppressive agency. The point is a familiar one and does not need any emphasis here (Berlin 1969, Essay 1).

Should we say, then, that the state ought to be concerned with the interpersonal, but not with the intrapersonal, requirements of discursive control among the individuals who are its members? A third problem suggests that this is not quite right either. The requirements mentioned all involve agency rather than the environment in which agency operates. This is understandable, given that we have been abstracting from environment up to this point in the book. But clearly the state can usefully concern itself with environment as well as agency. It can try to mitigate the effects of a harsh natural order or a harsh social system and ensure that people enjoy adequate opportunity sets in respect of which to make discursively controlled choices. This being so, the political ideal of freedom ought to reflect that possibility and ought to hold out the prospect of action on the side of environment as well as on the side of agency.

A political ideal of freedom, then, will be in one way more austere, and in another way more enriched, than freedom as discursive control. It will be more austere, so far as it will only bear on the interpersonal, not on the intrapersonal preconditions of discursive control, and only on the requirements of control in individual subjects. It will be more enriched, so far as it will articulate the requirements for enjoying discursive control on two fronts: not just on the side of agency, but also on the side of the environment where agency is exercised; not just on the side of interpersonal relations but also on the side of impersonally determined opportunities.

The contending ideals

What are the main candidates for the role of a political ideal of freedom? It has been traditional for some time to distinguish between two forms of the political ideal of liberty, one negative and the other positive, and to proceed as if these exhausted the field (Berlin 1969). But positive freedom is not an ideal that we have any reason to consider here; and negative freedom is not the only alternative to the positive ideal.

Positive freedom is sometimes equated with a psychologically demanding ideal – the rule of reason in the soul – of a kind with the psychological capacity required by discursive control. But in that sense it scarcely looks like an ideal that is usefully susceptible to political influence, as we have just seen. At other times positive freedom is equated with the ideal of incorporation in a democracy that is sometimes described, in Benjamin Constant's (1988) phrase, as the liberty of the ancients. But in this sense it does not constitute a form of political freedom so much as a means whereby we might hope to see freedom promoted or protected; we shall be discussing that means in the next chapter.

Negative freedom, as that is conceived in Berlin's dichotomy, is subject to a different but equally telling problem. It is identified with freedom from interference, where interference is generally taken to involve intentional obstruction or coercion (Miller 1993, 12–13). But, as we shall be seeing, interference is not the only politically visible and malleable way in which discursive control may be threatened and it is a big mistake to focus exclusive attention on it.

I prefer to taxonomize things on quite different lines. I distinguish between three plausible forms that the political ideal of freedom can assume. The first equates political freedom with non-limitation, the second with non-interference and the third with non-domination. The ideal of political freedom as non-limitation holds that all inhibitions on freedom, impersonal as well as interpersonal, are on a par and that people are free just to the extent that such limitations are absent. The other two ideals disagree, arguing that interpersonal inhibitions are more damaging to freedom and that impersonal inhibitions represent only a secondary evil; they may condition the enjoyment of freedom, as I put it, but they do not compromise freedom in the same way. Those two ideals differ among themselves, however, on the question of what the interpersonal inhibition on freedom involves. The one ideal holds that interpersonal inhibition is nothing more or less than interference – intentional or quasi-intentional interference – while the other represents it as domination.

I look in this chapter at these three different versions of the political ideal of liberty and try to argue in favour of the ideal of non-domination. The argument proceeds as follows. First I describe the ideal of non-limitation and reveal the problem that makes the ideal of non-interference preferable to it. Then I describe the ideal of non-interference and identify flaws that point us towards the ideal of non-domination. I spend some time elaborating the ideal of non-domination and explaining its merits, and I conclude the discussion by providing the historical background that entitles us to describe this ideal as republican in character.

One last observation, however, before proceeding. When we take an agent or agency like the state and identify an ideal with which it is to be concerned, there is always a question as to whether the ideal is supposed to bind the agency in a consequentialist or a non-consequentialist way. The issue is whether the agency should promote the ideal, even at the cost of not always complying with it in its own behaviour or relationships; or whether the agency should comply with the ideal, at whatever cost to its effectiveness in promoting it (Baron, Pettit and Slote 1997). The question for us, then, is whether the state that is charged with embracing the ideal of liberty should be required thereby to promote the ideal as best it can; or whether it is enjoined to comply with the ideal in its relationships with its citizens, and not to worry about how freedom fares overall.

Happily, we may set this question aside. My own view is that the state should be primarily required to promote political freedom, a requirement that will entail compliance with the ideal in most circumstances, but not in all (Pettit 1997a, chapter 3; Pettit 2001c). But I do not need to go into a defence of that position here, since the points to be made in this chapter can be endorsed by those who give a consequentialist or non-consequentialist reading to the demands of political freedom.

The ideal of non-limitation

The ideal of political freedom as non-limitation begins with the thought that there are different ways in which someone's freedom to do one thing rather than another may be curtailed by factors within the state's purview. Some involve intentional human agency, for example; others the unintended consequences of human agency; and others again the natural limitations imposed by disability, illness, poverty and the like. The ideal suggests that these are equally bad and holds that people will enjoy political freedom just to the extent that they escape the effects of all. It says that all forms of limitation, intentional and non-intentional – interpersonal and impersonal – impact on freedom in the same way and that political freedom should be taken as nothing more or less than non-limitation. A person will be politically free just to the extent that they avoid limitations of these kinds. And two or more people will be equally free just to the extent that they avoid limitations in the same measure, even if they differ in the proportion of interpersonal to impersonal limitations that they suffer.

This is an attractively simple theory of political freedom and is endorsed, at least implicitly, by many writers. Those who endorse it often begin with the common claim that freedom is non-interference – freedom is what Berlin's negative conception holds it to be – and then go on to the not so common comment that interference should be taken to include the non-intentional obstruction and restriction that can get in a person's way as well as the intentional (Cohen 1979; Steiner 1994). In standard usage, interference is restricted to acts of coercion and obstruction and the like which people perform intentionally or quasi-intentionally: that is, in such a way that they may at least count as negligent (Miller 1984; Miller 1993, 12–17). When the concept of interference includes non-intentional restrictions on freedom as well as interference in the ordinary sense, and freedom is identified with non-interference, then the ideal of political freedom espoused is that which I describe here as non-limitation.

The limitations that are said to take away political freedom on this approach are sometimes restricted to those that make free action impossible, by removing or enforcing certain options (Taylor 1982; Steiner 1994; Carter 1999). But there is no reason inherent in the theory why the category of limiting factors should not be extended further. There is no reason, for example, why factors that raise the costs of taking one or another option should not be said to reduce political freedom; they affect the ease with which people exercise discursive control, if not the range over which it is exercised. The factors that reduce political freedom in this way, as distinct from removing it altogether, would include acts of coercion whereby one person credibly threatens another as well as those natural events whereby an agent's taking a certain course is made more hazardous.

Although the ideal of political freedom as non-limitation is simple and straightforward, it does not look very attractive from the point of view of someone concerned about people's enjoyment of discursive control. Once we see discursive control as the key element in freedom, then we are bound to think that some limiting factors are worse than others, contrary to what this ideal proposes. Those interpersonal limitations that stem from the obstruction or coercion of others, for example, represent far deeper incursions on freedom as discursive control than comparable obstacles that stem from the impersonal environment of choice. They involve denying a person discursive control, and the status that goes with it, whereas the impersonal limitations do not: such obstacles restrict the domain of options in respect of which discursive control can be enjoyed but they do not deprive the agent of such control in the same way.

The point can readily be illustrated by considering the difference between a threat and a warning. The person who threatens to do damage to your car if you leave it parked in a certain spot may hold out exactly the same prospect of damage as someone who warns you that if you park your car there it is likely to be damaged, say in a coming storm. But there is an enormous gulf separating the two situations. In each you find that your choice is worse than you thought; there is a serious prospective cost attached to leaving your car parked where it is. But in the first scenario, unlike the second, there is also another problem: apart from indicating that there is a cost attached to leaving your car, the person who issues a threat challenges your very possession of discursive control in regard to the choice on hand.

The blindness of the ideal of non-limitation to this distinction has direct implications for the sort of state action it would tend to support. It would allow the state to do everything possible to cope with limitations on freedom due to handicap and illness, lack of education and information, insecurity and poverty, and on that account it may be found appealing; it would look for a very rich environment of opportunities. But the ideal would permit the state to coerce or manipulate or force people in this or that manner – even short of emergency circumstances where people's life or health is at risk – just so long as this was beneficial in the overall struggle against limitation: just so long as those interpersonal assaults on freedom promised to emancipate people from somewhat larger impersonal obstacles. Because it demonizes impersonal and interpersonal obstacles equally, the ideal would be likely to justify a state in treating people as less than properly discursive subjects.

This problem gives us reason to reject the ideal of non-limitation as a political counterpart to the ideal of freedom as discursive control. The reduction or removal of discursive control is intuitively much more damaging than a limitation in the number of choices that can be discursively made. It might be defensible for the state to resort to such an invasion of freedom in extreme circumstances where people's life or health is at stake. But short of extreme circumstances, no such assault on freedom could be justified by the mere fact that it makes it possible for the state to remove a non-intentional limitation that happens to restrict choice to a slightly greater degree. The lesson is that any ideal of freedom ought to regard interpersonal restrictions on a person's freedom as more serious than the impersonal restrictions that arise non-intentionally from the natural order or from the way things are socially organized.

The ideal of non-interference

Towards the concept of non-interference

This criticism is the cue for introducing the second candidate for the role of political counterpart to freedom as discursive control. That is the ideal, as it is ordinarily described, of freedom as non-interference. The ideal takes interference to be the paradigmatic or unique form of interpersonal inhibition on freedom and it holds that freedom primarily requires the reduction of such interference.

How exactly to understand interference? Some people will interfere with another, I suggest, so far as they intentionally or quasi-intentionally worsen the other's choice by means of one of the following initiatives: removing an option; raising the costs attached to an option; or denying the person knowledge of the options available or of the associated costs. Under this definition, obstruction and agenda-rigging are forms of interference, since they remove options. Coercion is a form of interference so far as it raises the costs of taking an option – this, as punishment may also do – or, to cover the case of a coercive bluff, denies the agent knowledge of those costs. And manipulation of an agent's psychology or belief-set will be forms of interference so far as they also deny the agent knowledge of options or costs.

The ideal of freedom as non-interference will have two components, if it is designed not just to demonize interpersonal interference but also to treat impersonal limitations as a secondary evil. It will hold that a person is politically free just to the extent that, first, they are not subject to interference by others; and second, they are not subject to limitations on the enjoyment of such non-interference. To the extent that a person satisfies the first requirement, they will enjoy formal freedom as non-interference. To the extent that they also satisfy the second requirement, they will enjoy effective or real freedom as non-interference (Van Parijs 1995). Formal freedom as non-interference requires the absence of the factor – interference – that inherently compromises such freedom, as we may put it. Effective freedom as non-interference also requires the absence of non-compromising factors – say, natural obstacles – that condition the extent to which people can make uninterfered-with choices; it requires, not just a capacity for acting without interference, but an environment of opportunity in which there is ample scope for the exercise of that capacity (Pettit 1997a, chapter 2).

Some theorists of freedom as non-interference, particularly in the so-called libertarian camp, argue that all the state should be concerned about is formal freedom, not effective. But this looks like an unmotivated circumscription of concern and I shall assume that the ideal of freedom as non-interference also licenses a concern for making formal freedom effective. This extra concern may be described, in John Rawls's (1971) way, as a concern for improving the value of formal freedom to those who enjoy it, through increasing their opportunities to exercise it: through lifting the restraints associated with handicap or inability or poverty or whatever.

Under the ideal of political freedom, so constructed, interference is taken as a way in which freedom is compromised, whereas limitation is represented as a way in which freedom is conditioned. The compromising of freedom by interference is cast as a more serious affront than its conditioning by natural or other unintended forms of limitation. And this prioritizing of interference serves to distinguish the ideal from the simpler ideal of non-limitation and to guard it against the criticism made of that ideal. The state will not be licensed to compromise people's freedom just because it thereby combats a form of conditioning that places a somewhat larger obstacle or cost in the way of choice. For the compromising of freedom will be taken as a more serious form of damage than an otherwise similar conditioning.

The priority accorded to removing or reducing interference over removing or reducing limitation may be more or less significant. At the limit it might be the lexical sort of ordering, under which no increase of interference, no matter how small, could justify any decrease in limitation, no matter how large (cf. Rawls 1971). Short of that limit it might involve weighting interference more heavily – more heavily in this or that degree – than limitation (Van Parijs 1995, 26). We abstract here from the precise kind of priority that is recommended.

How plausible is it to take the ideal of political freedom to be nothing more or less than an ideal of non-interference? The question is of the first importance, because the ideal of freedom as non-interference, understood in roughly the fashion I have described, is the dominant ideal in contemporary politics and political theory and has been in the ascendant since early in the nineteenth century. Libertarians take the formal component in non-interference to be the supreme ideal relevant to what the state should do and how the state should be. Liberals of a broader persuasion take one of two general lines. They understand the ideal as effective, not just formal non-interference, and take that richer ideal to be the supreme political ideal (Van Parijs 1995); or they argue that the ideal, formal or effective, combines with equality or the elimination of poverty or something of the kind to constitute the supreme political ideal (Rawls 1971).

There are two problems that I see with the ideal of political freedom as non-interference. The first problem is that it is not constitutionally rich enough to allow us to discern the possibility of a freedom-friendly state, and the second that it is not sociologically rich enough to allow us to see all the problems that such a state might address.

First criticism

The first problem is that by casting interference as the primary affront to political freedom, the ideal fails to make a distinction that is salient from the point of view of discursive control. This is the distinction, mentioned earlier, between the sort of interference that is forced to track the avowable interests of the interferee – this, in the way that Ulysses' sailors track his express interests when they keep him bound – and the sort that is downright hostile: the sort that is not forced to track the interferee's avowable interests and that typically reflects the interests or perceptions of the interferer. The first sort of interference is non-arbitrary, in the sense that it is controlled in a passive or virtual way by what the interferee thinks and wants. The second sort is arbitrary, in the sense that such control is lacking, and an arbitrary influence – typically, the interferer's own interest or judgement – is put in its place.

By failing to make this distinction – by painting all forms of interference with the same brush – the ideal of non-interference has to say that all forms of coercive law-making and administration are hostile as such to political freedom. The ideal is not constitutionally rich enough to give us reason for properly distinguishing and assessing different ways in which the state might be organized. The only concern it licenses is an interest in keeping state interference at the level where interference overall, public and private, is minimized and non-intentional limitations are satisfactorily reduced, by whatever criterion is thought relevant.

This position is blind to the contrast between states that differ, intuitively, in the degree to which the authorities have an arbitrary power over citizens. At one extreme are states where the authorities are not themselves ordinary citizens, where they are not popularly elected and are not subject to popular challenge, where they can rule case-by-case rather than according to general law, where they need not give any defence of their decisions, and where there are no countervailing forces to check their performance. At the other extreme are states where the authorities are themselves ordinary citizens before the law, where they are required to submit to popular election and criticism, where they can govern only according to the rule of law, where they have to defend their laws in public, and where they divide into different bodies – executive, legislative and judicial – that serve to keep one another in check. In the former case the state has an arbitrary power of interference over its citizens, in the latter it has a power of interference, as any state must have, but this power is far from arbitrary. The authorities will be powerfully motivated to pay serious attention to what the citizens may be presumed to want – in particular, to want in common – from government and to try to legitimate what they do by reference to common citizen interests. They will be motivated to relate to citizens as his sailors related to Ulysses, though the relationship will be made more complex by the fact that there are many citizens, with many points of view, while there is only one Ulysses. More on the implications of that complexity in the next chapter.

The commitment to treating state interference on a par with interference by other agencies is wholly counter-intuitive. For, rhetoric aside, there is a great difference between the relatively non-arbitrary power that a state may exercise in imposing a tax, or establishing a coercively enforced law, or even applying a penalty to a convicted offender, and the wholly arbitrary power that an individual or corporation assumes in obstructing or coercing someone for private benefit, in manipulating the choices before the person, or in creating an atmosphere in which the person will feel intimidated. To the extent that an agency's power of interference in one's life is checked by a requirement to track one's avowable interests – even just the interests one has in common with others in the same boat – to that extent, however limited it may be, the interference exercised does not challenge one's possession of discursive control in the same way as the interference of common offenders.

The position associated with the ideal of non-interference is not only constitutionally impoverished, in failing to support a preference for non-arbitrary over arbitrary interference. Because of being so impoverished – because of being so hard on all forms of interference, non-arbitrary as well as arbitrary – it will also make it difficult to justify the claim that a concern with effective non-interference would support a strongly redistributive, welfare state (*pace* Van Parijs 1995). The ills which such a state would be designed to counter might include interference by some in the lives of others but they will typically involve the impersonal limitations associated with handicap, inability, poverty and the like. There is much that the state might effectively do to combat these ills and thereby to improve people's enjoyment of discursive control: to extend the range or ease with which they exercise such control. But if interference is the primary affront to political freedom, and if all state action involves interference, then it is not going to be easy to justify a priority rule under which a good deal of state interference is allowed in order to cope with such ills.

My first criticism of the ideal of non-interference, then, is that the ideal is not constitutionally rich enough to recognize the difference between a relatively arbitrary state power and a relatively non-arbitrary one – both are powers of interference and to that extent bad – and that it thereby puts severe shackles on what the state can be asked or allowed to do. As we have just seen, for example, it makes it difficult to justify a demand that the state pursue welfare measures in any significant measure.

Second criticism

My second criticism of the ideal of non-interference complements this first line of attack. It is that not only is the ideal constitutionally too poor to allow for a suitably active state; it is sociologically too poor to recognize all that the state might be intuitively required to do. The first problem stems from the implication that all interference is bad, even interference that is relatively non-arbitrary. The second problem comes from the suggestion that only interference is bad and that there is no problem, from the point of view of freedom, with relationships in which interference does not actually materialize or is not particularly likely to materialize.

This suggestion runs in the face of something that we already discussed in the chapter before last. This is that it is possible to have your freedom as discursive control severely challenged by agents and agencies that never actually exercise any interference and that may elicit dispositions in you that make it very unlikely they ever will.

These are agents and agencies that have a power of arbitrary interference in your life but that rarely if ever exercise that power. They may have little reason to exercise that power, indeed, so far as they can depend on you to make efforts to keep them sweet, tailoring your actions to their expected wishes, and staying out of their way if you do not. While they may not assume the profile of interferers in your life they manage to control what you do in relevant areas with marvellous effectiveness. They operate in those areas like a master or *dominus* and what they exercise in relation to you may be well described as *dominatio* or domination.

Domination comes in many forms. Think of the child of the emotionally volatile parent; the wife of the occasionally violent husband; or the pupil of the teacher who forms arbitrary likes and dislikes. Think of the employee whose security requires keeping the boss or manager sweet; the debtor whose fortunes depend on the caprice of money-lender or bank-manager; or the small business owner whose viability depends on the attitude taken by a bigger competitor or a union boss. Think of the welfare recipient whose fortunes turn on the mood of the counter-clerk; the immigrant or indigenous person whose standing is vulnerable to the whims that rule politics and talk-back radio; or the public employee whose future depends, not on performance, but on the political profile that an ambitious minister happens to find electorally most useful. Think of the older person who is vulnerable to the culturally and institutionally unrestrained gang of youths in her area. Or think indeed of the young offender whose level of punishment depends on how far politicians or newspapers choose to whip up a culture of vengeance.

In all of these cases someone lives at the mercy of others. That person is dominated by those others in the sense that even if the others don't interfere in his or her life, they have an arbitrary power of doing so: there are few restraints or costs to inhibit them. If the dominated person escapes ill treatment, that is by the grace or favour of the powerful. The price of liberty in such a world is not eternal vigilance but eternal discretion. The person lives in the power or under the mastery of others: they occupy the position of a *dominus* in his or her life. And so far as the person is subject to domination of this kind, they are bound to censor and inhibit what they do, so that the net effect on their behaviour will be just as deep as any that active interference might have achieved. The self-censorship or self-inhibition that the person practises need not involve actively thwarting desire; it will occur just so far as there are any options, otherwise desired or undesired, that a wish to keep the dominating party sweet would stop them taking.

But won't interference in a person's life be made more likely by the fact of domination and won't the ideal of non-interference give us reason on that account to complain about it? Not necessarily. So far as domination by others leads a person to censor and inhibit what they do, it may be very unlikely indeed that those others will ever practise interference. Self-censorship and self-inhibition is not itself a form of interference and if it actually serves to make interference less likely, then adherents of the ideal of non-interference can find no grounds for complaining about it. On the contrary, indeed, they may even have to hail it as something that advances the ideal they embrace.

The second problem with the ideal of non-interference, then, is that it does not offer any grounds for making a political complaint about relationships where such domination obtains. At least it does not offer any grounds for complaint so long as active interference fails to be a likely prospect or, to be still more specific, so long as any active interference that is likely fails to warrant the interfering activities that a state response to the problem would require. The ideal is sociologically too poor to recognize the reality of domination as a way in which freedom as discursive control can be diminished. The most it can recognize is that the self-censorship and self-inhibition induced by domination is, like non-intentional limitation, a factor that restricts what people do.

The ideal of non-domination

Towards the concept of non-domination

As our criticism of the ideal of non-limitation served as a cue for moving to the ideal of non-interference, so these criticisms serve as the cue for introducing the ideal of non-domination. I want to argue that this ideal is much more appealing as an account of political freedom than the alternatives described; in particular, that it articulates nicely those requirements of discursive control that we might reasonably expect the state to monitor and do something about.

The ideal of non-domination starts with the notion of interference as we explicated it in the last section, holding that a person enjoys non-domination to the extent that they are not exposed to an arbitrary power of interference on the part of others. There are two respects, then, in which it contrasts with the ideal of non-interference. First, it does not indict interference as such, only interference that is arbitrary: interference that is not forced to track the avowable interests of the interferee. And second, it indicts not just the experience of arbitrary interference, but any exposure to a power of arbitrary interference, whether or not that power is exercised.

The arguments for making these two moves away from the ideal of non-interference, and for embracing the ideal of non-domination instead, have already been given in our criticisms of the earlier ideal. By targeting only arbitrary interference, the ideal of non-domination points us towards the constitutional challenge of designing a polity that can possess coercive and related powers but be so constrained that these powers of interference tend not to be arbitrary. By targeting exposure to arbitrary interference, and not just the experience of such interference, the ideal points us towards the sociological challenge of identifying those areas where without actually acting against others, some people keep others under their thumb; it directs us to areas where state action may be usefully employed to rectify domination.

A constitutionally rich ideal

The ideal of non-domination will be attractive under both of these aspects to anyone concerned about discursive control. To the extent that state action is not arbitrary – to the extent that it is forced to track people's common avowable interests – it does not represent an assault on people's possession of discursive control. It occurs in a context where the guiding assumption is that the action is justified only so far as it satisfies the interests that people can ascribe in common to themselves, even if on this or that occasion an individual might wish that it take a different direction: say, might wish that though the law be enforced, it not be enforced against them. The assumption is that people have discursive reason to endorse the action and that this is what makes the action legitimate.

To the extent that that assumption is true – and this may only be to a limited extent – the state will not have the effect of a mugger or a defrauder or a thief. And to the extent that the state signals the presence and relevance of the assumption, it will effectively recognize those over whom it claims authority as discursive subjects. It will reinforce them thereby in the possession of discursive control, for the state that declares its citizens to have such control is a state that can be held to account for removing or reducing that control, or for allowing it to be removed or reduced.

So far as the state interference involved in taxation, coercive legislation or the imposition of a penalty is non-arbitrary, it will resemble the action of Ulysses' sailors in keeping him bound to the mast. The sailors track Ulysses' avowable interests – as evidenced in his earlier injunction – in keeping him bound and empower those interests in a passive or virtual manner. The non-arbitrary state might claim in a similar fashion to be empowering the common avowable interests of those who live under it and to be giving them passive or virtual control over what it does, even what it does coercively. But why, it may be asked, is there need for coercion in these cases? In Ulysses' situation, coercion is necessary to guard against the bewildering effect of the sirens. And in the situation of the citizens, it is necessary to guard against the fact that although their common avowable interests may support a given form of state action, their self-serving interests may not do so on this or that occasion.

In making these points about the possibility of state action being non-arbitrary and of reinforcing people in their possession of discursive control, I am in danger of seeming to be a naïve idealist. Let me put the balance right, then, by immediately conceding that in actual states there is every likelihood that political power will be arbitrary in considerable measure. It may be arbitrary in countenancing the interests only of a majority, and it may be arbitrary in the ways in which its agents behave: in the self-serving or self-assertive ways in which government ministers, civil servants, police officers, or prison authorities conduct themselves towards those on whom they impact. The only point I want to make is that despite this melancholy reality – and despite the consequent appeal of minimizing state power – there is still an ideal in view here and it should keep us alert to the possibility of improving the constitution of the state rather than just despairing of it. We turn in the next chapter to a consideration of how that ideal should be pursued.

A sociologically rich ideal

The ideal of non-domination will not only be attractive for recognizing the possibility of the non-arbitrary or not so arbitrary state. It will also appeal for its recognition that discursive control can be jeopardized by exposure to a power of arbitrary interference, not just by the experience of such interference. To enjoy discursive control is to be proof against being silenced, or ignored, or refused a hearing, or denied the final say in one's own responses. It is, on the contrary, to be given recognition as a discursive subject with a voice and an ear of one's own. The long testimony of literature and history is that such control and such recognition is severly jeopardized under any conditions where one lives *in potestate domini*, in the power of another; and that this is so, whether or not that other ever exercises their power in active interference.

In at least the ordinary case, the presence of a power of arbitrary interference will be a matter of shared awareness among the parties to the relationship. This means that the weaker will have a motive, and will be commonly taken to have a motive, to keep the stronger sweet. And that in turn will jeopardize any possibility of a discursive relationship in which each enjoys full and equal control. Suppose that I am the stronger and you the weaker party. You will have a motive to censor and inhibit, or hide and deny, any speech or behaviour that might turn me against you. And, short of binding myself in a way that alienates my power, nothing I can choose to do will release you from this bondage and give you recognition as a proper discursive partner. If I try to treat you as if you were independent enough to be willing to speak or act against me, for example, this will be taken – and I must expect it to be taken – as a condescending or cynical gesture. The salient fact of my greater power will eclipse any such efforts to enact a fiction of equality.

There is a paradox lurking here, which we might describe as follows. No one can be given discursive control as a gift from others who are powerful enough to be able to withhold it. Let some others have that sort of power and nothing they do can effectively transfer such control. The only way for a person to enjoy discursive control is to command it: to be powerful enough in relation to others for the denial of such control – the denial of a voice or a hearing – to be impossible or excessively costly for others. The power whereby a person commands discursive control in this way need not be personal, of course. It may be the vicarious power that comes about through the commitment of the state to protect them against others, and to pursue and punish those who breach that protection.

Not only is the ideal of non-domination attractive, then, for pointing us towards the possibility of a state that respects and recognizes the discursive control of its citizens. It is equally attractive for pointing us towards a way in which discursive control may be jeopardized without the presence of any actual interference. It enables us to say, on the one hand, that state action need not be inimical as such to political freedom and, on the other, that state action may be required to put right problems that arise from the bare fact of asymmetrical powers of interference.

A third attraction

But the attractions of the ideal of non-domination are not yet fully in view. For what has to be added to these two considerations is that the ideal lends itself, like the ideal of non-interference, to a distinction between factors that compromise non-domination and factors that condition it. This feature shows why the ideal, like that of non-interference, is superior to the homogenizing ideal of non-limitation. And, as we must now see, it also adds in other ways to its appeal.

The factors that compromise non-domination will be any relationships of domination and any acts – say, the random attack of a mugger – that assume and enact such a relationship. But what factors will condition non-domination? What factors will reduce the range over which non-domination can be enjoyed or the ease with which it can be exercised?

The impersonal or non-intentional sorts of obstacles and costs that condition the enjoyment of non-interference will also condition the enjoyment of non-domination and they will be targeted as a secondary evil from the point of view of the ideal. But apart from such non-intentional limitations on agents, there is a second set of factors that will condition the enjoyment of non-domination, without compromising it, and that will count as a secondary evil. These are the restrictions imposed on agents in the enactment and administration of non-arbitrary laws. While such state action may not compromise people's non-domination, as we saw, it will certainly restrict their range or ease of undominated choice and in that way condition non-domination. Thus, while we may not have to indict non-arbitrary laws as compromises of freedom, in the way that the ideal of non-interference indicts them, we do have grounds for reluctance about imposing legal restrictions.

What form should this reluctance take? That will depend on the priority established between compromising and conditioning factors, understood from the point of view of the ideal of non-domination (Pettit 1997a, chapter 3). Non-arbitrary laws should be imposed only to the extent that worse compromises of non-domination are thereby avoided – worse compromises, according to whatever priority rule is followed – or worse forms of conditioning limitations reduced.

By recognizing two ways in which political freedom is jeopardized, the ideal of non-domination is also able to explain why exposure to arbitrary power, however bad in itself, is not quite so bad as the experience of arbitrary power: that is, suffering arbitrary interference. When one experiences arbitrary power in that sense then one suffers two distinct evils. On the one hand, the domination or compromising of freedom that was already present in exposure to that power. And on the other, the restriction or conditioning of freedom that is imposed by the act of interference. This second evil is the sort of evil that a corresponding natural event might have brought about, but without the first evil of domination (Pettit and Braithwaite 1994; Pettit 1997b).

The ideal of non-domination goes along with the ideal of non-interference, then, in identifying two ways, one more serious, one less serious, in which political freedom may be negatively affected. But it draws the boundary between those two sorts of factors, respectively compromising and conditioning, in different places from the ideal of non-interference. It recognizes relationships and assumptions of domination as ways in which freedom may be compromised, and the restrictions that stem from non-intentional and non-arbitrary (legal) limitations as ways in which it may be conditioned.

The fact that a concern for reducing factors that condition non-domination is built into the ideal means, as with the ideal of non-interference, that the ideal has an environmental as well as an agency aspect. It requires, not just that people enjoy the capacity for un-dominated choice – the capacity associated with free agency – but that they have access to an environment in which the opportunities for the exercise of that capacity are optimal. The environment should be as free or unfettering as it can be – it should offer a minimum of natural and social obstacles, including the obstacles represented by non-arbitrary laws – consistently with the desired reduction of domination.

The three attractions of the ideal of non-domination show why the ideal is so much more attractive than the ideal of non-interference. Like that ideal, it scores above the ideal of non-limitation in marking the difference between having one's possession of discursive control jeopardized and having one's enjoyment of discursively controlled choice restricted. Unlike that ideal, however, it is constitutionally rich enough to recognize the distinction between non-arbitrary and arbitrary power and to hold out the hope of making the state, even perhaps a welfare state, friendly to freedom. And unlike that ideal, it is sociologically rich enough to direct us to the diminution of a person's discursive control that may occur as a result of others having an unexercised power of arbitrary interference.

Although this presentation of the ideal of non-domination should be sufficient to make its appeal clear, in one respect I have left the ideal seriously underspecified. I have said nothing on how we should compare and rank the different forms of domination that compromise the ideal (see Taylor 1985, Essay 8). And I have said nothing on how we should determine the conditioning damage done, here by this restriction of opportunity, there by that (Sugden 1998). As I have left open the issue of how to prioritize the compromise of non-domination in relation to the conditioning of undominated choice, so I have also left open the question of how to measure the severity of different forms of compromise and conditioning. In short, I have said nothing on the measurement of non-domination.

The issue of measurement is going to be of the first importance in applied political theory but its investigation would take us too far afield (see Pettit 1997a). The exploration of the topic is likely to go quickly into matters of detail and context. How far the priority issue is troublesome will depend, for example, on how soon the state will reach a ceiling in promoting non-domination; if that ceiling is relatively low, then the state will naturally seek it out first and then devote its efforts to increasing opportunities for undominated choice. Again, how far different forms of domination, or how far different restrictions on undominated choice, damage a person will often depend on the sorts of things that are most valued in the local community. We cannot hope to explore such questions here, though we should take note of the need to deal with them in any full exploration of what the ideal requires.

This completes my case for why, starting from the theory of freedom as discursive control, we should be led to embrace the political ideal of non-domination. That ideal describes a concern that we can safely and efficiently put in the hands of the state. And it describes a concern such that if the state does well in furthering it, then the people who live under that polity stand an excellent chance of enjoying a high level of discursive control. We turn in the next chapter to a discussion of the institutional implications of designing a state so as to further the ideal of non-domination. But before turning to that topic, it will be useful to give the ideal some historical context.

The republican history of the idea

I have argued elsewhere that a political philosophy built around the ideal of non-domination should be described as republican in character (Braithwaite and Pettit 1990; Pettit 1997a). The reason is that we find this ideal of political freedom at the centre of the long republican tradition. That tradition begins properly in Rome, though it draws on the work of many Greek thinkers; it is reworked in the northern cities of Renaissance Italy; it appears in England at the time of the civil war and, modified to allow for constitutional monarchy, survives well into the eighteenth century; and, in its most dramatic incarnation, it provides the crucial, inspiring ideas behind the American and French revolutions (Pocock 1975; Sellers 1995; Skinner

1997). The tradition then goes suddenly to ground around the turn into the nineteenth century, being replaced by a set of ideas that came to be described, in a term that appeared at the time, as liberal in character.

In the republican tradition we find the two themes that distinguish the ideal of political freedom as non-domination. First, the argument that a person who is the slave or subject of another is unfree, even if that other never acts against them. And second, the argument that so far as the law of the land is non-arbitrary – and much is written about how it can be made non-arbitrary – to that extent it does not itself take away people's freedom. The first theme is that the non-interfering master takes away the subject's freedom; the second that the non-mastering interferer does not (Pettit 1997a, chapter 1).

The republicans in the tradition I am describing were, like everyone else at the time, extremely narrow in their view of who counted in politics. They restricted the body of the citizens to mainstream, propertied males. But the very fact of maintaining such a narrow view of the citizenry led them to embrace a very rich image of the freedom that those citizens might enjoy. Citizens could be expected to enjoy a status wherein no one was vulnerable to another; each could walk tall and look others squarely in the eye. Or at least citizens could be expected to enjoy this, so long as the state ensured that power and property was not too unequally distributed and so long as the state's own authority was checked and undominating. Republicans argued that checking the authority and power of the state required citizens to be vigilant against any faction taking the state over for its own ends and to be willing to take an active part themselves in politics. Hence the familiar republican emphasis on civic virtue and political participation (Sandel 1996; Pettit 1998).

A broadly republican view pervaded the English-speaking world from mid-way through the seventeenth century right down until the end of the eighteenth. That view was absorbed and transformed in the work of eighteenth-century French figures like Montesquieu and Rousseau and it was given a distinctively German form by the philosopher Immanuel Kant. The main intellectual challenge that was brought against it in the modern period appeared in the work of Thomas Hobbes in the 1650s. Hobbes was an absolutist about the state, believing that only a government with the absolute power of a Leviathan, as he described it, could hope to ensure peace in a time of religious and civil strife. In the attempt to defend that state – an anathema to contemporary republicans – he defined political freedom in a wholly new way and used the definition to argue that people could be just as free under Leviathan as under a republic.

According to Hobbes (1968), people are free so far as they are not interfered with: they are naturally or corporally free, so far as they are not actually stopped from doing what they will, as we saw earlier; they enjoy civil freedom, or the freedom of the subject, so far as they do not suffer the coercive threat of punishment. This enabled him to say that all laws, so far as they are coercive, take away liberty in the sense that includes civil liberty; the only freedom anyone enjoys is in the silence of the law: in the area where the law leaves people with personal discretion. And so he argued that people who live in a republic are made just as unfree by the laws of the republic as are those who live under a more or less absolute state. In each regime people are unfree so far as they are bound by the law, they are free so far as the law leaves them alone. 'Whether a Commonwealth be Monarchical, or Popular, the Freedome is still the same' (Hobbes 1968, 266).

Hobbes's redefinition of freedom as non-interference was effectively ridiculed by contemporary republican thinkers, in particular James Harrington (1992), and the conception of political freedom as non-domination remained firmly in place. It achieved perhaps its most dramatic impact on politics when it was used by England's American colonists to articulate their grievance against the mother country. The grievance, in essence, was that even if the English parliament did not interfere much in the lives of American colonists, it retained a power of arbitrary interference in relation to them that it did not have over English subjects: this, so far as the parliamentarians had themselves to live under English laws and taxes, whereas they did not have to live under those imposed in America. Such an arbitrary power clearly made the Americans unfree, by the republican understanding of freedom as non-domination. Richard Price (1991, 77) made the relevant point, as it was made by many others at the time. 'Individuals in private life, while held under the power of masters, cannot be denominated free, however equitably and kindly they may be treated. This is strictly true of communities as well as of individuals.'

The American grievance was well articulated by a friend of Price's, another pro-American Englishman, Joseph Priestley (1993, 140).

> Q. What is the great grievance that those people complain of? A. It is their being taxed by the parliament of Great Britain, the members of which are so far from taxing themselves, that they ease themselves at the same time. If this measure takes place, the colonists will be reduced to a state of as complete servitude, as any people of which there is an account in history. For by the same power, by which the people of England can compel them to pay *one penny*, they may compel them to pay the *last penny* they have. There will be nothing but arbitrary imposition on the one side, and humble petition on the other.

But the Hobbesian idea had not died completely and it was precisely in the opposition to the American cause that it was first revived. John Lind (1776), a pamphleteer writing on behalf of Lord North's government, used the idea of freedom as non-interference to justify colonial government in precisely the way Hobbes had used it to justify the government of Leviathan. Freedom, he says in a pamphlet directed against Price, is just 'the absence of coercion' (20). That means that 'all laws are coercive' (24). And so it follows that the freedom of the English is just as badly affected by law as the freedom of the colonists, in which case their complaint fails (114).

If the only use of the ideal of non-interference was to license colonial government, then it is doubtful whether it would have triumphed over the republican ideal, as it did in the decades after the American revolution. But the ideal of non-interference has another aspect that made it attractive to thinkers, even progressive thinkers, at the time.

Lind acknowledges in a footnote that he picked up his notion of freedom from 'a very worthy and ingenious friend' (17). This, it turns out, was Jeremy Bentham, who had written to Lind and had asked to be acknowledged as the source of the idea, on the grounds that it was to be 'the cornerstone of my system'; whether he had forgotten Hobbes, or chose to ignore him, is a moot point. Bentham wrote in his letter to Lind: 'It may have been half a year or a year or more, I do not precisely recollect the time, since I communicated to you a kind of discovery I had made, that the idea of liberty, imported nothing in it that was positive: that it was merely a negative one: and that accordingly I defined it "the absence of restraint"' (Long 1977, 54).

Bentham, certainly one of the most progressive thinkers of his time, did indeed make the idea of political freedom as non-interference into the cornerstone of his system. He argued famously that coercive laws should be introduced only so far as the interference they perpetrated was more than compensated for by the interference they prevented. One of those who followed Bentham was the Cambridge divine, William Paley, and he may have been even more influential in pushing the culture away from the ideal of non-domination and towards the ideal of non-interference. His 1785 book on 'The Principles of Moral and Political Philosophy' was a staple of nineteenth- and early twentieth-century reading and it provided a clear distinction between the two ideals – understood in roughly the way we have been taking them – and explicit arguments in favour of the new.[1]

---

[1] Paley differs in one respect from Hobbes and Lind, and indeed from Bentham. Freedom is not the absence of impediment and the absence of legal coercion as such – the absence of interference, *tout court* – but rather the absence of all interference

What made the ideal of political freedom as non-interference so attractive to progressive thinkers such as Bentham and Paley? They were not as likely as Hobbes or Lind to be influenced by the fact that the ideal could legitimate a despotic or colonial regime, though Paley did clearly recognize this potential. 'Were it probable that the welfare and accommodation of the people would be as studiously, and as providently, consulted in the edicts of a despotic prince, as by the resolutions of a popular assembly, then would an absolute form of government be no less free than the purest democracy' (Paley 1825, 166).

What is much more likely to have influenced Bentham and Paley, however, is this. They were progressives in taking the constituency of people with whom the state should be concerned to include women and servants, not just mainstream, propertied males. Notwithstanding their utilitarian commitment to the value of happiness, they could not reject the popular idea that the state should provide for the freedom of those in the constituency of its concern. And so they faced a problem. If they said that the state should provide for the freedom of people in general, and took freedom in the sense of non-domination, then they would have to argue in an impossibly radical vein that contemporary family and master–servant law should be overthrown; according to that law, after all, women and servants were inherently subject to their masters and incapable of enjoying non-domination. Their solution to that problem was to give up the ideal of non-domination in favour of the ideal of non-interference.

My evidence for this suggestion can be found in Paley's own book. He acknowledges that the idea of political freedom as non-domination 'agrees better with the signification, which the usage of common discourse, as well as the example of many respectable writers upon the subject, has affixed to the term' (Paley 1825, 164). But then a few pages later he argues, paradoxically, that that very idea of political

---

except that of beneficent laws. 'Civil liberty is not being restrained by any law, but what conduces in a greater degree to the public welfare' (Paley 1825, 23). But the shift in question was not much taken up and it had little impact on the issue that concerns us. The fact that freedom is equated with a form of non-interference – albeit a qualified rather than an unqualified form of non-interference – still makes for a significant break with the older conception of freedom as non-domination. And Paley was well aware of the break, contrasting his new view with the established, republican conception. 'There is another idea of civil liberty, which, though neither so simple nor so accurate as the former, agrees better with the signification, which the usage of common discourse, as well as the example of many respectable writers upon the subject, has affixed to the term. This idea places liberty in security; making it to consist not merely in an actual exemption from the constraint of useless and noxious laws and acts of dominion, but in being free from the *danger* of having such hereafter imposed or exercised' (Paley 1825, 164–5).

freedom belongs to a family of conceptions that are too radical to be taken seriously in politics: 'those definitions of liberty ought to be rejected, which, by making that essential to civil freedom which is unattainable in experience, inflame expectations that can never be gratified, and disturb the public content with complaints, which no wisdom or benevolence of government can remove' (Paley 1825, 168).

How could Paley say that a conception of political freedom that was in common usage, and that enjoyed the blessing of tradition, was nevertheless too radical to be taken seriously? He takes it to be too radical, I suggest, because he supports the expansion in the constitutency of the state's concern to include women and servants and he sees that in the context of that expanded constituency, the ideal would require the overthrow of all contemporary family and master–servant law. By adopting the new conception of political freedom as non-interference, he could avoid this problem, arguing that though women and servants are subject to their masters this subjection will not compromise their freedom, provided that they are not actually interfered with. That line of thought would have been naturally supported by the pious belief that Christian husbands would not exercise arbitrary obstruction or coercion against their wives and that economically rational employers would not practise arbitrary interference against their employees.

This historical suggestion, which is more fully documented elsewhere (Pettit 1997a, chapter 1), argues that it may be time to go back to the republican ideal of political freedom as non-domination. Why shouldn't the state be concerned to provide for this richer ideal in respect of the enlarged constituency of concern that liberals like Bentham and Paley rightly wanted to empower? Such early liberals may have had to trim back the ideal of political freedom as they expanded the constituency of political concern. They may not have done so in the public realm, where they generally opposed all forms of benign dictatorship, but they certainly did so in the private realm of family and workplace. But no such inhibition should tell with us now, since the political pursuit of non-domination for all, however demanding in itself, would not have the scandalous aspect that it must have had for them. It is time for a revival of the republican ideal and such a revival is already under way, of course, in many intellectual circles (Sunstein 1988).

Conclusion

We began this chapter by arguing that an ideal of political freedom should try to identify the requirements for the enjoyment of discursive control that the coercive state might be expected to be able to monitor and do something about. On the side of agency we argued that the ideal should try to combat interpersonal challenges to discursive control among individual, though not collective, subjects: that is, those interpersonal relations that jeopardize people's possession of such control. On the side of environment we argued that it should also set itself against unnecessary, impersonal restrictions on discursively controlled choice.

The first ideal of political freedom that we considered would say that the state ought to be equally concerned with removing impersonal limitations due to handicap or ignorance or poverty and interpersonal, more or less intentional assaults by others. This ideal of non-limitation will not impress anyone concerned with discursive control, since it reduces those factors that deny people the possession of control to the same level of significance as those factors that restrict the range or ease of discursively controlled choice.

The ideal of non-interference is designed to rectify this failure, so far as it says that intentional or quasi-intentional interference compromises political freedom, non-intentional limitation conditions it, and it is more important to remove or reduce interference than to remove or reduce limitation. But this ideal runs into problems in other ways. It is constitutionally impoverished in suggesting that all coercive action by the state is bad as such, regardless of how far state arbitrariness is reduced: regardless of how far the state is forced to track people's avowable interests. The ideal of political freedom as non-interference is also sociologically impoverished, because it suggests that actual interference is required for people to undermine one another's discursive control. This runs foul of the fact that if others have an arbitrary power of interference in someone's life then, short of that power being exercised, this can already lead to the person's losing discursive control.

The ideal of political freedom as non-domination is designed to get over these difficulties. It allows that the state may be a non-mastering interferer and so not a source of compromise to freedom – it will, however, be a source of conditioning – so far as the arbitrariness of state power can be reduced; how far it can be reduced is an open question. And it recognizes that non-interfering masters can jeopardize the freedom of their subjects so far as they have and are seen to have an arbitrary power of interference in the lives of those individuals. In these ways, then, it escapes the constitutional and sociological impoverishment of the ideal of non-interference. But it also escapes the problem raised for the ideal of non-limitation, for while it can recognize non-intentional limitations as an evil, it takes them as secondary, conditioning ills, on a par with non-arbitrary law, not as ills of the primary, compromising sort.

The ideal of political freedom as non-domination has deep historical roots. It is the ideal present in the Roman and neo-Roman tradition of republican thought. This ideal was replaced about the end of the eighteenth century by the characteristically liberal ideal of non-interference but the consideration that argued for that replacement among progressive thinkers – that the older ideal would be too radical an ideal for the populace as a whole – no longer applies. The time is ripe for a republican revival of the ideal of political freedom as non-domination.

7

Freedom and Democratization

Towards a republican political philosophy

Suppose we think of freedom as something that the state ought to advance among its members or citizens: we may or may not think that there are other concerns that it ought also to further. And suppose that we identify the political ideal of freedom with non-domination. Where will that lead us in political theory: that is, in the theory of what the state ought to be and do? Assuming that we follow the liberal tradition in forming an inclusive conception of the citizenry, then it will lead us towards a liberal or inclusive form of republican theory (Dagger 1997).

There are two kinds of power within any social world, each marked in a traditional Latin tag (Kriegel 1995). First, there is the *imperium* of the state, or public power. And second there is the *dominium* or private power of interference that certain agents, individual and collective, enjoy in relation to others. A republican philosophy of the kind envisaged would suggest that if the freedom as non-domination of individual citizens is to be furthered, then steps have to be taken for curbing each of these forms of internal power, as well as the power of any external enemies.

The republican state will be charged with putting such restrictions on private power that so far as possible – and this may not be as far as we would wish – people will be able to live in situations where others do not have arbitrary power over them. The republican state will seek to foster social forms of life within which each is able to look others in the eye, in a shared awareness of not being dependent on their good will, and no one stands at the mercy of any collective subject. People may choose to make themselves dependent on one another's good will, and this may be a source of fruitful relationships between them, but they will not have such vulnerability or dependency thrust upon them.

The devices whereby the republican state may reduce such vulnerability and encourage a forthright independence among people are various, and different devices may be suited to different conditions. In some circumstances the provisions of the welfare state may be appropriate, for example, while in others the institutions of a significantly more open market may serve people better. The ideal must be, in Amartya Sen's phrase, that each enjoys a robust capability of functioning in their local society: they are reliably able to achieve the access that local functioning requires to food and shelter and medical care, to education and information and a cultural network, to work and mobility and an address at which others may make contact with them, and so on (Sen 1985a; Nussbaum 1992; Pettit 2001a). The measures needed for providing people with such access, however, may vary greatly, depending on the circumstances of the society.

But whatever the state may be able to do by way of furthering freedom as non-domination in these ways – by way of curbing the effects of private power or *dominium* – and whatever it may do by way of countering external enemies, republicanism will insist that it should only be permitted to act within certain limits on public power or *imperium*. A state that acted beyond such limits – *ultra vires* – would be likely to constitute a worse threat to freedom as non-domination than any danger that it might be expected to remove. The first question for a republican philosophy, then, is to determine what limits have to be imposed on the state – what sort of agency the state has to be – if it is to be a force for republican good and not itself a source of serious bad.

This question has been at the centre of discussion within the republican tradition for as long as that tradition has existed. And the question, so it turns out, has always been conceptualized as an issue of freedom. What is it that makes for freedom in the constitution of a state, as Montesquieu (1989) would have put it? What is it that makes for a state that is consistent with the freedom of its citizens – their freedom as non-domination – and that is able to advance the cause of freedom in relation to other dangers, without becoming itself a danger of perhaps even greater significance? What is it, in short, that makes a state or polity free (Skinner 1997)?

This last chapter is devoted to that question. I first rehearse the danger that the state – any state – represents from the point of view of the freedom as non-domination of its citizens. Then I argue that from a republican point of view the only recourse is to make the state, so far as possible, non-arbitrary in its operation. A state will be non-arbitrary in this sense to the extent that it is forced to track the common avowable interests of the citizens, and only the common avowable interests of the citizens. I argue that the best hope for forcing the state to track such interests is to have a regime of electoral democracy in place and that the best hope for forcing the state to track only such interests is to put in place a regime of what I describe as contestatory democracy. The ideal of political freedom, as long traditions have emphasized, is intimately tied up with the ideal of democracy. The connection has sometimes been denied by liberal theorists of freedom as non-interference – they have suggested that a benign dictatorship may do even better than democracy in furthering non-interference (Berlin 1969, Essay 1; Paley 1825, 166) – but it becomes undeniable under a republican conception of freedom as non-domination (Pettit 1999a).

The danger of *imperium*

Wherever people form a collective subject, on the model presented in the fifth chapter, that subject is always going to represent a danger to their freedom as non-domination. In order to pursue a collective purpose the integrated collectivity will have to collectivize reason, as we put it in that chapter. And in order to collectivize reason it will have to be organized in such a way that the views and votes of individuals on some issues – even when those individuals are separately quite rational – can be ignored and overridden. We looked at a particularly radical case of this where, on pain of collective unreason, the votes of all members on a particular issue had to be overturned: this was the issue of whether or not to forgo a pay-rise.

Not only do collectivities inevitably represent this general sort of threat to their individual members. They will often represent a specific and pointed threat so far as their members collectively give them the power to impose an annual fee or contribution, to enforce a code of behaviour, and to punish members for a failure to pay their contribution or abide by the code. This casts many collectivities in the role of a centralized power that individual members can only challenge at their peril.

But notwithstanding these undoubted facts, there is no great need to worry about the power of most collectivities: not at least about the power of collectivities in relation to their members. With collectivities other than the state, individual members have the formal right of exit and in the bulk of cases that right can be exercised without excessive cost. That being so, we may assume that those members who do stay in place do not experience the collectivity as a dominating presence in their lives. It may have a limited right of interference with their affairs, being able to ignore certain votes and to impose the measures just mentioned. But the fact that people do not leave its ranks suggests that in pursuing such interference the collectivity tracks the avowable interests – presumptively, the common avowable interests – of the members. And the fact that people can leave its ranks should the collectivity offend against such interests means that this is no accident: the collectivity is forced, on pain of suffering mass emigration, to track the common avowable interests of its members. The collectivity may be an agent of interference in the lives of members, then, but it is only an agent of non-arbitrary interference. That is why it does not have the presence of a dominating power.

Did the state or polity relate to its members – broadly speaking, its citizens – in this way, then its *imperium* would not represent any particular danger to people's freedom as non-domination. But of course the state is very different from other collectivities. Assuming a monopoly of legitimate force in its territory, the state has a coercive power of charging members a fee: that which is levied in tariffs and taxation; of enforcing a code of behaviour: that which is embodied in law and regulation; and of punishing those who offend against that code, say by imposing fines, imprisonment or even execution. And not only is the state coercive in these ways; it is also inescapable. It is the one sort of collectivity that offers members only a purely formal right of exit: a right of exit that means nothing except in the relatively unlikely event that another state – ideally, a state that differs significantly from the first – will accept them.

Being coercive and inescapable, there is a real danger that the state will be an arbitrary, dominating power in the lives of citizens. So far as it is coercive it will represent a power of deep interference in their affairs. So far as it is inescapable, there is no guarantee that it will be forced to track the common avowable interests of citizens in how it exercises that power of interference. Thus while the state may be essential for all sorts of reasons – not least, because it can guard against the danger of *dominium* to people's freedom as non-domination – it will itself represent a serious threat to people's enjoyment of such freedom. The *imperium* of the state is powerful and ubiquitous and special measures are obviously going to be needed if it is to be turned into a freedom-friendly power.

In the title of a well-known study, Albert Hirschman (1970) identifies the three great options in political life as exit, voice and loyalty. Exit is not available with the state and loyalty is not going to achieve anything by way of ensuring that the state is not arbitrary and dominating. So the only remaining alternative among these options is voice; specifically, the voice of authorization and contestation that is available to ordinary people under democratic arrangements.

I want to argue that Hirschman gives us the right cue in suggesting that the exercise of voice may be the strategy to explore in seeking a means of containing the state. I believe that properly understood, democratization is the only feasible way of guarding against the state's being arbitrary and dominating in the way it treats its citizens. Specifically, I believe that democratization can make it much more likely than it would otherwise have been that the state will be forced to track the common avowable interests of its citizens, and only the common avowable interests of its citizens.

Common avowable interests

How should we think of people's common avowable interests? A well-functioning democracy, as I go on to argue, will serve as a search procedure for identifying and empowering such interests. Common avowable interests cannot usefully be defined, however, just as those that such a democracy would identify and empower; that would make it impossible to criticize a democracy for failing to identify or empower them effectively. So how then should we conceive of common avowable interests? That the interests are avowable means that they are conscious or can be brought to consciousness without great effort. But what is involved in saying that they are common?

The definition of common interests that I find most persuasive holds that a certain good will represent a common interest of a population just so far as co-operatively admissible considerations support its collective provision (Pettit 2000a). Co-operatively admissible considerations are those that anyone in discourse with others about what they should jointly or collectively provide can adduce without embarrassment as relevant matters to take into account (Habermas 1984, 1989; Elster 1986). They are not selfish or sectional considerations, for example, of the kind that some parties to the discussion would have to see as calls for special treatment and as calls that they had no particular reason to heed. Assuming that there are many co-operatively admissible considerations available to the potential citizens of a common state — why form a common state if there are none? — we can think of the common interests of the citizens as those things that such considerations would argue for collectively providing.[1]

This conception of common interests is grounded in two assumptions, neither of which is particularly troublesome. First, that there really is a distinction between co-operatively admissible and co-operatively inadmissible considerations. And second, that there is a fact of the matter as to what these support. The first assumption is borne out by the relative ease with which conversational practice polices the distinction between what in a given context are relevant reasons and what irrelevant. The second may seem to run afoul of the possibility that while co-operatively admissible considerations can offer support for certain initiatives, they are liable to offer equally strong support for rival sets of initiatives: typically, sets of initiatives that would benefit different groups differently. But this possibility need not be an insurmountable problem.

The reason is that in many situations there will always be a further co-operatively admissible consideration available: viz, that everyone is worse off not agreeing at all than agreeing on one or other of the rival schemes and that some measure ought to be adopted, therefore, to break the tie. The situations where people will take this view are those situations of compromise where no one feels that their position is wholly undermined by the failure to get their preferred solution. The measure adopted for resolving a stalemate in such a situation of compromise may be to toss a coin, for example; or to go to adjudication of some kind; or of course to put the issue to a majority vote in the electorate or parliament.

What sorts of goods are likely candidates for common interests, and in particular candidates that are likely to be identified and empowered

---

[1] This way of defining common interests is broadly contractualist in spirit; it owes much in particular to the interpretation of Rawlsian contractualism (Rawls 1971) developed in the work of T. M. Scanlon (1982) and Brian Barry (1995). It rejects the idea that common interests are to be defined as those private interests that happen to be shared by everyone in a community; such a least-common-denominator definition would make common interests so elusive and unstable as to be of no normative significance (Goodin 1996). Without departing too far from our sense of what makes for a genuine interest, and what makes for an interest's being really common — so at least, it seems to me — the definition offers us a firmer and potentially more useful way of thinking about common interests.

as common interests in democratic practice? Perhaps the most salient examples are those procedural and institutional arrangements that are necessary for solving familiar game-theory predicaments (Hardin 1982). The co-ordination predicament, where everyone prefers that all choose the same alternative – drive on the right or the left – and is otherwise indifferent between alternatives. Or the compromise predicament where everyone prefers that all choose the same alternative – say, that all operate under certain rules of ownership and transfer – but among the different alternatives, they divide on which should be the option selected (Vanderschraaf 1998; Bellamy 1999). Or the assurance predicament, where everyone prefers that all choose a certain alternative but no one wants to choose it in the absence of an assurance that others are going to do so too. Or the exchange predicament – in one version, the prisoner's dilemma – where everyone prefers that all take a certain course rather than all doing anything else but where everyone prefers not to have to take that course themselves; each prefers to exploit or free-ride on the efforts of others (Pettit 1986).

Many such predicaments may lend themselves to spontaneous resolution in the course of social evolution (Skyrms 1996). But where they are unresolved, or not satisfactorily resolved, co-operatively admissible considerations will surely argue that collective action should be taken to provide a resolution. Thus those procedural and institutional arrangements that allow for the resolution of such predicaments are likely to count as common interests. And so of course are those substantive goods that are attained as a result of the resolution: external defence, internal harmony, and the like.

But common interests, on the definition adopted here, may also prove to require redistributive measures. Redistribution may be in the common interest because everyone wants to be protected against a certain sort of difficulty – say, medical or legal or financial – and only those currently in such difficulty benefit. Or it may be in the common interest because while everyone wants a certain sort of good – say, to be able fully to enjoy membership in his or her cultural group (Kymlicka 1995) – providing that good may require spending more resources on some than on others. Or it may be in the common interest because certain disadvantaged groups cannot be expected to co-operate without compensation for certain disadvantages that they suffer. That a group has certain interests in common does not presuppose that members already enjoy equal economic standing or identical cultural affiliations; the required commonality of interests is wholly consistent with economic, social and indeed ethnic diversity (Pettit 2000b).

Forcing the state to track common avowable interests, and only such interests

The suggestion that I now want to pursue is that the strategy of democratization – voice – can be used to try and force the state to track all and only the common avowable interests of citizens and that it can help thereby to stop the state's *imperium* from becoming an arbitrary sort of power. It is plausible as an abstract idea that if people are given a voice – given an audible and powerful voice – then they can use it both to articulate all the common avowable interests that the state ought to be furthering and to identify and denounce any interests it furthers that are not truly common and avowable interests. But we need to give the idea more concrete form before it can have any hold. We need to spell out the ways in which democratic voice can be organized so as to force the state to track all and only the common avowable interests of the people.

That the state should be democratically forced to track all the common avowable interests of the people means that there should be democratic institutions which make it possible to search out and authorize policies whose implementation promises to advance common avowable interests. That the state should be forced to track only the common avowable interests of the people means that equally there should be democratic institutions which make it possible to scrutinize the policies identified, and the other factors that influence how policies materialize, to try to weed out those that do not answer to such interests.

Democratic institutions must have a positive search-and-identify dimension, then, and a negative scrutinize-and-disallow dimension. They must conform to what Daniel Dennett (1996) calls a generate-and-test heuristic. The search-and-authorize dimension – the generative mechanism – will help to ensure that all policies whose implementation might advance common avowable interests get a hearing. And the scrutinize-and-disallow dimension – the testing mechanism – will help to ensure that only policies and modes of policy-making that really answer to common avowable interests survive and have influence. The first dimension will guard against false negatives, by allowing every possible common-interest policy into consideration. The second dimension will guard against false positives, by subjecting the policies adopted, and their mode of implementation, to a rigorous testing and filtering procedure.

The two-dimensional structure envisaged has analogues in a variety of areas. One is provided by the way in which control is exercised over the text that appears in a newspaper or journal. The original text is actually provided by the respective authors of the pieces, be they journalists or outsiders who submit pieces for publication. But the text that finally appears is determined by the hand of the editor or editors; they select from submissions and, with any piece accepted, they require abbreviated or otherwise amended versions. The authors determine all the candidates for publication that come the way of the newspaper or journal. But only the candidates that satisfy the editors ever get to be actually published.

By analogy with this case, what democratic institutions have to do is, first, to establish an authorial dimension of control – control by ordinary people – for searching out and generating a rich supply of presumptive common-interest policies; and second, to establish an editorial dimension of control – again, control by ordinary people – for rigorously scrutinizing and eliminating those candidate policies and those modes of policy-implementation that do not advance common avowable interests. The lesson of the two-dimensional structure is that people will have to be able to determine both the general policies that government considers and the policies and modes of policy-implementation that are allowed to shape the things that government finally does.

The authorial dimension in democracy

How are the people to be authors of those candidate common interests that get to be articulated in politics? Such an authorial role has to be implemented, clearly, by electoral institutions whereby policies and policy-making agencies are popularly discussed and chosen from among a range of alternatives; in particular, from among a range of alternatives which anyone in principle can help to determine. It is only by recourse to electoral means that we can hope to ensure a generous supply of candidates for consideration as matters of common avowable interest.

The electoral procedures that we associate with real-world democracy allow for the periodic, popular election of certain authorities: at the least, the legislators. They ensure both that the periods between elections are not very long and that the elections are popular in the sense that all competent adults have electoral rights – they can stand for election and they can vote in elections – and are able to make their voting decisions without undue pressure (Przeworksi 1999). And in most cases they leave open the possibility that the very rules under which those in government are selected, as well as the rules under which they operate, can themselves be put to the electoral test: they can be amended by the elected politicians themselves or by the people in a referendum.

Under these electoral institutions, the governed people have an important authorial role in relation to political decision-making. They choose the personnel who will author the laws and decisions to be introduced by government or who, at the least, will supervise their authorship by bureaucratic officials. In this way they are the indirect authors of whatever policies those personnel put forward in office.

That the people are the indirect, electoral authors of such policies suggests in itself that the policies endorsed will generally be worth considering as candidates for matters of common avowable interest. It would certainly be surprising if none of the policies collectively authored by the people had a connection with such common interests. But in any case democratic electoral institutions should serve in other respects to reinforce this effect and to make popular elections a plausible means of generating a rich supply of candidates for matters of common interest.

The reason, roughly, is this. Those who stand for political office will have an incentive to enhance their chances of election and re-election by promoting any cause that can attract general support. And any cause that answers to a common avowable interest will attract general support. Thus those who stand may be expected to be on the look-out for matters of common avowable interest that they can espouse. And so the policies that people are invited to author will tend to include all half-plausible candidates for being matters of common avowable interest. There should be relatively little danger of politicians and people failing to detect any matters of common avowable interest. False negatives should not be a major problem.

These comments are, of necessity, rather brief and under-argued. The point is not to provide a detailed defence of democratic electoral institutions, as we know them. Rather it is to show that under such institutions people are enabled, however imperfectly, to play the first, authoring role required by the two-dimensional ideal of democracy.

But if democracy encompassed nothing more than electoral institutions, then however well it did in generating a rich supply of candidates for matters of common interest — for avoiding false negatives — it would be ill-equipped to guarantee the avoidance of false positives. It might seem to guard against the adoption of policies for the furtherance of goods that do not answer in any way to the interests of ordinary people or that do not answer to avowable interests. But it would offer relatively inadequate protection against the adoption of policies that represent majority interests alone. And it would do little or nothing to guard against the influence of a hostile elite in the specification and implementation of such policies.

The first of these worries, which is a familiar theme in the republican and liberal tradition, is that the democratic majority can support as a matter of common interest something that is not truly a common concern: it may be a policy that discriminates significantly against some minority. The second of the worries is that the democratic elite in government – and these range from politicians to prison wardens – can implement policies in a way that does not answer to common interests. The first is the traditional worry about the tyranny of the democratic majority, the second a worry about the tyranny of the democratic elite.

The second concern is probably more important than the first. The people are only the indirect authors of the policies that are put up as candidates for matters of common interest, so that governmental policy-making can be influenced by factors which are such that it is not in the common avowable interest of people that they have an influence. Policies are specified in detail, and implemented, by the successful party or parties in government and, ultimately, by the public service that those in government try to oversee. Thus it is possible that in the specification and implementation of common-interest policies, for example, those in government will not be guided just by common interests. The implementation of policies may be designed to serve a particular electoral, bureaucratic or just personal advantage. And policies that appear to represent common interests in the indeterminate rhetoric of an election may materialize in the fine print of legislation and regulation as policies that serve only the ends of this or that special-interest lobby.

This latter development is particularly possible, of course, if the elected government is in the debt of such a lobby for its support in the course of the electoral campaign or indeed for its support over the term of government. The organization or association in question may be able to damage the government through adverse media publicity, for example, or through taking actions – say, closing down operations in electorally sensitive locations – that reflect badly on government.

Even if electoral institutions offer a reliable means of producing a generous supply of candidates for matters of common interest, then – even if they reduce the risk of false negatives – still they do not incorporate a reliable means of ensuring that only matters of common avowable interest shape what happens in and at the hands of government. The authorial control that they would give ordinary people needs to be complemented by an independent measure of editorial control.

The editorial dimension in democracy

How might such editorial control be implemented? The control in question cannot be exercised collectively, in the manner of electoral, authorial control; whatever problems arose in the first dimension will recur in the second. The editorial control that democracy requires – the control designed to ensure, ideally, that only matters of common avowable interest have an influence on government – has got to be exercised by individuals or groups at a non-collective level.

How much can we say about the mode of non-collective, editorial control that democracy might incorporate? There are three points that can be registered, it seems to me, with a reasonable degree of confidence.

First point: the impossibility of a veto system

The first point to be registered is that while editorial control must operate at non-collective levels, it cannot plausibly take the form of a veto. Not an individual veto. And not the group-level veto envisaged in some past arrangements: for example, in the veto that the tribunes of the plebs could exercise in republican Rome or in the veto given to the assembly of the people in James Harrington's republican vision of *Oceana* (Harrington 1992).

The reason why no such veto can work is this. Matters of common avowable interest can often be advanced in different ways, where one way of advancing it is more costly for this group, a second more costly for that, and where the different groups therefore will prefer different approaches. It may be a matter of common avowable interest that the tax system should be made more efficient, that a new power station should be constructed, or that various anti-pollution measures should be implemented. But any way of advancing such a cause is bound to hurt some more than others. There will always be a minority who are negatively affected by any improvement in the tax system, a minority who live in the vicinity of a new, much needed power station, and a minority who depend for their livelihood on industries hard hit by important anti-pollution legislation.

If people had an individual power of veto then every such initiative could easily be stymied – certainly it would become more difficult to realize – as people each tried to push the relative costs of the initiative elsewhere. And by parity of reasoning many an initiative of this kind could become difficult to access if different groups within the society had a power of veto; where groups were differently affected, the worst hit would be likely to block the initiative in the hope of inducing others to bear the costs. There might be a possibility of resolving stalemates by bargaining, of course, but that can be no consolation in the present context, for bargaining would scarcely serve to guard against false positives; on the contrary, it would be likely to support coalition-building that is damaging to those left out.

Second point: the possibility of contestation

The second point to be registered is that short of the veto, there is still an important power of challenge that can be invested in individuals or groups. This becomes salient by analogy with the power of challenge – challenge as distinct from veto – that some real-life editors enjoy. Take the sort of journal, or even newspaper, that is run on fairly co-operative lines: say, because it is actually owned by those who write for it and work on it. With such a publication the editors may not be given the right to veto outright any piece authored by one of the writers. But clearly they can still exercise a great deal of editorial control. Instead of vetoing a piece they do not like, they can contest its publication before a meeting of the owners or before a meeting of a board appointed by the owners. They can argue that the journal or newspaper in question has such and such standards, or such and such a role, and that the piece in question does not fit. And they can expect to succeed in this sort of challenge whenever they make what is accepted as a good case.

Short of giving individual people or groups of people a power of veto over government, it might be possible to give them a power of contestation on parallel lines to the case just envisaged. All we have to assume is that where there are electorally supported policies, or modes of policy-implementation, that do not promise to promote common avowable interests, then:

1 this is capable of being established in debate and argument;
2 it is possible to have bodies set up – perhaps under an electorally approved arrangement – that can be relied on to give a fair hearing and discussion to the different arguments and to pass compelling judgements;
3 the judgements of such bodies can be given suitable authority in relation to the decision-making of government; and

4 it can be a matter of common belief in the society that clauses 1–3 are true, so that minorities need not be fated to distrust the bodies in question.

The element in these assumptions that is likely to be challenged is the claim made in the second, and presupposed in the fourth, that it is possible for certain bodies to be impartial on matters where the population is divided. It may be said that since the bodies imagined are likely to reflect the society as a whole, there is little reason to think that they will not divide on the same lines as the electorate or the elected representatives; thus they may be expected to support whatever the electors or representatives proposed.

But this objection supposes that members of such a body are bound to make a judgement dictated by whatever interest may be thought to have influenced electors and representatives. And that is clearly not so. They will be asked to judge on the factual issue of whether the policy as identified and implemented is supported by common avowable interests and only by such interests. For example, they may be asked to judge on whether the change to the tax system is dictated only by the common interest in making the system more efficient, and not in part by the interest of an effective coalition in pushing the relative costs of change onto a minority. The question will be the factual one as to whether the change proposed does indeed make a good claim to be in the common interest, so that the negative effect on the minority can be regarded as just an unhappy accident.

It requires a determined cynicism – and a cynicism that is apparently not shared in democratic electorates (Tyler et al. 1997) – to believe that faced with deciding such a factual issue, any body that is representative of the society as a whole will divide on the same interest-bound lines that are taken to have divided electors or representatives. But even if we are cynical, there is an important reason why such a body should prove impartial, and should be generally expected to prove impartial. This is that in a society where divisions remain relatively civil, the members of such a body will stand to win the good opinion of most of their fellows only so far as they are seen to discharge their allotted brief. We may assume, as the established tradition has it, that people care a lot about the opinion that others have of them (Lovejoy 1961; Pettit 1990; Brennan and Pettit 1993; McAdams 1997; Pettit 1997a, chapter 7; Brennan and Pettit 2000). And we may expect that it will be possible to organize relevant bodies in such a way that this desire for esteem will provide motivation enough for members to act impartially.

Third point: the feasibility of a contestatory regime

We have seen that while the editorial dimension of democratic control cannot require a veto, it may operate effectively under a regime where government decisions are always contestable. But the prospect of a contestatory regime may not be all that attractive; it may seem to hold out the spectre of endless disputation and a chronic inability to get things done. The third point I want to make at this stage, however, should dissipate that spectre. It is that there are ways of achieving the control that democratic contestability would give to ordinary people, short of allowing a society to get bogged down in never-ending contestations.

Consider the way in which things are likely to evolve with the editors of our imagined journal or newspaper. A regime of frequent contestation, involving regular challenges before the editorial board, would be very likely to prove both time-consuming and inefficient: many of the challenges would be of the same sort, for example, and would be routinely upheld. We can readily envisage steps being taken, then, to reduce the contestatory load. There are two steps, in particular, that spring to mind.

The first would be for the editors and editorial board to agree on the conclusiveness of certain grounds for challenge, on the need for submissions to be prepared for consideration according to certain guidelines, on the expectation that no contributor be in the pay of certain interests, and perhaps even on specific constraints that any published piece ought to meet, and to lay out these points of agreement in the form of procedures that writers can take for their guidance. The procedures might rule out the publication of any material of an offensive kind, for example; they might require that an advance outline of every submission be cleared in advance; they might stipulate that contributors should declare any personal interests in the matter on which they are writing; and the like. The promulgation of such a policy would involve the pre-emptive acceptance of certain contestations, in the sense that it would have the effect of removing certain submissions – or at least reducing the incidence of certain submissions – that would be contested, and successfully contested, by the editors. It would create procedural resources designed to facilitate the contestation that actually occurs.

The second step that the editors and editorial board might take in order to make a contestability regime effective would be to allow room for *ex ante* as well as *ex post* contestation. Instead of allowing only the contestation whereby the editors challenge a finished submission before the editorial board they might allow editors to have a say at an earlier stage by inviting authors to seek editorial input and advice whenever they are worried about the possibility of objection. They might introduce consultative as well as procedural resources in support of *ex post*, appellate contestation.

Not only would procedural and consultative resourcing reduce the need for appellate contestation by the editors. Such resourcing would also facilitate whatever contestation occurs at the appellate stage. For if the editors can argue that a given piece offends against clearly stated editorial procedures, or that it breaches an agreement made in consultation with the authors, that will strengthen the contestatory case that they can make against it. Procedural and consultative measures should serve at once to reduce the need for, and enhance the effectiveness of, appellate contestation.

Moving back now to the political world, it should be obvious that there is room for giving people resources of contestation at three levels. It is possible to give people procedural and consultative resources as well as the appellate resources originally considered.

Procedural resources

The procedural resources that democracies typically institute, to go to the first category, come in two broad kinds. On the one hand, there are procedural constraints on the content of government decisions, in particular laws. And on the other, there are procedural constraints on the process whereby decisions and laws get to be authorized.

The most important content-related constraint is embodied in the principle of limited government, as we might call it. This principle is not often spelled out in the documents of those regimes that we would be happy to describe as democratic but it is almost always built clearly into the practice. It says, roughly, that there is a limit to the range of matters on which government can rule. The strictest version is incorporated in the harm principle put forward in John Stuart Mill's essay 'On Liberty': according to this, government is warranted in interfering in the lives of individuals only to prevent them from harming others (Mill 1978; Feinberg 1986). Less strict versions, all of them vague in the detail of what they require, prescribe that government ought to be restricted to dealing with issues that are, broadly, in the public domain and ought to respect the privacy of individuals.

But the principle of limited government, however understood, does not exhaust the content-related constraints that most democracies impose on those in power. Almost all democracies recognize, formally or otherwise, that no laws should be passed, no decisions taken, that offend against any of a variety of individual and group expectations. Those expectations may be encoded in a bill of rights or implied in a founding constitution. But equally they may just be registered informally as matters of convention such that a parliament that tried to remove them could expect widespread resistance. Thus they may be matters of common law, so long tested and tried that no parliament would contemplate setting them aside (Dicey 1960). Or they may be matters subject to 'ordini' as distinct from 'leggi', in the language of Machiavelli (1965); matters of custom or 'ethos' as distinct from law or 'nomos' in the even older, equally influential language of Polybius (1954).

So much for procedural constraints of a content-related kind that democracies generally impose on government. Other procedural constraints restrict the process rather than the content of governmental decision-making. I have a number of familiar restrictions in mind, nothing very esoteric, and I list them here without detailed commentary.

1   Rule of law. The law-based decisions of government have got to be general and apply to everyone, including the legislators themselves; they must be promulgated and made known in advance to those to whom they apply; they should be intelligible, consistent, and not subject to constant change; and so on (Fuller 1971; Ten 1993).
2   Separation of powers. The legislative, executive and judicial functions should be sufficiently separate to guarantee at least two things: the independence, in most of their operations, of the courts; and the requirement that those in executive government have to get parliamentary approval – the approval of legislators – for the main initiatives they undertake (Gwyn 1965; Vile 1967).
3   Deliberative democracy. The decisions of those in government should always be backed by reasons, whether the decisions be judicial, executive or legislative in character; and the validity and relevance of the reasons offered ought to be subject to parliamentary – and, inevitably, community – debate (Cohen 1989; Sunstein 1993; Gutmann and Thompson 1996; Pettit 2001b).
4   Bicameral approval. There ought to be two houses of parliament, distinct in the basis on which they are elected or in the mode of election to them; and the approval of each ought to be required in the course of most legislation, so that the different mix of interests represented by the two houses has each got to be satisfied.

5 Depoliticized decision-making. Subject to the possibility of review in extreme cases, certain decisions are best left by elected governments to bodies and officers who are appointed on a statutory basis for a set period of time. These are decisions in which elected politicians are likely to have self-seeking interests, inimical to the public interest; they are best put at arm's length on the grounds that no one should be judge in their own case: *nemo judex in sua causa*. Examples recognized in many jurisdictions include decisions on public prosecution; decisions on redrawing electoral boundaries; decisions on interest rates; and even decisions on certain planning issues.
6 Independent accountability. There should be provision for the auditing of government accounts by an independent authority, with the reports of that authority available for debate in parliament and community.
7 Freedom of information. Subject to a time embargo in certain sensitive areas, there ought to be provision for members of the public, including the press, to access documentary information on the data and arguments that carry weight in decisions by public bodies (Manin 1997).

Without going into detail, it should be obvious that the procedural constraints just reviewed, whether content-related or process-related, are well understood as providing ordinary people with pre-emptive resources of contestation against government decisions. To the extent that government decisions are required to satisfy these constraints, they are less likely to reflect matters that are not truly of common interest. False positives should be a somewhat lesser problem than they might otherwise have been. So at any rate I assume.

Consultative resources

Consultative opportunities have long been available, at least as a matter of formal right, in matters where government requires parliamentary support. Parliament can be petitioned by members of the public to act on a certain matter. Individual parliamentary representatives can be accessed by their constituents or by this or that lobby group. And parliamentary inquiries and committees can often be accessed in a more formal, often public manner. But much government is now conducted, whether we like it or not, in domains where parliamentary control is not available or parliamentary scrutiny is almost certain to be ineffective. Thus the traditional avenues of public access provide ordinary people with only very limited consultative resources.

The reason why government escapes effective parliamentary control and scrutiny is that, on pain of infeasibility, administrative decisions in contemporary democracies cannot all be implemented via regular legislation. They have to be taken under delegated or subordinate legislation that gets very little parliamentary scrutiny. Or they have to be left to the discretion of the relevant agency or officer.

But most contemporary democracies have developed some means whereby the public, on an individual, organizational or associational basis, are enabled to have an input into such legislatively under-examined decision-making; and these measures are often applied to decision-making more generally. Thus we find that provision is made, sometimes under a statutory, legislated requirement, for the establishment of advisory, community-based bodies that administrative agencies have to consult; for the setting up of public hearings and inquiries relevant to this or that proposed venture of government; for the publication of proposals – say, in 'green' or 'white' papers – and the eliciting of responses from members of the public; and for the conduct of focus-group research, or research of a related kind, into public opinion on issues where the government intends to take action.

These initiatives, together with the traditional modes of access to parliament, represent consultative resources that are of the first importance from the point of view of preventing government from succumbing to false positives. They give concrete form to the old injunction *audi alteram partem* (Cane 1996; Skinner 1996) – hear the other side – and they offer at least some prospect that government will be dissuaded from taking action in cases where the line proposed does not answer to common avowable interests; in particular, where it promises to treat a minority in a deleterious way.

Of course, as already noted, many government decisions, even decisions that are prompted by common avowable interests, will be relatively more damaging for one group than for others and that group may be expected to protest at the consultative stage. But if its voice has been fully heard – and that may be tested in later appeals – then members of that group may feel some greater confidence that though they suffer more than others, that is just bad luck and not a result of their being treated as less than equals. They can agree that it is in the common avowable interest of members of the community that a power station of a certain sort be constructed, for example, and they may come to see that, though they are hurt by the decision, the best place to locate the power station is indeed in their own neighbourhood (Pettit 1997a, 198–200).

Appellate resources

In any regime that we would be happy to describe as a democracy, it goes without saying that citizens must be able to challenge officers of government in the courts on matters of private law, as it goes without saying that officers of government may be charged with offences against the criminal law. Like ordinary citizens, government officials and bodies are capable in proper democracies of being sued for torts, breaches of contract, breaches of trust, and the like.

But democracies go much further than this in allowing ordinary citizens to challenge those in government. They allow citizens to appeal to parliament for an inquiry into the doings of government, whether the inquiry take the form of a parliamentary question or a full-scale investigation by a parliamentary committee. That is implicit in arrangements already described. And, over and above that, they provide citizens with a capacity to challenge government initiative on three more or less distinct counts: for its legality under public law; for its substantive merit; and for its general propriety (see Cane 1996 for an overview).

To challenge government action for its legality under public law is to apply for the judicial review of the action in question (Cane 1996, 8). The challenge may be brought under the head of a written constitution or international covenant, or on grounds that the action offended against natural justice, was not within the authority of the agent, was in some other way unreasonable, and so on. The remedy that the courts can offer in the case of a successful challenge is to quash the relevant decision of government, to order the government to perform appropriately, or to prohibit it from continuing on its current path.

The courts, in particular the high court or supreme court, are the forums in which people can challenge the government on grounds of legality. But in most democratic jurisdictions bodies of a different kind – they are often described as tribunals – provide people with the opportunity to challenge government on a different count, to do with the substantive merits of decisions taken rather than their strict legality. These tribunals are often specialized, with one tribunal dealing with land use, another with education, another with immigration, and so on. They are associated with the rise of administrative law over the past fifty years and they differ from the courts in being able to substitute their own decisions for the decisions of government that are under challenge.

Not only may people in most democracies contest government initiatives for their legality and their merit. They may also bring challenges of 'maladministration' – charges of neglect, inattention, delay, arbitrariness, and so on – of a kind that the courts and the tribunals won't always be able to hear. These are brought before those complaints officers, some specialized, some not, who are generally described as 'ombudsmen'. Ombudsman figures are able to investigate a complaint and publish a report and, while they do not have a power to enforce a remedy, they are often effective in securing compensation, and even a change of practice on the part of government agents.

These avenues of challenge represent, from our point of view, potentially important resources of contestation. They may not all work well and may require significant amendment. Some may even work for ill – say, the institution of judicial review – in being overcautious and overcensorious of electoral and parliamentary choice (Waldron 1999). But they do represent an attempt to guard people against false positives: that is, to guard against those in government forming or implementing policies in a way that is responsive to something other than the common avowable interests of their citizens. They are designed, however imperfectly, to protect people from the danger of government officials and bodies behaving in a corrupt or factional manner.

The emerging perspective

The proper step at this point would be to try and outline a list of reforms that ought to be made in the actual institutions of democracy. This would give a better critical edge to our examination of how far democracy – two-dimensional democracy – can guard against the *imperium* of the state becoming arbitrary and dominating. And it would emphasize that the forgoing discussion is not intended as a paean to existing democracy but is meant only to demonstrate why institutions of a broadly democratic sort are so important to freedom as non-domination.

It is not possible in the compass available, alas, to say anything in this vein on where democracy should go from here (see Pettit 2000a for a little more). But short of providing a manifesto for democratic reform, our discussion should still be useful in providing a perspective on issues of reform. It furnishes us with a picture of the role that democracy ought to play if it is to be the protector of our freedom under the state: that of empowering the common avowable interests of ordinary people, and nothing else besides. And it gives us a view of the rationale of existing democratic institutions, electoral and non-electoral. They can be seen as serving to guard, however imperfectly, against the two dangers identified: on the one hand, false negatives – the failure in certain cases to recognize genuine matters of common avowable interest – and on the other, false positives – the empowerment of factors other than common avowable interests in the realm of policy-making.

I suggested earlier that those who have worked with the republican conception of freedom as non-domination have always sought a characterization of the free constitution or the free state. The idea has been that while the state is going to be essential for protecting individuals against one another's *dominium*, and against external enemies, it is only a very particular sort of state that will itself respect the freedom of its citizens, giving them a free, undominated status in its own regard, as well as a free, undominated status *vis-à-vis* one another; it is only a very particular sort of state whose *imperium* will rescue people from subjection without itself exercising subjection against them.

What we have been looking at is a particular vision of the free constitution or state. Under the image defended, the free state has to be a democratic state, and in particular a state that is democratic in two dimensions, electoral and contestatory. There are enough republican antecedents of the ideas marshalled in this image to describe it as itself a distinctively republican story (Pettit 1997a, chapter 6; 1999a). But the important point about the image is that it is drawn, not out of slavish fidelity to the republican tradition, but out of reflection on what exactly is going to be required of a state that protects its people from domination without itself becoming a dominating instrumentality.

Conclusion

We argued in the last chapter that the political ideal of freedom – the ideal of freedom that should be held up for the state to further – is that of non-domination. We began this chapter by noting, however, that any state which is given the task of furthering people's non-domination will itself be a power that threatens to dominate them. It may protect them against private power or *dominium*, as it may protect them against external enemies, but it will itself have such public power or *imperium* that it may represent an even worse danger of domination.

The problem with the state is that it has a coercive power of interference and that its members are not in a position to exercise an effective power of exit; in these respects it contrasts with most other collective entities. Thus there is no guarantee on this front that it will not be arbitrary and dominating: no guarantee that it will track the common avowable interests of its members. How then to guard against this danger? Starting from a contractualist conception of common interests as those goods that co-operatively admissible considerations suggest should be collectively provided, we argued that if democracy is going to work in the way envisaged, then it must force the state to be guided by people's common avowable interests, and only their common avowable interests. And then we looked at how each of these effects might be secured.

On the first front, the idea defended was that having an electoral democracy would help to ensure that most plausible candidates for being common avowable interests get an airing and, if compelling, tend to get endorsed. In this way electoral democracy would guard against false negatives: against failures to recognize certain common avowable interests and get them taken into account by the state. But electoral democracy does not promise to do so well in respect of false positives: that is, in respect of the representation of sectional interests as matters of common avowable interest. And so we argued that electoral democracy needs to be complemented by a contestatory form of democracy that enables people as individuals and groups to raise an effective voice against policies and practices that do not, by their lights, reflect common avowable interests. We argued, in particular, that people should be provided with procedural, consultative and appellate resources of contestation. A quick overview of the institutions of democractic societies reveals that the point is recognized in practice.

This account of democratic practice, electoral and contestatory, is not intended as a defence of existing democracy. The point is that a two-dimensional democracy represents the right sort of response to the problem raised about the *imperium* of the state, not that democracy is free of imperfection: on the contrary, our analysis immediately suggests ways in which existing democracies can be improved. The democratic state, properly understood, has a claim unique among constitutions to be described as the free state. It is the only state imaginable that can claim to protect people against domination without itself becoming a dominating instrumentality.

Conclusion

I argued in the Introduction that there is good methodological reason to explore the possibility of a comprehensive theory of freedom in place of two compartmentalized theories, one addressed to free will issues, the other to issues of political liberty. The argument was that the two areas are conceptually connected; that the intuitions in each area allow of different, more or less equally satisfactory ways of being equilibrated and systematized; and that because a single, unified theory will be required at every point to fit with intuitions across both domains, it may prove easier to find a single candidate, or a small family of candidates, that scores clearly ahead of competitors.

How does this claim look in the light of the position which we have been led to embrace in the course of the preceding seven chapters? What marks has the aspiration for a unified theory left on our approach? And how far can we associate them with the tighter methodological constraints imposed by that aspiration?

I suggest that the main features of the position adopted can be explained, at least in some part, by requirements imposed by the search for a unified theory. I did not comment on this methodological aspect of things in the body of the text, as it would have been repetitious and tiresome to do so, and it may be useful to put that omission right in this Conclusion. I list ten features of the position defended and try to show how each reflects in some way the holistic constraints imposed on a unified theory. The review presupposes a familiarity with the text and is not intended as a stand-alone summary; the conclusions to the individual chapters will serve better in that role.

1 The construal of freedom in the agent and of political freedom

The desire to have a comprehensive theory led us at the very beginning to think of freedom in the agent as something involving every aspect of agency, not just the particular phenomenon associated with talk of free will, and to equate the political ideal of freedom with the requirements of freedom in the agent that can usefully be put in the charge of the state. The different aspects of agency that we took freedom to involve are, first, the free choice of action; second, the presence of a free self that can identify with that choice, not just look on it as a bystander; and third, the power of a free person who is secure against the pressure of others to act as they might wish.

2 The prioritizing of the responsibility connotation

While I gave many independent arguments for why it is useful to conceptualize freedom as fitness to be held responsible, one striking feature that recommends it – as I mentioned in the Introduction – is that it applies quite clearly on the side both of free will and of political liberty, and that it underlines the conceptual unity in talk of freedom across those two areas. It also serves, as I argued, to give us a good sense of what it means for an action or self or person, as such, to be free; it means that the action, self or person is compatible, in itself, with the agent's being fit to be held responsible.

3 The testing of theories of freedom in the agent

The three theories of freedom in the agent that we considered – freedom as rational, volitional and discursive control – were each tested for how well they fit with the assumption that when an agent acts in full freedom then the control of the action, the constitution of the self, and the status of the person must be compatible with the agent's being fit to be held responsible. This mode of testing, motivated by the aspiration for a unified theory, is more demanding than that which any compartmentalized approach would require. It puts more constraints in place than it is normal to impose on a theory of free agency or free will.

4 The importance given to freedom of the person

The mode of testing to which the three theories were exposed is distinctive as well demanding. It requires a satisfactory theory to explain how the freedom of an agent can be vulnerable to the presence of others who, without actually impeding action, coerce or intimidate the agent with a view to getting their own way. This intuitive constraint helped to make the case for looking first at what freedom in the person – freedom in the person's relations to others – requires and then for seeing how far the satisfaction of those requirements coheres with a satisfactory account of freedom in self and action. It meant that there is little prospect that a non-social theory of freedom – say, the theory of freedom as rational or volitional control – can prove satisfactory; any such theory, as we saw, is bound to have a problem in explaining why hostile coercion or intimidation is an offence against freedom. It directed us, more or less unambiguously, towards the theory of freedom as discursive control.

5   *The explication of freedom in the self*
According to the theory of freedom as discursive control, what makes for freedom in the person is their having the ratiocinative and relational capacity required for being authorized as a discursive partner: their being conversable, in at once a psychological and a social sense. The theory could only prove satisfactory, however, so far as we found it possible – a further constraint – to identify being a free self with being the type of self that is consistent with being discursively authorized. And this we did find possible, arguing that being a free self is just being the type of self that can non-elusively own, and effectively live up to the legacy of commitments generated in discursive relationships.

6   *The explication of freedom in action*
The approach adopted also required us – another constraint – to be able to represent performing a free action as operating in a way that is consistent with having the authority of a conversable person. And this too we were able to do. We equated performing a free action with performing as the type of agent in which one is cast under discursive authorization: the type that can be expected to act as discursive considerations require. This is a type of agent who can be held responsible to such reasons, in the sense of being praised for living up to them and blamed for not doing so. And it is a type of agent of whom we can always say that they could have done otherwise. If they did well, we will mean that had the reasons supported another course, they would have taken that instead. If they did ill, we will mean that this was an accident and that only an untypical malaise or malfunction led them not to act up to type: not to act as the reasons required.

7   *The construction of a theory of collective freedom*
If freedom is to be theoretically reconstructed in a comprehensive and unified way, then we have to be able to explain within that theory how it is possible to speak of free collectivities as well as of

free individuals. That constraint means that whatever theory of freedom we adopt for individual agents, it must prove capable of applying to collective agents as well. The theory of freedom as discursive control proved able, happily, to meet this requirement. As we argued, the theory applies in a quite literal sense to those groups and groupings that impose the discipline of reason at the collective level and that count as social integrates, not just social aggregates.

8   The argument for non-interference against non-limitation

Among the main issues between theorists of political liberty is the question of whether political freedom is equally compromised by natural and intentional obstacles and the related question of whether it is compromised by the natural or intentional imposition of costs as well as by the actual blocking of choice. The aspiration for a unified theory makes it imperative to construct the political ideal of freedom so that something is inimical to it to the extent, and only to the extent, that it reduces or removes discursive control. And that led us to argue that the intentional imposition of costs or blocks on the choices of another – interference, properly so called – is more inimical by far than non-intentional limitation. It gave us a line on one of the deepest divisions in current political theory.

9   The argument for non-domination against non-interference

The same train of reasoning, directly sourced in the search for a unified theory of freedom, argued in turn that non-arbitrary interference – interference designed, ideally, to track the avowable interests of the interferee – is not any more serious than non-intentional limitation; it conditions but does not compromise freedom. And it argued equally that while the experience of arbitrary interference compromises freedom, so does the mere fact of being vulnerable to such interference: so does the mere fact of being dependent on the good will of powerful, potential interferers. In arguing for these positions, the train of reasoning supported the republican conception of political freedom as non-domination.

10   The relevance given to democracy, electoral and contestatory

The political ideals of freedom that respectively privilege non-limitation and non-interference make the connection between freedom and democratization wholly contingent, contrary to the traditional equation between the free polity and the democratic polity. But, as we would want in a comprehensive theory, the line taken here secures that equation in a very satisfying way. The democratic state – the state that is democratic in electoral and contestatory ways – is designed to track the common avowable interests of those who live under it, so we argued, and only such common interests. And that means, under the ideal of non-domination, that so far as a state is democratic – a matter, inevitably, of imperfect degree – to that extent it will be non-arbitrary and will not compromise the freedom of its members. Its coercive laws and decrees and other initiatives will condition people's choices, as natural limitations do, but the state will not compromise people's freedom in the manner of a dominating presence.

I hope that this brief review of features that characterize the position defended here will help to bear out the case for thinking about freedom comprehensively, not just in a compartmentalized way. Like any author I would like the substantive things I say here to make a small mark on the long sort of conversation in which we philosophers find purpose and pleasure. But I would be particularly happy if the book served to persuade some others that the conversation about freedom took a wrong turn when, rejecting the classic precedent set by the likes of Hobbes and Kant, it broke up into isolated discussions of free will and political liberty. If there is any topic where philosophical conversation would benefit from going more expansive and connected, freedom is surely it.

References

Ayer, A. J. (1982). Freedom and necessity. In G. Watson (ed.), *Free Will*. Oxford, Oxford University Press.
Baier, A. C. (1997). *The Commons of the Mind*. Chicago, Open Court.
Baron, M., P. Pettit and M. Slote (1997). *Three Methods of Ethics: A Debate*. Oxford, Blackwell.
Barry, B. (1995). *Justice as Impartiality*. Oxford, Oxford University Press.
Bellamy, R. (1999). *Liberalism and Pluralism: Towards a Politics of Compromise*. London, Routledge.
Berlin, I. (1969). *Four Essays on Liberty*. Oxford, Oxford University Press.
Berofsky, B. (1987). *Freedom from Necessity*. London, Routledge.
Bilgrami, A. (1998). Self-knowledge and resentment. In B. S. C. Wright and C. Macdonald (eds), *Knowing Our Own Minds*. Oxford, Oxford University Press.
Braithwaite, J. and P. Pettit (1990). *Not Just Deserts: A Republican Theory of Criminal Justice*. Oxford, Oxford University Press.
Bramhall, B. (1962). Liberty and necessity. In S. M. and J. Walsh (eds), *Free Will*. New York, Prentice-Hall.
Bratman, M. (1999). *Faces of Intention: Selected Essays on Intention and Agency*. Cambridge, Cambridge University Press.
Brennan, G. (1999). Collective irrationality and belief. Mimeo. Canberra, Research School of Social Sciences, Australian National University.
Brennan, G. and P. Pettit (1993). Hands invisible and intangible. *Synthèse* 94: 191–225.
Brennan, G. and P. Pettit (2000). The hidden economy of esteem. *Economics and Philosophy*. Vol. 16, 77–98.
Burge, T. (1998). Reason and the First Person. In B. S. C. Wright and C. Macdonald (eds), *Knowing Our Own Minds*. Oxford, Oxford University Press.

Cane, P. (1996). *An Introduction to Administrative Law.* Oxford, Oxford University Press.
Carter, I. (1999). *A Measure of Freedom.* Oxford, Oxford University Press.
Chapman, B. (1998a). Law, incommensurability, and conceptually sequenced argument. *University of Pennsylvania Law Review* 146: 1487–582.
Chapman, B. (1998b). More easily done than said: rules, reason and rational social choice. *Oxford Journal of Legal Studies* 18: 293–329.
Cherniak, C. (1986). *Minimal Rationality.* Cambridge, Mass., MIT Press.
Chisholm, R. M. (1982). Human freedom and the self. In G. Watson (ed.), *Free Will.* Oxford, Oxford University Press.
Cohen, G. A. (1979). Capitalism, freedom and the proletariat. In A. Ryan (ed.) *The Idea of Freedom.* Oxford, Oxford University Press.
Cohen, G. A. (1993). Equality of what? On welfare, goods, and capabilities. In M. C. Nussbaum and A. Sen (eds), *The Quality of Life.* Oxford, Oxford University Press.
Cohen, J. (1989). Deliberation and democratic legitimacy. In A. Hamlin and P. Pettit (eds), *The Good Polity.* Oxford, Blackwell.
Constant, B. (1988). *Political Writings.* Cambridge, Cambridge University Press.
Dagger, R. (1997). *Civic Virtues: Rights, Citizenship, and Republican Liberalism.* Oxford, Oxford University Press.
Darwall, S. (1999). Reciprocal recognition: the second-person standpoint in moral thought and theory. Mimeo. Ann Arbor, Department of Philosophy, University of Michigan.
Davidson, D. (1980). *Essays on Actions and Events.* Oxford, Oxford University Press.
Davidson, D. (1984). *Inquiries into Truth and Interpretation.* Oxford, Oxford University Press.
Dennett, D. (1984). *Elbow Room: The Varieties of Free Will Worth Wanting.* Cambridge, Mass., MIT Press.
Dennett, D. (1987). *The Intentional Stance.* Cambridge, Mass., MIT Press.
Dennett, D. (1996). *Kinds of Minds: Towards an Understanding of Consciousness.* London, Weidenfeld and Nicolson.
Dicey, A. V. (1960). *An Introduction to the Law of the Constitution.* London, Macmillan.
Dworkin, G. (1970). Acting Freely. *Nous* 4: 367–83.
Dworkin, G. (1988). *The Theory and Practice of Autonomy.* Cambridge, Cambridge University Press.
Elster, J. (1986). The market and the forum: three varieties of political theory. In J. Elser and A. Hillard (eds), *Foundations of Social Choice Theory.* Cambridge, Cambridge University Press.
Feinberg, J. (1986). *Harm to Others.* Oxford, Oxford University Press.
Fischer, J. M. (1994). *The Metaphysics of Free Will.* Oxford, Blackwell.
Fischer, J. M. (1999). Recent work on moral responsibility. *Ethics* 110: 93–139.
Frankfurt, H. G. (1988). *The Importance of What We Care About.* Cambridge, Cambridge University Press.

Frankfurt, H. G. (1999). *Necessity, Volition, and Love.* Cambridge, Cambridge University Press.
French, P. A. (1984). *Collective and Corporate Responsibility.* New York, Columbia University Press.
Fuller, L. L. (1971). *The Morality of Law.* New Haven, Conn., Yale University Press.
Gilbert, M. (1989). *On Social Facts.* Princeton, N.J., Princeton University Press.
Goffman, E. (1975). *Frame Analysis: An Essay on the Organization of Experience.* Harmondsworth, Penguin Books.
Goodin, R. E. (1996). Institutionalizing the Public Interest: The Defense of Deadlock and Beyond. *American Political Science Review* 90: 331–43.
Gorr, M. J. (1989). *Coercion, Freedom and Exploitation.* New York, Peter Lang.
Gutmann, A. and D. Thompson (1996). *Democracy and Disagreement.* Cambridge, Mass., Harvard University Press.
Gwyn, W. B. (1965). *The Meaning of the Separation of Powers.* The Hague, Nijhoff.
Habermas, J. (1984, 1989). *A Theory of Communicative Action, Vols 1 and 2.* Cambridge, Polity.
Hardin, R. (1982). *Collective Action.* Baltimore, Md., Johns Hopkins University Press.
Harrington, J. (1992). *The Commonwealth of Oceana and A System of Politics.* Cambridge, Cambridge University Press.
Hirschman, A. O. (1970). *Exit, Voice, and Loyalty: Responses to Decline in Firms, Organizations, and States.* Cambridge, Mass., Harvard University Press.
Hobbes, T. (1968). *Leviathan.* Harmondsworth, Penguin Books.
Hobbes, T. (1998). *On the Citizen.* Cambridge, Cambridge University Press.
Honneth, A. (1996). *The Struggle for Recognition.* Cambridge, Polity, and Cambridge, Mass., MIT Press.
Honoré, T. (1999). *Responsibility and Fault.* Oxford, Hart Publishing.
Hurley, S. L. (1999). Responsibility, reason, and irrelevant alternatives. *Philosophy and Public Affairs* 28: 205–41.
Jackson, F. (1998). *From Metaphysics to Ethics: A Defence of Conceptual Analysis.* Oxford, Oxford University Press.
James, S. (1984). *The Content of Social Explanation.* Cambridge, Cambridge University Press.
Kane, R. (1996). *The Significance of Free Will.* New York, Oxford University Press.
Klein, M. (1990). *Determinism, Blameworthiness and Deprivation.* Oxford, Oxford University Press.
Kornhauser, L. A. (1992a). Modelling collegial courts. I. Path-dependence. *International Review of Law and Economics* 12: 169–85.
Kornhauser, L. A. (1992b). Modelling collegial courts. II. Legal doctrine. *Journal of Law, Economics and Organization* 8: 441–70.

Kornhauser, L. A. and L. G. Sager (1986). Unpacking the court. *Yale Law Journal* 96: 82–117.
Kornhauser, L. A. and L. G. Sager (1993). The one and the many: adjudication in collegial courts. *California Law Review* 81: 1–59.
Korsgaard, C. (1996). *The Sources of Normativity*. New York, Cambridge University Press.
Korsgaard, C. M. (1999). Self-constitution in the ethics of Plato and Kant. *The Journal of Ethics* 3: 1–29.
Kriegel, B. (1995). *The State and the Rule of Law*. Princeton, N.J., Princeton University Press.
Kukathas, C. and P. Pettit (1990). *Rawls: A Theory of Justice and its Critics*. Cambridge, Calif., Polity Press and Stanford, Stanford University Press.
Kutz, C. (2001). *Complicity: Ethics and Law for a Collective Age*. Cambridge, Cambridge University Press.
Kymlicka, W. (1995). *Multicultural Citizenship*. Oxford, Oxford University Press.
Lewis, D. (1969). *Convention*. Cambridge, Mass., Harvard University Press.
Lewis, D. (1983). *Philosophical Papers, Vol. 1*. Oxford, Oxford University Press.
Lewis, D. (1986). *Philosophical Papers, Vol. 2*. Oxford, Oxford University Press.
Lewis, D. (1996). Elusive knowledge. *Australasian Journal of Philosophy* 74: 549–67.
Lind, J. (1776). *Three Letters to Dr Price*. London, T. Payne.
List, C. and P. Pettit (2000). Mimeo: The aggregation of reason: an impossibility result. Canberra, Australian National University.
Locke, J. (1975). *An Essay Concerning Human Understanding*. Ed. P. H. Nidditch. Oxford, Oxford University Press.
Long, D. C. (1977). *Bentham on Liberty*. Toronto, University of Toronto Press.
Lovejoy, A. O. (1961). *Reflections on Human Nature*. Baltimore, MD., Johns Hopkins University Press.
Machiavelli (1965). *The Complete Work and Others*. Durham, N.C., Duke University Press.
Manin, B. (1997). *The Principles of Representative Government*. Cambridge, Cambridge University Press.
McAdams, R. H. (1997). The origin, development and regulation of norms. *Michigan Law Review* 96 (2): 338–433.
McGeer, V. and P. Pettit (2001). The self-regulating mind. *Language and Communication*.
Meijers, A. (1994). *Speech Acts, Communication and Collective Intentionality: Beyond Searle's Individualism*. Utrecht, de Jonge.
Mill, J. S. (1978). *On Liberty*. Indianapolis, Hackett.
Miller, D. (1984). Constraints on freedom. *Ethics* 94: 66–86.
Miller, D., ed. (1993). *Liberty*. Oxford, Oxford University Press.
Montesquieu, C. de S. (1989). *The Spirit of the Laws*. Cambridge, Cambridge University Press.

Moore, G. E. (1911). *Ethics.* Oxford, Oxford University Press.
Nozick, R. (1969). Coercion. In P. S. S. Morgenbesser and M. White (eds), *Philosophy, Science and Method: Essays in Honor of Ernest Nagel.* New York, St Martin's Press.
Nozick, R. (1981). *Philosophical Explanations.* Oxford, Oxford University Press.
Nussbaum, M. (1992). Human functioning and social justice. *Political Theory* 20: 202–46.
O'Leary-Hawthorne, J. and P. Pettit (1996). Strategies for free-will compatibilists. *Analysis* 56, 191–201.
Oshana, M. (1997). Ascriptions of responsibility. *American Philosophical Quarterly* 34: 81–102.
Otsuka, M. (1998). Incompatibilism and the avoidability of blame. *Ethics* 108: 685–701.
Paley, W. (1825). *The Principles of Moral and Political Philosophy, Vol. 4, Collected Works.* London, Rivington.
Parfit, D. (1984). *Reasons and Persons.* Oxford, Oxford University Press.
Perry, J. (1979). The essential indexical. *Nous* 13: 3–21.
Pettit, P. (1986). Free riding and foul dealing. *Journal of Philosophy* 83: 361–79.
Pettit, P. (1990). *Virtus normativa*: a rational choice perspective. *Ethics* 100: 725–55.
Pettit, P. (1991). Realism and response-dependence. *Mind* 100: 587–626.
Pettit, P. (1993a). *The Common Mind: An Essay on Psychology, Society and Politics*, paperback edition 1996. New York, Oxford University Press.
Pettit, P. (1993b). A Definition of physicalism. *Analysis* 53: 213–23.
Pettit, P. (1995). The virtual reality of homo economicus. *Monist* 78: 308–29.
Pettit, P. (1997a). *Republicanism: A Theory of Freedom and Government.* Oxford, Oxford University Press.
Pettit, P. (1997b). Republican theory and criminal punishment. *Utilitas* 9: 59–79.
Pettit, P. (1998). Reworking Sandel's republicanism. *Journal of Philosophy* 95: 73–96.
Pettit, P. (1999a). Republican liberty, contestatory democracy. In C. Hacker-Cordon and I. Shapiro (eds), *Democracy's Value.* Cambridge, Cambridge University Press.
Pettit, P. (1999b). A theory of normal and ideal conditions. *Philosophical Studies* 96: 21–44.
Pettit, P. (2000a). Democracy, electoral and contestatory. *Nomos* 42: 105–44.
Pettit, P. (2000b). Minority claims under two conceptions of democracy. In D. Ivison, P. Patton and W. Sanders (eds), *Political Theory and the Rights of Indigenous Peoples.* Cambridge, Cambridge University Press.
Pettit, P. (2000c). Groups with minds of their own. Mimeo. Canberra, Australian National University.
Pettit, P. (2001a). Capability and freedom: a defence of Sen. *Economics and Philosophy* 17: 1–20.

Pettit, P. (2001b). Deliberative democracy and the discursive dilemma. *Philosophical Issues* (suppl. to *Nous*).
Pettit, P. (2001c). Non-consequentialism and political philosophy. In D. Schmidtz (ed.), *Nozick*. Cambridge, Cambridge University Press.
Pettit, P. (2001d). Two Sources of Morality. *Social Philosophy and Policy* 18, 2: 102–28.
Pettit, P. (2001e). Embracing objectivity in ethics. In B. Leiter (ed.), *Objectivity in Law and Morals*. Cambridge, Cambridge University Press.
Pettit, P. (2001f). The capacity to have done otherwise. In P. Cane and J. Gardner (eds), *Relating to Responsibility: Essays in Honour of Tony Honoré on his 80th Birthday*. Oxford, Hart Publishing.
Pettit, P. and J. Braithwaite (1994). The three Rs of republican sentencing. *Current Issues in Criminal Justice* 5: 318–25.
Pettit, P. and M. Smith (1996). Freedom in belief and desire. *Journal of Philosophy* 93: 429–49.
Pocock, J. G. A. (1975). *The Machiavellian Moment: Florentine Political Theory and the Atlantic Republican Tradition*. Princeton, N.J., Princeton University Press.
Polybius (1954). *The Histories*. Cambridge, Mass., Harvard University Press.
Price, R. (1991). *Political Writings*. Cambridge, Cambridge University Press.
Priestley, J. (1993). *Political Writings*. Cambridge, Cambridge University Press.
Przeworksi, A. (1999). A minimalist conception of democracy: a defense. In C. Hacker-Cordon and I. Shapiro (eds), *Democracy's Value*. Cambridge, Cambridge University Press.
Quinton, A. (1975). Social objects. *Proceedings of the Aristotelian Society* 75.
Rawls, J. (1971). *A Theory of Justice*. Oxford, Oxford University Press.
Raz, J. (1986). *The Morality of Freedom*. Oxford, Oxford University Press.
Rovane, C. (1997). *The Bounds of Agency: An Essay in Revisionary Metaphysics*. Princeton, N.J., Princeton University Press.
Ruben, D.-H. (1985). *The Metaphysics of the Social World*. London, Routledge and Kegan Paul.
Runciman, D. (1997). *Pluralism and the Personality of the State*. Cambridge, Cambridge University Press.
Sandel, M. (1982). *Liberalism and the Limits of Justice*. Cambridge, Cambridge University Press.
Sandel, M. (1996). *Democracy's Discontent: America in Search of a Public Philosophy*. Cambridge, Mass., Harvard University Press.
Sartre, J.-P. (1958). *Being and Nothingness*. London, Methuen.
Scanlon, T. M. (1982). Contractualism and utilitarianism. In A. Sen and B. Williams (eds), *Utilitarianism and Beyond*. Cambridge, Cambridge University Press.
Scanlon, T. M. (1998). *What We Owe To Each Other*. Cambridge, Mass., Harvard University Press.
Searle, J. (1995). *The Construction of Social Reality*. New York, Free Press.
Sellers, M. N. S. (1995). *American Republicanism: Roman Ideology in the United States Constitution*. New York, New York University Press.

Sen, A. (1983). Liberty and Social Choice. *Journal of Philosophy* 80: 18–20.
Sen, A. (1985a). *Commodities and Capabilities*. Amsterdam, North-Holland.
Sen, A. (1985b). Well-being, agency and freedom. *Journal of Philosophy* 82: 169–221.
Skinner, Q. (1996). *Reason and Rhetoric in the Philosophy of Hobbes*. Cambridge, Cambridge University Press.
Skinner, Q. (1997). *Liberty Before Liberalism*. Cambridge, Cambridge University Press.
Skyrms, B. (1996). *Evolution of the Social Contract*. Cambridge, Cambridge University Press.
Smith, M. (1997). A theory of freedom and responsibility. In G. Cullity and B. Gaut (eds), *Ethics and Practical Reason*. Oxford, Oxford University Press.
Stalnaker, R. C. (1984). *Inquiry*. Cambridge, Mass., MIT Press.
Steiner, H. (1994). *An Essay on Rights*. Oxford, Blackwell.
Stoljar, S. J. (1973). *Groups and Entities: An Inquiry into Corporate Theory*. Canberra, Australian National University Press.
Strawson, G. (1994). The impossibility of moral responsibility. *Philosophical Studies* 75: 5–24.
Strawson, P. (1982). Freedom and resentment. In G. Watson (ed.), *Free Will*. Oxford, Oxford University Press.
Stump, E. (1996). Persons: identification and freedom. *Philosophical Topics* 24: 183–214.
Stump, E. (1997). Aquinas's account of freedom: intellect and will. *Monist* 80: 576–97.
Sugden, R. (1998). The metric of opportunity. *Economics and Philosophy* 14: 307–37.
Sunstein, C. R. (1988). Beyond the republican revival. *The Yale Law Journal* 97: 1539–90.
Sunstein, C. R. (1993). *The Partial Constitution*. Cambridge, Mass., Harvard University Press.
Sunstein, C. R. (1997). *One Case at a Time*. Cambridge, Mass., Harvard University Press.
Swanton, C. (1992). *Freedom: A Coherence Theory*. Indianapolis, Hackett.
Taylor, C. (1985). *Philosophy and the Human Sciences*. Cambridge, Cambridge University Press.
Taylor, M. (1982). *Community, Anarchy and Liberty*. Cambridge, Cambridge University Press.
Ten, C. L. (1993). Constitutionalism and the rule of law. In R. E. Goodin and P. Pettit (eds), *A Companion to Contemporary Political Philosophy*.
Tuomela, R. (1995). *The Importance of Us*. Stanford, Calif., Stanford University Press.
Tyler, T. R. (1990). *Why People Obey the Law*. New Haven, Conn., Yale University Press.
Tyler, T. R., R. J. Boeckmann, H. J. Smith and Y. Y. Huo. (1997). *Social Justice in a Diverse Society*. Boulder, Colo., Westview Press.
Van Inwagen, P. (1983). *An Essay on Free Will*. Oxford, Oxford University Press.

Van Parijs, P. (1995). *Real Freedom for All*. Oxford, Oxford University Press.
Vanderschraaf, P. (1998). The informal game theory in Hume's account of convention. *Economics and Philosophy* 14: 215–47.
Velleman, J. D. (1992). What happens when someone acts? *Mind* 101: 461–81.
Vile, M. J. C. (1967). *Constitutionalism and the Separation of Powers*. Oxford, Oxford University Press.
Waldron, J. (1999). *Law and Disagreement*. Oxford, Oxford University Press.
Wallace, R. J. (1996). *Responsibility and the Moral Sentiments*. Cambridge, Mass., Harvard University Press.
Watson, G. (1982). Free Agency. In G. Watson (ed.), *Free Will*. Oxford, Oxford University Press.
Watson, G. (1996). Two Faces of Responsibility. *Philosophical Topics* 24: 227–48.
Wolf, S. (1990). *Freedom within Reason*. Oxford, Oxford University Press.

Index

action
   free 34–6, 63–4, 121, 176, 177
   theory of 36–42, 49, 57–60, 90–3, 93–102, 125
agency 30, 42, 127, 143, 150
agent
   collective 105–6, 114–21, 177, 178
   free 3, 6, 40, 176
   reason-responsive 98, 99
anthropocentric property of freedom 25–30, 31
authorization, discursive 17, 77, 84, 95–8, 141, 177
Ayer, A. J. 9, 44, 57

Baier, A. 117
Baron, M. 129
Barry, B. 156n
beliefs 43, 44, 48, 57, 81, 98
   lower-order 58
Bellamy, R. 158
Bentham, J. 147–9
Berlin, I. 24, 127, 128, 130, 154
Berofsky, B. 9
Bilgrami, A. 27

blame 12, 15, 100–2
Boeckmann, R. J. 165
Braithwaite, J. 143, 144
Bramhall, B. 24
Bratman, M. 106
Brennan, G. 106, 165
Burge, T. 81
bystander problem 10, 42, 49, 50, 56, 79, 80, 87–90, 120

Cane, P. 170, 171
Carter, I. 46, 130
Chapman, B. 106
Cherniak, C. 36
Chisholm, R. M. 10, 51
citizenship 145, 148–9, 152
coercion 62, 130–2, 155
   friendly 74–7
   hostile 45–6, 48, 61, 72–5, 77, 79, 103
   state 174
Cohen, G. A. 130
Cohen, J. 168
collective subjects 5, 104–5, 105–6, 109, 111–12, 125, 154, 177
   freedom of 5, 115–21, 123–4
   integrated 116–19, 120

purposive 111–12
  reality of 114–15
collectivization of reason 109–14, 154
concept-bound property of freedom 29, 31
Constant, B. 128
constituency 145, 148, 149, 152
consultation 169, 170
contestation 164–5, 166–7, 178
  appellate resources 171–2
  consultative resources 169–70
  procedural resources 167–9
  resources of 167–73, 174
control
  active 38, 53, 91, 121
  virtual 38, 39, 53, 76, 91, 93, 121
  discursive *see* discursive control
  rational *see* rational control
  volitional *see* volitional control

Dagger, R. 152
Darwall, S. 72
Davidson, D. 9, 22, 36, 41, 93n
decision-making 107–9, 111–12, 169
democracy 159, 160–7, 168, 170, 172–3, 178
  resources for 167–73
democratization 5, 152–74
Dennett, D. 24, 35, 159
desires 43, 44, 48, 57, 81, 98
  first-order 51, 54
  higher-order 55, 61–3
  lower-order 55, 58, 61, 90
  second-order 51, 53, 54, 56
Dicey, A. V. 168
dilemma, discursive 106–11, 114, 123
discourse, etymology of 67
  practical 68
  restricted 73–5
discourse-friendly relationships 69–71, 101, 103, 120
discursive control 70–2, 88, 91
  and action, free 90–102
  and adverse influences 77–9

and collective subjects 119–21, 124
and person, free 66–79
and friendly coercion 75–7
and hostile coercion 72–4
and non-domination 138, 139–41, 150
and self, free 79–90
and theory of freedom 5, 34, 41, 90, 125, 176–8
  conditions for 86, 88
  freedom as 65, 90, 100, 127
  ratiocinative and relational aspects of 70–3, 79, 93n, 103, 77
  virtual 76–7, 93, 121
discursive interaction 67–9, 85
discursive reflection 91–3
domination 78, 128, 129, 137, 138; *see also* non-domination
dominium 152, 153, 173
Dworkin, G. 51

electoral procedures 160–2, 165, 174, 178
Elster, J. 156
environment of choice 30, 45, 66, 127, 133, 143, 150

Feinberg, J. 167
first-person aspect of freedom 10, 56, 80, 116–17; *see also* bystander problem
Fischer, J. M. 7, 22
fitness to be held responsible 5, 11–25, 47, 97–100, 176
  conditions for 14–16, 57, 59, 63, 83
  freedom as 26–7, 31, 48, 65
Frankfurt, H. 8, 10, 22, 50–2, 53–5, 57–60, 61–4, 86, 90, 121
freedom
  and responsibility 18–25
  anthropocentric property 25–30, 31
  bystander problem of 10, 42, 49, 50, 56, 79, 80, 87–90, 120

freedom (*cont.*)
  collective 177–8
  concept-bound property 29, 31
  connotations of 1, 6–8, 28, 30, 60, 94, 97, 176
  conundrums of 8–11
  first-person aspect of 10, 56, 80, 116–17
  modal problem of 9–10, 95–7, 99, 100
  objectivity of 25–9, 31
  ownership connotation 6–8, 10, 20, 28, 30, 50, 60
  personal 127
  perspective-dependence of 28, 31
  political ideal of 125–9, 133, 149, 150, 176
  recursive problem of 10–11, 97–100
  responsibility connotation 9, 11–14, 60, 94, 97, 176
  state concern with 126
  theory of 1, 3, 4, 33–4, 175–9
  underdetermination connotation 2, 3, 6–11, 20, 28, 30, 94, 97
French, P. A. 110
Fuller, L. L. 168

Gilbert, M. 106, 117
Goffman, E. 69
Goodin, R. 156n
Gorr, M. J. 46
government 168–9
groups 110–11, 113, 116; *see also* collective subjects; integrates, social
Gutmann, A. 168
Gwyn, W. B. 168

Habermas, J. 156
Hardin, R. 158
Harrington, J. 146, 163
Hirschman, A. 156
Hobbes, T. 1, 46, 80, 145–8, 179
holistic methodology 3, 4, 33–4, 175, 179

Honneth, A. 17, 24, 72
Honore, T. 19
Huo, Y. Y. 165
Hurley, S. L. 11

identity, personal 82–5, 86, 118
imperium 152–6, 159, 172–4
institutions, democratic 159–62, 167, 168, 172–4, 178
integrates, social 113, 114–20, 123; *see also* collective subjects
intention 35, 36, 41, 89, 99, 115, 119
interests, common 134, 135, 139–40, 153–4, 156–63, 165, 170, 179
interference 129, 130, 132–8
  arbitrary 135–41
  freedom from 128
  state 139, 174
  see also non-interference

Jackson, F. 9, 27
James, S. 106
jurisprudence, doctrinal paradox in 106–7, 123

Kane, R. 11
Kant, I. 1, 145, 179
Klein, M. 11
Kornhauser, L. A. 106, 107
Korsgaard, C. 51
Kriegel, B. 152
Kukathas, C. 127
Kutz, C. 122
Kymlicka, W. 158

Lewis, D. 9, 26, 39, 67
liberalism 134, 151
libertarianism 133, 134
liberty
  negative 128, 130
  political 2, 3
  positive 128
  see also freedom
limitation 128, 129–32, 133; *see also* non-limitation

Lind, J. 147, 148
List, C. 107, 110n, 112
Locke, J. 82
Long, D. C. 147
Lovejoy, A. O. 165

Machiavelli 168
McAdams, R. H. 165
McGeer, V. 40
Meijers, A. 106
methodology, holistic 175, 179
Mill, J. S. 167
Miller, D. 128, 130
modal problem of freedom 9–10, 95–7, 99, 100
Montesquieu, C. de S. 145, 153
Moore, G. E. 9

non-domination 5, 128, 129, 178
  concept of 138, 139
  freedom as 139–41, 149, 150, 153, 154, 173
  history of 144–9
  ideal of 138–44, 148, 151
non-interference 128, 129, 142–3, 178
  concept of 132–4
  criticisms of 134–8
  freedom as 130, 146, 147–9
  ideal of 131, 132–8, 150, 151
non-limitation 46, 128, 129–32, 143, 150, 178
Nozick, R. 23
Nussbaum, M. 153

O'Leary-Hawthorne, J. 6, 26
objectivity of freedom 27–9, 31
Oshana, M. 14
Otsuka, M. 22
ownership connotation of freedom 6–8, 10, 20, 28, 30, 50, 60

Paley, W. 147–9, 154
paradox, doctrinal 106, 107, 123
Parfit, D. 84

parliament 168, 169, 170
permissibility 100–2
Perry, J. 81
person 80, 116
  collectivity as 118, 119, 123–4
  free 21, 34, 48
  freedom of 77, 103, 125, 176
  theory of free person 44–6, 60–3, 65–72, 72–9, 86
personal identity 82–5, 86, 118
Pettit, P. 28, 40
  and free agent 6, 9, 25, 26, 129
  and response-dependence 28
  and responsibility 7, 22, 27
  collective subjects 114, 127, 156
  discursive dilemma 106–7, 110n, 112
  discursive interaction 68, 72
  domination 78, 142, 143, 154
  intentionality 35, 97
  interests 165, 171
  republicanism 144, 145, 153, 168, 172, 173
  virtual control 38, 76–7
Pocock, J. G. A. 144
political philosophy, republican 152–4
political theory 175
  measurement in 144
polity 125, 155; *see also* state
Polybius 168
power 78, 79, 152, 153, 164
  arbitrary 135, 137–8, 141, 142, 146
  separation of powers 168
praise 12, 15, 100–2
Price, R. 146
Priestley, J. 146
problem
  discursive 67
  modal 9, 10, 95–7, 99, 100
  recursive 10–11, 97–100
Przeworski, A. 160

Quinton, A. 105, 114, 115

ratiocinative aspect of discursive control 70–3, 79, 93n, 103, 177
rational control 5, 53, 66, 103, 176
  and action, free 36–42
  and person, free 42–4
  and self, free 447
  freedom as 32–48, 49, 58, 60, 73, 87–8, 94
  necessity of 47, 48, 90
Rawls, J. 2, 7, 33, 34, 133, 134, 156n
reason, collectivization 110–14, 154
reasoning 68, 96, 111
  group 106–9, 115, 119
recursive problem 10–11, 97–100
reflective equilibrium 2, 7, 33, 34
relationship aspect of discursive control 70–2, 79, 103, 177
relationships 66, 119, 141
  discourse-friendly 69–71, 101, 103, 120
republicanism 5, 151, 152, 173
  history of 144–9
resources of contestation 164–7
  appellate 171–2
  consultative 169–70
  procedural 167–9
responsibility 4, 18–25, 27, 44, 50, 121–3
  and action, free 40, 42
  collective 122, 124
  connotation of freedom 6–9, 11–14, 30, 60, 94, 97, 176
  developmental considerations 16, 17
  individual 122, 124
  recursive character of 10, 11, 30, 41, 59, 94, 97–100, 103
  see also fitness to be held responsible
Rousseau, J. J. 145
Rovane, C. 70, 82, 116, 119
Ruben, D.-H. 105
Runciman, D. 116

Sager, L. G. 106, 107
Sandel, M. 85, 145
Sartre, J.-P. 9, 51
Scanlon, T. M. 7, 76, 156n
Searle, J. 30, 106, 117
self 80, 86, 87, 116, 123
  collectivity as 118, 119
  elusive 88, 89, 120
  free 21, 34, 48, 57, 63–5, 85, 103, 124, 176
  freedom in 125, 177
  theory of 42–4, 49–57, 79–87, 87–90, 125, 177
self-identity 82–5, 88, 118
Sellers, M. N. S. 144
Sen, A. 24, 77, 153
Skinner, Q. 78, 144, 153, 170
Skyrms, B. 158
Slote, M. 129
Smith, H. J. 165
Smith, M. 7, 22, 25, 68, 72, 97
Stalnaker, R. C. 35
state 5, 125–6, 136, 155, 173
  concern with freedom 126–7
  power of 140, 174
  republican 152–4
  tracking of common interests 153–4, 159–60
Steiner, H. 46, 130
Stoljar, S. J. 110
Strawson, P. 7, 11, 12, 101
Stump, E. 51
subject 126
  collective 105, 106, 114, 115–21, 123–5, 154, 177
  see also collective subjects; integrates, social
subjection 78, 79; *see also* domination
Sugden, R. 143
Sunstein, C. R. 111, 149, 168
Swanton, C. 20

Taylor, C. 143
Taylor, M. 46, 130
Ten, C. L. 168

theory of freedom, method of 1, 3, 4, 33–4, 175–9
Thompson, D. 168
threat 74, 131
Tuomela, R. 106, 117
Tyler, T. R. 25, 165

underdetermination connotation of freedom 2, 3, 6–11, 20, 28, 30, 94, 97
unified theory of freedom 1, 3, 4, 33–4, 175–9

Van Inwagen, P. 9
Van Parijs, P. 133, 134, 136
Vanderschraaf, P. 158
Velleman, J. D. 53
veto 163–4
Vile, M. J. C. 168

volitional control 5, 34, 47, 66, 73, 88, 103, 176
and action, free 57–60
and person, free 60–2
and self, free 50–7
freedom as 49–64, 87, 94
necessity of 63, 90
volitions
higher-order 58, 59, 61, 63, 90
second-order 55, 56

Waldron, J. 172
Wallace, R. J. 7, 12, 14, 27
'wanton' 52, 86, 121
Watson G. 7, 14, 53
will, freedom of 2, 3, 50–2; *see also* volitional control
Wolf, S. 7, 22